What the Ind
LEGENDS: PIONEERS OF THE
AMUSEMENT PARK INDUSTRY

"Reading this book is like taking a private tour through the minds, private thoughts and the great visions of the giants who created this industry. O'Brien writes with the knowledge of an insider with the access of a personal friend."

- BOB ROGERS, CHAIRMAN/CEO, BRC IMAGINATION ARTS

"Students of the amusement park industry will never have a better opportunity to become acquainted with these legends!"

- *AMUSEMENT TODAY*

"Tim's profiles colorfully bring to life those individuals who had the vision and determination to take a dream and turn it into reality. His words remind us that even the largest and most dominant amusement parks began with individuals who typically went against the grain for the simple but noble goal of creating a lifetime memory of joy."

- JIM SEAY, PRESIDENT, PREMIER RIDES

"This is a very well written book with incredible details on incredible people. Tim's writing style makes it feel like you are sitting right there with him during the interview. Excellent job!"

- ALAN RAMSAY, PRESIDENT, CLM ENTERTAINMENT

"Tim's appreciation of and his dedication to the history of this industry is unsurpassed by any writer today. His writing is both fun to read and historically accurate!"

- RICK DAVIS, FOUNDER AND CO-DIRECTOR,
DARKRIDE & FUNHOUSE ENTHUSIASTS

RIPLEY's

LEGENDS

PIONEERS
of the
AMUSEMENT PARK
INDUSTRY

VOLUME ONE

by TIM O'BRIEN

First Printing
ISBN: 978-1-893951-13-6
Library of Congress Control Number (LCCN): 2006933834

Second Printing, 2007

Cover, Page and Text Design: Jennifer Wright

For additional copies of *Legends: Pioneers of the Amusement Park Industry, Volume One,*
ask your local bookseller to order it for you, or visit www.amazon.com

DEDICATION

To the Best and Greatest of Men,
I Dedicate these Volumes.

-Benjamin Disraeli-

CONTENTS

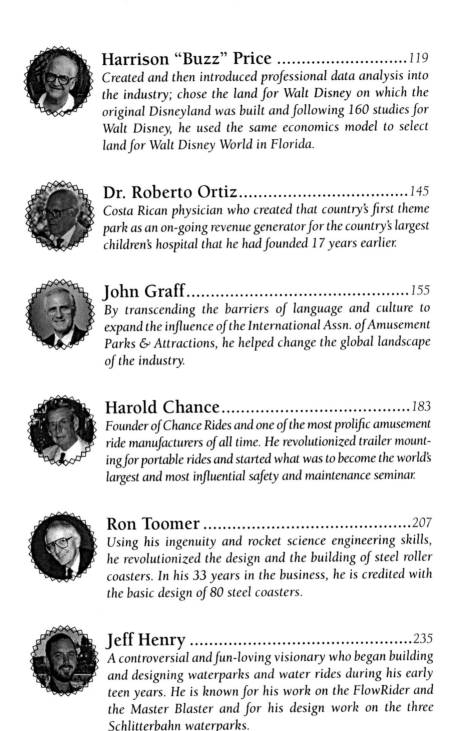

ACKNOWLEDGEMENTS

When word got out that I was writing biographies of the amusement industry's top pioneers - doors, file cabinets, and hearts across the country were opened to my efforts. Thanks to everyone who helped me in the research process and a special thanks to the 10 pioneers featured in this volume for agreeing to spend so much time with me and for enduring my incessant questioning.

As one can imagine, thousands of photographs have been taken of these legends through the years and I scrutinized hundreds to come up with the ones you will find in this book. I credited the photographer when possible, but unfortunately, most of the photos I found did not have the photographers name attached. Many of the photos in the book came from my personal collection and two industry scribes, Paul Ruben of *Park World* magazine and Gary Slade of *Amusement Today* also contributed a few. To them, a hearty thanks.

A big thank you also goes out to Bob Masterson, president of Ripley Entertainment, for his strong desire to preserve the history of this industry. If it were not for his passion of the past and the support he has shown by having Ripley Publishing issue these books, much of the industry's colorful history would certainly be lost to us all. Thanks Bob!

And of course, I acknowledge you, the reader and the buyer of this book. Thanks for doing your part to help us capture the history and the work of these amazing pioneers who made our industry what it is today! Enjoy!

FOREWORD

There are very few businesses in this world whose sole purpose is to put smiles on people's faces. Amusement parks are one of those amazing industries.

For centuries, these fun spots have served as an escape from the worries of everyday life. However, the parks of today would be far from the family fun palaces they are if it were not for the unique breed of pioneers who literally created this industry.

It takes a special person to succeed in the amusement park industry: someone willing to spend 12 hours or more a day in the scorching summer heat dealing with the often difficult general public; someone willing to risk their livelihood on their new innovation, usually an untested concept; and someone who has the foresight to identify the next great industry trend.

The people profiled in this book all embody those special characteristics and in their own way each one contributed to the success that the amusement park industry enjoys today. Tim O'Brien has selected an excellent group of individuals to launch this series and he has highlighted not only the special qualities of the pioneering men themselves, but has provided us with an illustrious and mostly heretofore undocumented history of the parks, products and companies these pioneers created.

It is a pleasure to be a part of this book. As someone who has researched the amusement park industry for three decades, I have developed a special admiration for the unique personalities who make the amusement business special. Tim shares my passion for this industry and his long hours of research and writing, along with his keen observation of the industry should give you a special appreciation for these pioneers. Enjoy!

Jim Futrell,
Historian: National Amusement Park Historical Assn.
Author: *Amusement Parks of Pennsylvania; Amusement Parks of New Jersey; Amusement Parks of New York*

INTRODUCTION

Welcome to the first volume of *Legends: Pioneers of the Amusement Park Industry*, a new series by Ripley Publishing that pays tribute to the greatest of the great - those who made the amusement park industry what it is today. I think you'll agree that this first collection of Living Legends is really an innovative and interesting grouping.

To kick off the series, I have chosen 10 larger than life characters whom I have had the privilege of knowing for at least 15 years. Interviewing them for this book was more like talking with old friends than conducting a formal interview. As a veteran photojournalist in the amusement industry, I had the opportunity to interview these guys long before they had reached legendary status.

The first time I met them, they were just hard working men who had been around for a long time and were successful in what they were doing. They were pioneers, yes, but becoming a legend was the last thing any of them had on their mind. They had too much work to do.

One factor all 10 had in common as they blazed their respective pioneering trails was there were no road maps to follow. They did it their way with gut instincts leading the charge. They learned as they went, and yes, they made mistakes, but amazingly few. All somehow possessed an innate skill and a clear vision for what they were attempting and where they were headed. Maybe that's why they are now considered legends.

Buzz Price had no data bank to refer to when he conducted the original feasibility study for Disneyland or when he directed Walt to the location in Anaheim where the park was built. **Ron Toomer** had no g-force numbers or more than a basic knowledge of friction when he left the space industry and joined Arrow Development Company to design the world's first Runaway Mine Train roller coaster for Six Flags Over Texas. He had never ridden a coaster until he designed and built one.

When you read the chapter on the Father of the Waterpark Industry **George Millay**, you'll not only become acquainted with this remarkable man personally, but you'll learn of his amazing visionary skills that led to the creation of three SeaWorld marine parks, Magic Mountain theme park, and seven Wet'n Wild waterparks. You'll read of **Harold Chance's** pioneering journey through life as you also learn the history of Chance

Rides, a ground-breaking American ride manufacturer and one of the most prolific ride builders ever.

You'll discover how **Carl Hughes** of Kennywood Park became the first non family member to reach top management at the park and at the same time you'll be treated to a short primer on the history of the International Assn. of Amusement Parks & Attractions (IAAPA), the group that Hughes helped develop into the world's largest amusement industry trade association.

To most, **John Graff** is known as the now-retired top official of the IAAPA; but few know of his pioneering efforts in theme park law and contract work when in the early 1970s he became the first lawyer for the parks division of the Marriott Corporation. **Dr. Roberto Ortiz,** a physician in Costa Rica raised funds to create that country's first modern theme park as an on-going revenue generator for the country's largest children's hospital that he built 17 years earlier. Today, the park contributes nearly $300,000 a year to the operating funds of the hospital.

Marty Sklar, who started working for Walt Disney four weeks before Disneyland opened in California in 1955, has attended the opening of and contributed to the creation of all 11 Disney parks worldwide. His creative instincts and managerial skills took him to the top rung of the Walt Disney Imagineers, where he has worked for more than 50 years.

You'll meet **Bo Kinntorph,** the affable Swede from Liseberg Park who was the first non-American president of IAAPA and who is widely recognized as the one who made the IAAPA the truly inter-national organization it is today. **Jeff Henry,** from the family who created and still owns the Schlitterbahn waterpark resorts, took his "crazy ideas" and became one of the world's most productive and creative waterpark ride builders and park designers in the history of the waterpark industry.

This group of pioneers is an amazing lot. At the time of publication, all but George Millay are still alive. We lost George in February 2006 to a battle with cancer. Buzz Price is the oldest at 85, coming in two months older than Carl Hughes and four months older than Harold Chance. Jeff Henry is the youngest at 51.

My approach to the writing of these industry celebrities is casual, somewhat whimsical and at times a bit irreverent. The style I chose follows more of an oral history approach than the traditional biblio-graphic style. It was the best way to communicate the colors, quirks and personalities of this particular group.

When I started this project, I thought it would be a breeze to locate and interview the guys – after all, most of them have retired or have slowed down. Surely they would have ample time to talk with me. Boy was I wrong. I soon learned that catching up with the "older generation" wasn't as easy as it sounds. Time after time I would call only to find out from their wives that (Insert Name) was either out back in their home workshop, at the doctor or was taking a nap. I was always informed of a specific time I could call back. However I soon learned their schedules and all is well. Thanks for reading and I hope you enjoy!

Tim O'Brien,
VP Publishing & Communications
Ripley Entertainment Inc.
October 2006

ANOAUITB

(A NOTE ON ACRONYMS USED IN THIS BOOK)

The amusement industry loves its acronyms and this book is overflowing with them. Here's a primer on some you'll find inside:

AIMS – Amusement Industry Manufacturing & Suppliers International
AREA – American Recreation Equipment Assn.
ERA – Economics Research Associates
HPC – Harrison Price Company
HBJ – Harcourt Brace Jovanovich
IAAPA – International Assn. of Amusement Parks & Attractions
OABA – Outdoor Amusement Business Assn.
PRC – Planning Research Corporation
SLA – Showmen's League of America
SRI – Stanford Research Institute
TEA – Themed Entertainment Assn.
WDI – Walt Disney Imagineering
WED – Walter Elias Disney Enterprises
WWA – World Waterpark Assn.

GEORGE MILLAY

"I love to eat fish, but fishing bores me.
I caught a fish once, that's enough."

Most people consider themselves lucky if they have one tremendous idea during their lifetime. George Millay was full of tremendous ideas and he cashed in on nearly all of them.

No one other than George can lay claim to the invention of two major types of theme parks - the modern marine park and the waterpark - each a major industry in itself. Today, nearly 200 million people visit a marine park or a waterpark each year worldwide – as a result of George's vision and tenacity. U.S. waterparks alone attract nearly 70 million people annually.

Following a successful restaurant career that made him a millionaire, he sold his stock and created SeaWorld in San Diego in 1964, the first themed sea life park. He built two more SeaWorld parks, in Ohio and Florida before being forced to resign from the company in 1974. He then went to work on his next big idea, a new concept that only he could envision at the time, a pay-one-price park full of water rides, attractions, pools and slides. In 1977, he opened Wet'n Wild, the world's first waterpark. It premiered in Orlando, a few miles down International Drive from SeaWorld, a park which George built just four years earlier.

Before selling the company to Universal in 1998, he had built a total of seven Wet'n Wild parks, including four international parks. In addition to the SeaWorld and Wet'n Wild parks, he created the Magic Mountain amusement park in Valencia, Calif. in 1971, as a part of the

The MILLAY File

GEORGE DANIEL MILLAY

Born: July 4, 1929 in San Diego at 11 p.m.

Died: Feb. 6, 2006

Married: Anne Reul, January 1963

Children: Patrick, Garrick, Chrislyn, & Gavin

Education: San Francisco's St. Ignatius High School, 1947; Naval aerographer school, Lakehurst, N.J., 1948; UCLA with BS in meteorology, 1955

Claim to fame: Created two genres of theme parks – the modern themed sea-life park and the waterpark. During his career he conceptualized and then helped design and build three SeaWorld parks; California's Magic Mountain theme park; FunSphere family entertainment center; and seven Wet'n Wild waterparks. He is the unchallenged Father of the Waterpark industry.

Mentor: David Tallichet, his partner in the Reef Restaurant. "During the time I spent with Dave, I learned the skills needed to approach bankers and to make a deal. He taught me how to work with city managers and commissioners and he taught me the skills of being a promoter and developer, all of which made it possible for me to create SeaWorld."

Being a pioneer: "Yes, I do see myself as a pioneer, but the feeling is mixed. I see a lot of pioneers as losers. Poor creative wretches who had great ideas but fate and good common sense weren't with them. I have been lucky."

Favorite saying: From Shakespeare, "Our doubts are our traitors and make us lose the good we oft might win by fearing to attempt."

George's personal motto: ILLEGITIMI NON CARBORUNDUM – Don't let the bastards grind you down.

Favorite show creation at SeaWorld: The Sea Maids production in the Theatre of the Sea pavilion at SeaWorld California. "It was beautiful, innovative, very calming to watch, and very, very popular with the guests."

First big payday: In 1968 when Specialty Restaurants (of which the Reef Restaurant was then a part) went public. "I took home a check for nearly $2 million. On the plane flying home, I kept pulling out the check and staring at it. I couldn't believe my good fortune."

Awards and kudos: International Assn. of Amusement Parks & Attractions Hall of Fame, 1994; World Waterpark Assn. Hall of Fame, 2000; Themed Entertainment Assn. Lifetime Achievement Award, 2003; World Waterpark Assn. Lifetime Achievement Award, 2004; proclamation officially declaring him Father of the Waterpark Industry from the World Waterpark Assn., 2004.

SeaWorld group, and in 1993, he created FunSphere, a hybrid family entertainment center next to his Wet'n Wild park in Arlington, Texas.

In 1994, he was inducted into the IAAPA Hall of Fame and in 2000, he was voted into the World Waterpark Assn. (WWA) Hall of Fame, the only person to make it into both of those prestigious Halls of Fame. However, the most significant kudo he ever received came in 2004 when the WWA bestowed upon him the official designation - "Father of the Waterpark Industry."

George Millay was a true pioneer in two major genres of outdoor entertainment and he learned everything the hard way – by trial and error. That's how pioneers do it. There was no one for him to turn to for answers; there was no one out there to copy.

The man tagged as having one of the most creative brains in the amusement park industry, died on Feb. 6, 2006 from complications of lung cancer. It was one of the few battles he lost in his lifetime.

Born in the USA

George joined the world on July 4, 1929, a true Yankee Doodle Dandy by anybody's standards. His mother was an Irish immigrant, his father a WWI Navy veteran. He was born in San Diego, moved to San Francisco, and when his father was called out of retirement and shipped off to Pearl Harbor, George and his family followed.

He was walking to church the morning of Dec. 7, 1942, a day he always remembered, a day that formed a decades-long sense of mistrust, even hatred at times, for the Japanese. "I saw the attacks, the explosions and afterward, I saw the pain and suffering of those involved. It hurt me deeply," George recalled. "That mistrust mellowed over the years and I gained an admiration for their culture and organizational skills. Through the years, I've had many successful business dealings with the Japanese and spent a great deal of time in that country."

Within three months of the attack, George, his brother and mother moved back to San Francisco where he graduated from high school. He followed in his father's footsteps and served in the Navy, returned back to California and worked his way through UCLA, where his true entre-preneurial skills were honed.

A $300 loan from his father helped George buy an old dump truck while in college and by using his fraternity brothers as laborers, he built up a lucrative part time business. Things went so well, he purchased another truck and with his fleet of two made a great deal of money – for a college kid. "I was Mr. Big Time and I actually considered staying in the trucking business," George said. Instead, he had a short lived career as a bond and mutual fund salesman and then as a stockbroker.

During the planning and construction of
the world's first SeaWorld in San Diego,
George sported a dandy mustache, which he shaved the
day his first son was born in December 1963.

George Meets His Mentor

While cold calling one day searching for new accounts, he met a
man who would change his life forever, David Tallichet, who George
considered to be his mentor. Tallichet was a hotel manager with dreams
of owning his own restaurant but didn't have the money. George assured
him that if the idea and business plan were good, money could always
be found. It wasn't long before Tallichet delivered both and challenged
George to raise the money. Less than a year later, in August 1958, the
two opened the 4,000 square foot Hawaiian-themed Reef Restaurant in
the Port of Long Beach, California. The restaurant was a huge success

from the day it opened and thanks to its success, George made his first million dollars. If it had not been for that successful restaurant, it is doubtful there would have ever been a SeaWorld or a Wet'n Wild.

He always looked back on the time of planning and financing of the Reef as "the kindergarten" of a life of creativity. "I think meeting Dave Tallichet was the luckiest thing that ever happened to me." Several years later when George left to build SeaWorld, Tallichet used the Reef as the mothership of a hugely successful restaurant chain - Specialty Restaurants.

The Seed is Planted for SeaWorld

A failed attempt at building a "submarine bar" at the Reef Restaurant seeded the SeaWorld concept. George had thought an underwater bar, with big windows and great views of the fish would be a good addition to the Reef. He consulted with Kenny Norris, then curator of both fish and mammals at Marineland in Palos Verdes, north of Los Angeles. Poor visibility in the waters of Long Beach Harbor proved to be an issue and the idea was scrapped. Norris then shared with George his own dream of "building a little marine park."

That casual reference piqued George's interest and it led to questioning Norris about the marine park business. Once he looked at the research Norris gathered, George was even more excited. He called Norris and asked him if he still wanted to build a park in San Diego and when he said he did, George said, "OK, let's build one." During initial talks with San Diego officials, he discovered the city had been making overtures to several developers to build something similar on Mission Bay.

Within six months of George and Norris coming up with the idea for a marine park, the city of San Diego put out a request for proposals for a marine park, and George and his assembled team submitted one of the three tendered.

Throughout his life, George always had the knack of knowing when he needed help and had a talent of being able to surround himself with the right people to get the job done. Realizing he needed assistance on this major project, he brought two fraternity brothers into the fold. To help in financing and projecting cash needs, Milton Shedd was asked to join. Dave DeMotte was brought on board as secretary-treasurer and numbers man.

George started dating his future wife, Anne Reul on a casual basis while he was putting the finishing touches on the Reef Restaurant. While they were dating, but before moving permanently to San Diego to work on SeaWorld, George would make the drive from Long Beach to San Diego, sometimes several times a week, on business errands for

Paine Webber, a company for which he continued to work during the Reef Restaurant days.

On one of those day trips to San Diego, Anne rode along with George to keep him company and they started talking about his dreams for a marine park and that he would soon be moving to San Diego. That meant a long distance romance between the two, something neither wanted, so they decided to get married, a ceremony that took place in 1963, a year before SeaWorld opened.

The Boys Won the Competition

The team of Millay, Mott and Shedd won the right to build the marine park and in doing so, was given one of the first commercial land leases ever on Mission Bay, in a city park on the southern end of the bay. The deal for the 21 acres called for a lease payment of $35,900 for the first year, escalating to $43,800 for year three and beyond. In addition, the park would pay the city 2.5% on all gross admission revenues, 3% on all food and beverage sales, and 7% on all other revenues.

Within two months of winning the right to build the park, George left Paine Webber to devote his full time efforts on SeaWorld. Financially, he was doing OK and was still getting nearly $130,000 a year out of the Reef Restaurant, enough of a cushion that he didn't have to worry if his marine park project didn't pan out.

The architects at Moffatt and Nichol, the same ones who helped George on the unsuccessful submarine bar idea, were initially contracted to help George create a vision for the marine park. Norris, George

Legend on a Legend

"George Millay taught me what to do as well as what not to do. In the big picture he had it right!"

JEFF HENRY, PIONEERING WATERPARK DESIGNER
AND RIDE MANUFACTURER (PROFILED ON PAGE 235)

and the team from Moffatt and Nichol all struggled to come up with a concept. They went down a number of paths. At first, they thought SeaWorld would be a boat tour with guests using a 50-passenger boat to go from one animal habitat to another, but as planning continued, it became clear that if the park received the number of guests it needed to make it financially, transporting the guests on boats would be a logistical nightmare.

George and Anne Reul on one of their first dates at the
Coconut Grove in Los Angeles in 1961. They married in early 1963.

George had many ideas on what the park could look like, but it was his future wife Anne who helped him focus. If anything, she over analyzed everything and would pull no punches when telling him what she thought. She was a ying to his yang. She notes that he never got upset with her questions or thoughts. "He would always let me roll until his interest flagged and he had already gone quickly onto the next subject, which of course happened all the time," Anne laughs.

John Moffatt, a senior partner with the firm, became quite interested in the park and saw early on that the planning was floundering for a

"C'MON OUT, HENRY! THAT WASN'T MR. MILLAY...
BESIDES... YOUR HAIR'S NOT THAT LONG!"

**This cartoon jokes about George's no-tolerance policy
against male employees wearing long hair.**

direction. He felt the project needed new, more creative energy and introduced George to Ben Southland, the senior partner and senior planner for Victor Gruen Associates, the second largest architectural firm in the world at that time. Southland took on the project and his firm was given the task of designing the park and refining the vision. Money became more important than ever at this point. Total financing wasn't in place and George was still funding the entire project, and a man of Southland's reputation didn't come cheaply. By this time George had already invested nearly $70,000 of his own money.

Never a fan of architects, George always said finding Ben Southland was a lucky happening. "He's one of the few architects I have liked in my life," he said. "Maybe out of 100 architects I've known, I've gotten along with five or six of them, and in general, I'm not a big fan of architects."

Neither was Walt Disney. During a visit to SeaWorld in 1966, Disney made a comment to George about the park's need of a new pool area and a bigger stadium. George told him he already had architects working on it. Disney stopped walking, grabbed George's arm and looked directly at him and said. "Remember one thing, there's nothing more dangerous in this world than an unsupervised architect. Stick your nose in and keep it in there!"

Little by Little, a Vision Emerges

Slowly, Southland and his team started coming up with a design, consisting of acres of gardens and strategically placed unique buildings that would house the shows and exhibits. George is quick to give credit for most of the original design ideas to Norris and Southland, including the ponds, the flowing rivers, waterfalls and rockwork – the elements for which SeaWorld San Diego is famous.

In the beginning, raising money was tough, but between Shedd and George, more than $1 million was raised before they hit a wall. George became worried. Construction was set to start in less than a year and all approved loans were dependent of getting a specific amount of equity, which they didn't have. Shedd eventually was responsible for raising half the equity, but George became frustrated and Shedd's contacts were tapped out. SeaWorld was an unknown, and themed marine parks were a new, unknown and unproven concept.

Once again, as He would do many times over a 40-year period, God smiled down on George. Marineland, which had been a privately-held corporation, decided to go public and put out a prospectus showing that the park was a goldmine. Armed with that information, Shedd and George trekked back to potential investors and within 45 days, all financing for SeaWorld was in place.

Living With George

"It's like living with a moving storm, thunder and lightning included."

ANNE MILLAY ON WHAT IT WAS LIKE
LIVING WITH HUSBAND GEORGE
FOR 43 YEARS.

SeaWorld was built and opened for approximately $3.5 million and the first year was a disaster, both operationally and financially.

A pre-opening feasibility study projected 400,000 visitors the first year. Only 200,000 came and the park lost $400,000.

Business was quite tenuous that first year and many times George had to dig deep into his own pockets to make payroll. He took no salary from SeaWorld during its construction or the first year of its operation, depending totally on his checks from the Reef Restaurant to support his family.

The Shows

George was involved in all facets of the creation of the park and signed off on everything. He took special interest in the shows. "I knew shows were going to be very important, something that set us apart and above all other aquariums and sea life parks," George said. "We knew if we wanted return business year in and year out, we needed to come up with something new and appealing at regular intervals that would also fit into our water and sea theme." One of his favorite show concepts was the SeaWorld Sea Maids. It was one of the original shows and made its debut on the park's opening day, March 21, 1964.

Brutal but Loyal

"George was brutal in his management style but he was relentless and totally blind in his loyalty and his friendship."

GARY ZUERCHER,
RIDE MANUFACTURER

The Theater of the Sea was architecturally unique and seated 1,200 people who all faced a large four-sided glass tank. The production in that facility starred four Sea Maids, two dolphins and one seal. The entire show took place under water and was seen from all four sides, making it a challenge for the producers. The 22-minute scripted show with music and special lighting was a success from the start and being a Sea Maid at SeaWorld quickly became the choice job for young ladies. Each day from four to 10 times, depending on the crowds, the girls entertained guests from inside the large tank.

George conceived the Sea Maid idea after watching the mermaids at Florida's Weeki Wachee Springs, the only other location where a similar show was produced. Unlike the mermaids, the Sea Maids wore masks and had small air tanks attached to their waists. "I also insisted the show be staged indoors where we could control not only the weather, but the water quality as well," George noted.

George, at right, escorted Walt Disney through SeaWorld in 1964, the park's first year.

The Peacock Fiasco

His attempts at creating unique shows weren't always successful. Take for instance what has become known in the SeaWorld annals of history as the peacock fiasco. George went to Japan and observed a production in which kimono-clad Japanese women each walked peacocks to the top of a mountain peak and at a designated time, released the peacocks, which then flew back down the hill and landed in front of the crowds, all choreographed to a music track. George was excited and came back with the idea to do something similar at SeaWorld.

He told Frank Todd, his top bird guy, about the show and one morning before most of the employees had arrived at the park, George had Todd take three peacocks to the top of the sky tower while five members of the top management team gathered at the base. George wanted them to see for themselves the beauty he saw in watching flying peacocks.

George and Dave DeMotte display a $500,000 check from Newhall Land and Farming Company, a partial payment for construction work at Magic Mountain, November 1970.

"Release the peacocks," George yelled up to Todd. All three of them dropped like rocks. They hit the ground at the feet of the executives and all died instantly. Bob Gault, now a top executive at Universal Studios Florida, was working at SeaWorld when this happened. He recalls

George's reaction to the fiasco as one of the funniest things he has ever seen. According to Gault, George just stood there looking down at the birds shaking his head. "Gee, it didn't look like that in Japan," George softly noted.

Twenty years later at a dinner party attended by several of those who had witnessed the peacock drop, George brought the subject up. "To this day I can't figure out why the peacock act worked in Japan but it didn't work here," George said to the group in casual conversation. Former SeaWorld executive Jan Schultz started laughing and explained to George that Todd had clipped the wings of the peacocks. "He sacrificed those three so he wouldn't have to have dozens of peacocks performing that show four or five times a day," Schultz told him. "If I had known that at the time," George recalled, "I would have fired his ass on the spot."

With a Little Help from the Disney Guys

The name SeaWorld was born at Disneyland Hotel in Anaheim, Calif., but George was always quick to point out that the concept was born in the minds of three people: George Millay, Ken Norris, and Ben Southland. Disneyland's marketing director Ed Ettinger, who also served, with Walt's blessing, as a SeaWorld consultant, met with George at the hotel to go over several things, including a name. "He thought SeaWorld was the most descriptive and the easiest to recognize and remember," George recalled. "I liked it and jumped on it, applying for federal and state registration immediately and quickly developed our first logo."

Creative Guy!

"George Millay will go down in history next to Walt Disney as the most creative person ever in our industry."

LARRY COCHRAN, FORMER
SIX FLAGS PRESIDENT

George said Walt Disney's permission to tap into the minds of many of his top executives was not only generous, but very beneficial. The seeds of many of George's original concepts and ideas came from his unofficial consultants at Disney. "Walt visited the park twice and on both times, he was immediately recognized and mobbed by the crowds. He always was eager to share ideas with me and to tell me the truth about what he thought of our park. The last time he visited, he came over to our house for dinner and my little son, Patrick, was in his highchair and spilled stuff on Walt, and Walt just laughed. What a humble man he was," George noted.

The Arrival of an Icon

In early 1965, George took a call that led to the acquisition of Shamu, one of the most powerful theme park icons of all times. The young female killer whale had been caught in a net in Puget Sound, near Seattle, and Ted Griffin, who had caught her, called George after his failed attempt to sell the whale to Marineland. No other Orca had ever lived long in captivity and it was believed that it was too dangerous to keep one. George struck a deal that would give Griffin $25,000 on delivery and another $10,000 if she lived for a year. Of course, the rest is history. Not only did George and his team's pioneering efforts keep Shamu alive, but made it possible that now, more than 40 years later, captive killer whales live and breed in captivity throughout the world.

It's not easy being a pioneer, as George and his team would attest. Virtually everything they did, from the design of the park, to the transportation of Shamu, was being done for the first time. Successes during those early years far outweighed the failures, as they always did for George. A chapter on his failures, tragedies and disappointments would be a short one.

Hair: An Important Issue

When it came to hair length on a man, George was about as traditional and mainstream as a businessman could be. He admired Walt's successful operation and he strongly supported the strict dress code at Disneyland. SeaWorld opened with a strict - some called it draconian - dress code. Stories of George's run-in with "long hairs" are legendary. If he saw hair on an employee that he thought was too long, he would approach the young man, hand him a couple dollars and tell him to go get a haircut and not come back until he did. After a while, too many people were missing too much work, going off property to get a haircut.

As a result, the first barber shop in a theme park was built by George. A retired military barber, who was given the name "Nick" by the employees because of his shaking hands and bad cut jobs, was hired and haircuts were initially given free to anyone who needed one. Once Nick's reputation was known and once employees realized they had no choice but to conform to the hair laws set forth by George, or go visit Nick, the number of hair infractions decreased significantly.

SeaWorld Expands to Ohio

One sunny San Diego afternoon in 1967, George received a call from Earl Gascoigne, VP marketing at Cedar Point, Sandusky, Ohio. He said the park's owners, Emile Legros and George Roose wanted to have George visit the park, see the area and to consider building a SeaWorld in Northern Ohio.

George liked the idea, but didn't like the area the Cedar Point executives had pitched for the park. By mid-1968, he had found land that he liked in Aurora, Ohio, south of Cleveland and worked out a deal to purchase part of the acreage next to Geauga Lake, adjacent to the

Dad's Quite the Guy

"He was an over-achiever. Whenever he entered a room, he was usually the most intelligent man in there. My dad was extremely smart, but he also had the guts to pursue things in life. He acted on what he wanted and was an amazing risk taker."

GAVIN MILLAY, SON

GEORGE MILLAY, 1965.

Geauga Lake amusement park, then owned by Gascoigne and several other former Cedar Point executives.

Harrison "Buzz" Price was hired to conduct the feasibility study, all the permits were acquired, and construction began. The process of getting the Ohio park built was a bit easier than getting the San Diego park on its feet. The construction, most of which took place in the dead of winter, was a challenge to Ron Harper, head of construction who had joined the SeaWorld team in 1968, but the park opened on time.

Ron Harper, right, head of construction, and George, flank Florida Governor Rubin Askew during a visit to Tallahassee in early 1973 to discuss the opening of SeaWorld Florida. Gar Millay, left, and Jeff Harper, in front, went along to meet the governor.

Price, who had conducted the original studies on Disneyland, had projected that first year attendance in Ohio would be 550,000. The park opened on Memorial Day 1970, and by the time Shamu had made her final jump that season, 1.1 million visitors had packed the park.

George said that first year could only be considered a phenomenal success and it far exceeded all projections. To handle the unexpected crowds, portable toilets had to be brought in, the Shamu Show had to be presented 10 times a day instead of five, the restaurants kept running out of food and beverage, and plans to expand were put on the front burner.

A Mountain of a Challenge

As SeaWorld Ohio was being built, and as SeaWorld executives were talking about building a third park in Orlando, Fla., George was visiting with Ben Southland and mentioned that one of his executives was hot on building a theme park based on rides, not marine life. Southland knew of a company with a huge expanse of land in the north of the San Fernando Valley, in Valencia, just north of Los Angeles that was looking for partners to help develop their acreage.

Southland introduced George to Tom Lowe, CEO of the Newhall Land and Farming Company, a wealthy land, cattle and oil company. SeaWorld had a great name and reputation by then and wherever George or his executives went, they were treated with respect. With that reputation preceding him, George didn't have to sell himself or the company to Lowe. Within a short time, the two had struck up a deal and selected the property on which to build a ride park.

It was a 50-50 partnership. Each partner put up $2 million and with that $4 million in equity, Newhall Land and Farming had the responsibility to raise the additional $18 million needed to build the park. In the end, it cost nearly $25 million to open Magic Mountain, now owned by Six Flags.

The renowned Los Angeles park designer and industry legend, Randall Duell, along with his design team of project architects, including Ira West (who later took over the company upon Duell's death), were sent to the property to design the park. Buzz Price conducted the feasibility study, and Doc Lemmon, a former GM at Cedar Point, was hired as the first GM of Magic Mountain. Cost overruns, construction and ride delivery delays, as well as office politics, hampered the development of the park.

One certainly won't find details of Magic Mountain's opening weekend in a scholarly dissertation entitled "How to Open an Amusement Park." On opening day three of the major rides weren't operating, the landscaping wasn't completed, there wasn't enough shade, there was a shortage of working water fountains, the parking lot wasn't large enough and thousands were turned away from the grand opening party to which they were invited.

Jan Schultz, Magic Mountain's VP of marketing during construction, said that on opening day, "basically there was not enough of anything in the park, except for people." He had recommended that the opening be delayed until the park was ready, but officials insisted on opening it on May 29, 1971, a date that had been set months before.

Magic Mountain Gets an Unkind Moniker

On opening day, the entertainment editor of the *Los Angeles Times,* along with his wife, showed up to do a story on the park. They were escorted onto the Funicular that would take them to the top of the mountain and give them a panorama of the park. About half way up the mountain, the Funicular came to an abrupt stop and said reporter tumbled to the floor breaking his leg. It took emergency crews nearly an hour to get him down and into the ambulance. His wife planned to follow in her car, but when she went to where they had parked, she realized it had been stolen.

George missed opening day because he was in Ohio watching the much bally-hooed water ski show make its premier at SeaWorld on the opening day of that park's second season. Informed of the fiasco at Magic Mountain, he could only shake his head. Everyone waited for the story to appear in the paper. A week later it did. The reporter wrote: "The owners call in Magic Mountain. It should really be called Tragic Mountain."

Imagine spending nearly a half-million dollars to promote the opening of a $25 million park and have the entire world laughingly call it Tragic Mountain within a week of opening. The nickname stuck, mostly within the company.

For many reasons, not just from the bad press, Magic Mountain didn't do well during its first season, losing nearly $800,000. By the end of 1971, George and the SeaWorld board knew they needed to get out of Tragic Mountain. A deal was struck, giving SeaWorld back its initial $2 million investment and an additional $1 million over a five-year period. "Needless to say, we were delighted to get out of Magic Mountain with our shirts," George said. Little could he have realized at the time, but that Magic Mountain debacle was the beginning of the end of his career at SeaWorld. Board chairman Milt Shedd, a member of the original SeaWorld team and George's fraternity brother, started discussing his doubts about George with other board members and they in turn began to see that George Millay was not omnipotent. The drama of George's demise played out in the boardroom less than six months later.

Shamu & George Head to Florida

While the development action was taking place at Magic Mountain and SeaWorld Ohio was packing them in, George was dedicating most of his time to the new SeaWorld Florida in Orlando. First, he made what he called "one hell of a good deal" on the property. "We bought 100 acres for $2,000 an acre and got an option on an additional 10 acres for 10 years at $10,000 an acre," George recalled.

George the Teacher

"George taught me the fundamentals of the theme park business. His ethics were always strong and he had a heart as big as Texas. Under that rough exterior was also a guy with a heart of gold."

BOB GAULT, PRESIDENT, UNIVERSAL ORLANDO

"By the time we approached the SeaWorld Florida project, we were the class of the industry and we could hire anybody we wanted and as a result, we assembled one hell of a team," he said, noting that the best part of this project was that they were starting with a big, flat palmetto field and were able to master plan it properly right from the beginning.

Construction crews began falling behind almost immediately and it wasn't long before a great deal of acrimony was taking place on the labor side with the sub-contractors. One major problem was the expectation of SeaWorld officials on how long it should take to get things done. The difference between the work ethic of Florida workers and the workers in Ohio became the problem. It's hot and humid in Florida and the speed in which things get accomplished in construction is much slower than in the Northern states. The difference created a "huge frustration level" during construction for George, who couldn't understand why things couldn't move faster.

On Dec. 21, 1973, at 10 a.m., SeaWorld Florida opened to the public. Because of the colder-than-normal winter that year, attendance for the first several months was terrible. Total gate count for the first year was 800,000 people against a projection of one million.

Keeping His Customer's Cool While Losing His

It was during the construction of SeaWorld Florida, during those hot, humid days, that George first started thinking of a water-oriented family leisure park concept. "Anyone who goes to Central Florida in the middle of summer and walks around on hot asphalt for a couple of hours soon realizes there must be a better way to be entertained. It had me thinking," he said.

Once George realized that the heat would be a potential problem with his SeaWorld guests, he decided it would be a nice touch to air condition the outdoor stadiums, which added another $4 million to the construction price, causing the total cost of the project to come close to $27 million.

Made in the Shade

"Nobody should ever say they have it made, if they do they're not too bright."

GEORGE MILLAY

Shedd didn't like the additional expenditures and continued planting doubts in the board's mind about George's ability to lead the company.

The conditions of the time were not kind to George's reputation as a big spender. The park opened in the middle of nation-wide gas rationing. Family auto trips as well as commercial airline flights were cut back due to the gasoline and jet fuel shortage and Florida tourism tanked as a result. Disney World severely felt the pressures as well.

During the same period, interest rates grew beyond belief. When George first borrowed the money for the Florida facility, he borrowed at 8% interest. It was at 14% by the time the park opened. The higher rates meant additional interest payments of nearly $750,000 per year.

"I don't think we had projected more than a million dollars a year in profits for the first couple of years, so it was a dangerous thing that was going on, a real dangerous thing," he said.

SeaWorld stock dropped from $63 to $30 per share during the same period. Everything combined only fueled Shedd's claim that the company needed an accountant and money man at the helm, not a "creative" guy. George said his "perceived" reputation for big spending was absolutely not true, noting that sometimes he had to spend more money because, "I never wanted to do anything unless we did it right. We needed to present something to the public that was well designed, well maintained and original. Sometimes to do that it involves money that you just can't accurately project."

Shamu is treated to a drink, courtesy of George and Chimp, in 1967.

George Ousted from His Own Creation

The board's first move against George was in November 1973, a month before the park's opening. His activities were curtailed and he was forced to report to various directors before spending or creating nearly anything. By early February (1974), the board had "promoted" George to chairman, effectively taking him out of the day-to-day decision-making process. In the meeting in which George was promoted, Dave DeMotte, another SeaWorld founder and former fraternity brother, became president. George said he quickly saw where the meeting was heading and got up and left. "I was stunned, shaken, confused and really pissed off," he recalled. "I owned more stock than anybody on the board and here they voted me out of there." He had lost his power and his control of the company and only went back to the park once after that February meeting.

Three months later, a week before the May board meeting, George sent Shedd a letter officially resigning from a chairmanship he had never accepted in the first place. That action officially closed the doors, and at that point, George Millay, the founder and most of the brains behind the SeaWorld concept, was no longer a part of the company he had created.

Giving up his $60,000 annual salary, his car and his insurance was difficult for this high rolling executive. Those were tough times in the world and he sensed there were going to be tough times ahead for him as well. He didn't know where he was going or what he was going to do. All he knew for sure was that he wanted no part of the organization that no longer believed in him and his dreams.

Top of the Line

"George was a creative, brilliant guy. You don't have to go too far down the list from Walt Disney to get to George Millay. Yeah, you can throw P.T. Barnum in there, and you can throw Henry Ford in, but George will always be in the top five!"

JAN SCHULTZ, RETIRED SEAWORLD EXECUTIVE
AND LONG TIME FRIEND AND EMPLOYEE OF GEORGE

He was bitter and he was hurt and it was another 30 years before he ever entered another SeaWorld park. He walked through the gates again in September 2004 when he returned to the original SeaWorld in San Diego to promote "The Wave Maker," his biography that was to be released later that month.

George Creates the World's First Waterpark

Fast forward to late spring 1974. George is out of SeaWorld, has rested well and is in a fresh creative state of mind. He's germinating ideas for what is to soon become the world's first waterpark.

It was a brand new concept, one never tried before and there were many questions to be answered. What should a gated water recreation facility consist of? What would it entail? How much of a critical mass of attractions would need to be created to attract the hundreds of thousands of paying customers needed? Would people pay money to go swimming? Those were just a few of the unknowns that pioneering George had to ponder and he loved every minute of it.

The water attraction idea he first conceived during the hot, humid Central Florida summer while building SeaWorld kept coming back to George. He had developed a few ideas, but he was still several attractions short of having a critical mass, one for which he could sell a one-price ticket. Orlando was his choice to build such a facility, the closer to Walt Disney World the better, he thought.

On a family vacation during the summer of 1974, George spotted a gunite water flume at a campground in Placerville, Calif., and when he saw how much the kids were enjoying it he knew water slides had to be one of his park's elements. In August 1974, he was told of a new concept called a wave pool that had been built in Decatur, Ala. The next day he was in that wave pool, having fun and by the end of that day, he realized he had found the key missing star element he needed. He already had ideas for slides and a variety of pools and he knew he would need some sort of children's water oriented playground.

After leaving SeaWorld, George set up office in his boat at the dock in front of his penthouse condo on Mission Bay in San Diego. He would often walk to his office in the morning in his pajamas with a cup of coffee in one hand. He hired architect George Walsh, the designer of two of the SeaWorld parks to help with the design, and brought on board Bill Dunn as mechanical engineer. The three created rough drawings of what George thought a waterpark should be. Don Stewart of Buzz Price's company, Economics Research Associates, conducted the feasibility study for the new park concept.

John Shawen, a former Disney financial planner was the first full time employee of the company that would become Wet'n Wild. He went to work for $1,500 a month and a promise that if the park was built, he would get at least 2% of the deal to start with. To put that deal in perspective, when George sold Wet'n Wild to Universal in 1998, Shawen became an instant millionaire. George said of Shawen, "He was my right hand, keeping me orderly. He has a very disciplined mind, and he was good for me to talk with because he's the exact opposite of me. He was perfect for the job."

Between 1974 and 1976, George sold off about a third of his SeaWorld stock in order to finance his waterpark dreams. Before a single investor stepped forward, George had nearly $500,000 of his own money in the project. He spent night and day thinking, dreaming and getting excited about his new concept, which in a way, probably saved his life. He remained very bitter and embarrassed about the SeaWorld situation, but his mind was now refocused. "I didn't shed any tears but I lost many a good night's sleep for a couple years. Had I not been blessed with the ability to get Wet'n Wild going and have it be successful, I think I would have been a very sorry, bitter man for the rest of my life," he said. The creation of and the quick success of Wet'n Wild was a salve.

Goodbye George, My Friend

"Tonight as I eat my corned beef and cabbage, I will send a nod to our unforgettable friend George Millay who proved without a doubt that the Irish make the best of friends."

HARRISON "BUZZ" PRICE, ST*. PATRICK'S DAY, 2006, A POSTHUMOUS SALUTE TO HIS FRIEND GEORGE (PROFILED ON PAGE 119)

By early 1976, George had a concept, proposals, investors, proformas and feasibility studies. He also had an option on 17-acres on International Drive in Orlando, near SeaWorld. But he had no name for the park. Rollie Crump, another early hire, was the first one to put wet and wild together. Crump was sitting on the floor in the office and he started talking. "The thing is wet, yeah, and it's kind of wild." Everyone

George thanks Robert Goulet for singing the
National Anthem at the opening of Wet'n
Wild Las Vegas, 1985.

in the room looked up and liked the idea, but it was several months later as George was explaining the park to a prospective investor using Crump's explanation, that the name was officially tagged.

Turn on the Water!

Wet'n Wild Orlando, the world's first waterpark, was built for $3.5 million and opened in March 1977. Business was slow and officials knew almost immediately that the park's scope wasn't large enough. The number of elements and the entertainment value were not enough to give it the breadth and value to make it a standalone park. George went back to his investors and came up with enough to keep the park afloat, and after the successful second season, the park was off to the races!

In 1983, the second Wet'n Wild opened, in Arlington, Texas. Two years later, Wet'n Wild Las Vegas opened. George built FunSphere, a new family entertainment center next to the park in Arlington in 1993, and then through franchise agreements, built his first international waterpark in Cancun, Mexico in 1996, followed by three in Brazil – Salvador in 1996, Sao Paulo in 1997, and Rio de Janeiro which opened a year after George sold the company in 1999.

In spring 1998, George and his executives decided to put the company up for sale. He didn't actually put it on the market. Instead, thinking that SeaWorld would scoop them up immediately, he went to them first. George was flabbergasted when he received an immediate "no thanks" from them. He then called a more agreeable Universal Studios and within a week, a letter of intent was drafted. They shook hands on a deal in April, and the final papers weren't signed until September 30. The deal closed for $41 million, paid off in three equal distributions over a two-year period.

George as a Cancer Survivor

George survived three severe bouts with cancer during his life, but lost his fourth battle on Feb. 6, 2006. The first three operations left his face disfigured and cost him his right ear, his right eye, and most of his right cheek. His first operation was in 1978, the second in 1979, and the third, in October 2003. The last operation, the one that cost him his eye, took place on Oct. 6, 2003, two days after he received the Lifetime Achievement Award from the Themed Entertainment Assn. (TEA). Less than a month later, wearing a black eye patch, George was on a panel of industry legends at the IAAPA Convention & Trade Show in Orlando.

Legend on a Legend

"How will George be remembered? As an original. As a great entrepreneur. As someone with lots of guts who was willing to take great risks, and as a creative innovator. In many ways he was a throwback to a time in our business that we have moved away from, the days of P.T. Barnum."

MARTY SKLAR, FORMER CREATIVE HEAD OF WALT DISNEY IMAGINEERING (PROFILED ON PAGE 89)

In October 2004, he was honored with the Lifetime Achievement Award from the World Waterpark Assn., at its annual convention in Fort Lauderdale. George was the keynote speaker at that convention and along with his Lifetime Achievement Award, he was presented with a proclamation officially recognizing him as the "Father of the Waterpark Industry," a title that he had unofficially held for decades. George will hold that official distinction forever. There can be only one father.

George did not rest on his laurels after selling Wet'n Wild. He received a U.S. Patent in 2001 for Sea Venture, an underwater observation ride for aquariums. In 2003, he worked with Ripley Entertainment on an unsuccessful proposal to build an aquarium, restaurant and other attractions at the Port of San Diego.

In 2004 and 2005, George again worked with Ripley Entertainment to acquire the rights to a former military building in San Diego to build a Hispanic-themed dinner theater. The California Coastal Commission quelched that idea in mid-2005. The commission put such strong restrictions on the property that the planned attraction would not financially be feasible.

George had been diagnosed with lung cancer on April 5, 2005 and had undergone chemotherapy in mid summer as he and the Ripley team were creating the model for the dinner theater. He felt he would whip the cancer again and saw the collapse of the theater project as an opportunity to take a short break that would "give me a chance to get better" before jumping into another challenge. As the year waned, "he never outwardly admitted it, but I think he knew this one was going to get him," his son Pat noted.

He died in his sleep with the family at his bedside, in the home he and Anne had built on Mission Bay, less than a mile from SeaWorld.

BIBLIOGRAPHY

MOST OF WHAT APPEARS IN THIS CHAPTER ABOUT GEORGE MILLAY WAS TAKEN FROM "THE WAVE MAKER," MILLAY'S OFFICIAL BIOGRAPHY WRITTEN BY TIM O'BRIEN. FOR A DETAILED BIOGRAPHY OF SOURCES, CONSULT THE ACKNOWLEDGEMENTS LISTED IN THE BACK OF THAT BOOK. THE BIOGRAPHY WAS PUBLISHED IN 2004 BY RIPLEY PUBLISHING, AND IS WIDELY AVAILABLE FROM THE MAJOR INTERNET BOOK STORES.

ADDITIONAL INTERVIEWS
Interview with Anne Millay, by email, April 20, 2006
Interview with George Millay, by Tim O'Brien, Dec. 11, 2005
Interview with Pat Millay, by Tim O'Brien, March 22, 2006

Hall of Fame committee chairman Carl Hughes, left, presented George with his IAAPA Hall of Fame Living Legend award in November 1994.

PHOTO: TIM O'BRIEN

CARL HUGHES

*"I didn't get a pay raise but it was
a big title and I got a free drink."*

The first "Living Legend" inducted into the IAAPA Hall of Fame, Carl Hughes, was the first to cross many of the industry's thresholds. He learned most of what he knows from on-the-job training, and surprisingly was a top executive not born into the industry, a rarity during the era in which he rose to prominence.

Ironically, this legend didn't even step foot into an amusement park until he was 23 years old and was already writing press releases for Kennywood Park, near Pittsburgh, as a part time job.

Carl was a big-time sports reporter for the *Pittsburgh Press* and worked as Kennywood's lone publicist, writing and mailing press releases. He had no intention of giving up a good sports gig at the city's top paper to work at an amusement park.

One day in early 1956, Carl received a call from Brady McSwigan, Kennywood's president, offering him a full-time job. What McSwigan was offering was less than Carl was making at the newspaper combined with what he was bringing in for the part-time work at the park. Carl turned him down, saying he had a family to be concerned about and he wouldn't change jobs for that kind of money.

McSwigan called again a couple of weeks later, telling Carl he would match whatever he was making between the two jobs. "Brady," Carl recalls telling McSwigan, "I would be giving up a job I really love and would still be making the same amount of money. I don't mean to insult you but that offer is just not good enough."

Kennywood opened in May 1956 as it had for the previous eight years, with Carl as the part-time publicist. Several weeks into the 1956 season, Carl received yet another call from McSwigan early one evening. "Carl, what are you doing?" he asked.

"I was about to have dinner," Carl replied.

After dinner could you run out to the park? Carl (Henninger, then general manager/vice president) and I would like to talk with you," McSwigan explained.

Later that evening, Carl walked out of their office as the park's new assistant manager. "Nobody ever had that title before and nobody has had it since. I was a lone sales person in a one person office with nobody to manage, but the title sounded good," Carl laughed.

The HUGHES File

CARL OWENS HUGHES

Born: July 18, 1921, at home in South Fork, Pa.

Married: Anny Coleman, March 12, 1955

Children: 2 daughters, Mary Lou and Lynn

Education: Geneva College, Beaver Falls, Pa., degree in economics, 1943

Claim to fame: First non-owner to become president of IAAPA, 1974; first non-family member to head up Kennywood Park, 1975; first Living Inductee into the IAAPA Hall of Fame, 1990

Military: Army, 1946 & 1947. Stationed in the Phillipines at the Philrycom Printing Plant and Publishing Depot.

First industry job: Writing publicity releases for Kennywood Park, West Mifflin, Pa., 1948, while working full time as a sports reporter for *Pittsburgh Press*.

Full time in industry: May 1956, as assistant manager at Kennywood

Rise to the top: Became Kennywood GM, 1960; VP & GM, 1964; President, 1975; President & Chairman, 1985; Chairman only: 1990

Retired: 2000

Hobbies: "Reading has always been my hobby, but I never had time to read a great deal until I retired. Now, I read all the time. I especially like mysteries and historical books."

The offer was good enough that he knew he couldn't turn it down - nearly 20% more than he had been making. They also promised him a certain amount of "ghost" stock, shares that he would not own but from which he would collect yearly dividends. During his entire career at Kennywood, Carl never actually owned stock and the ownership has stayed within the McSwigan and Henninger families to this day.

Through the years, he worked his way to the top position at Kennywood, joined the IAAPA and worked his way to the top rung of the association and in 2000 retired from the park business at the peak of his game. He now lives at the top of the highest mountain in Pittsburgh.

Carl's Route to the Top

Carl Owens Hughes was born in South Fork, Pa. in 1921, the son of a prominent small town banker. He was employed part time at the bank while growing up and went off to college where he earned a degree in economics, all the while expecting to graduate and go home and follow in his father's footsteps.

Although an avid fan of virtually all sports, Carl was never an athlete. His left eye didn't work properly and left him with little to no hand-to-eye coordination. To be a part of the high school sports scene, he volunteered as manager of the basketball team; a position he held until he discovered his writing skills. He soon dropped his athletic activities to become editor of his high school newspaper.

The combination of his love for athletics and his writing and communication skills came in handy at Geneva College in Beaver Falls, Pa., where he received tuition in exchange for his duties as sports publicity director. For spending money, he worked in the school's dining room.

Carl earned a reputation as a strong and perceptive writer and during his senior year in college, Beaver Fall's daily newspaper offered him a part-time job covering high school sports. "I worked all three jobs – the dining room, as the publicity director, and for the local newspaper - all at the same time and occasionally I went to class," he laughed. "Needless to say, I was delighted to get out of college."

Upon graduation, instead of going back to South Fork, Carl headed straight to Pittsburgh and began his search for bank employment. With his degree in economics and his work experience at his father's bank, Carl felt confident he would easily land a banking position, which he soon did. He was offered a position for $35 a week, a salary that he says was "pretty darn good" for someone right out of college in 1943.

But Wait a Minute, I Already Have a Job

The same afternoon in which he was offered the bank position, but before he officially accepted it, he stopped by the *Pittsburgh Press* sports offices to say hello to several of the reporters he had known from his sports work at Geneva College. "I stopped in just to say hello and to let them know I was in Pittsburgh and that I had graduated. The fellow who had the college sports beat said he was leaving for the Navy the following week and that the paper was looking for his replacement. He suggested I talk with Chet, the sports editor."

It was during the war and the paper "was running out of writers," said Carl. "I walked across the hall and talked to the sports editor who asked me when I could start and I asked him when he wanted me, and he said how about Monday and I said fine. He offered me $25 a week and I said I'd take it and I never regretted it. I starved, but I loved every minute of it. I had an aunt who lived in Pittsburgh and I ate at her house every Sunday night and I think I ate enough for half a week each time I ate there."

> ## CARL, THE STRAIGHT TALKER
>
> *"Carl always stuck to the point and I could always count on him to keep a board of directors meeting on track. There was no fooling around at the table when he was in control."*
>
> BOB BLUNDRED, FORMER IAAPA EXECUTIVE DIRECTOR

Carl Learns the Art of Pugilism

His first beat assignment at the paper was boxing. "I was the fight writer and up to that point I had never seen a boxing match in my life," laughed Carl. While others worried about being drafted into the war, he had no such worries at the time. Because of his eye condition, he received a 4F status. However, that surprisingly changed after the war.

"In 1946, when the war ended, they suddenly decided they needed me and I spent the next two years in the Army. I wound up in the

Bob Ott passes the IAAPA presidency to Carl Hughes in 1974.

Philippines and was chief clerk for the Philrycom Printing Plant and Publication Depot. We printed Christmas cards, maps, and all kinds of Army manuals. It was great because we were the only ones who had air conditioning, because of all the printing presses."

Carl returned home in 1948 to a promised job in the sports department of the *Pittsburgh Press*. He got his boxing beat back and picked up the college football beat as well.

Carl Meets Kennywood

Before Carl went into the Army and before he ever visited Kennywood for the first time in 1944, he was already "unofficially" working for the park. He was writing press releases and getting paid by John Hollihan, the graduate assistant of athletics at Duquesne University who was handling Kennywood's publicity on the side.

"He mentioned to me one day that he wasn't any good at creating press releases, and suggested that I do all his writing and that he would continue to mail everything out, and he would split the pay with me," Carl said. "I forget how much he paid me, but it wasn't much. I had only been out of college for a year, so the extra money helped."

While Carl was in the Philippines, Hollihan went to work full time with the Pittsburgh Steelers as business manager and had to give up his part time job. Shortly after Hollihan quit his PR stint for the park, Carl received a note from Brady McSwigan, Kennywood President, asking him to be the park's part time publicity person when he returned from the Army. Carl accepted, but noted he still had a year left in the Army. McSwigan said he would wait.

Carl received the Life & Top Alumni Award from Geneva College in 1974.

When he returned home and went back to his job at the newspaper, Carl took over the PR chores of the park as planned, but rarely visited it. "They had an office downtown and I went there and did my stuff," he said.

Carl recalls that one of his earliest Kennywood memories was taking a date to the park. "I wasn't making much money, but I got an unlimited supply of free tickets, so it was the right place to go. I remember the lights and the rides and the streetcar ride there, but that's about it."

Anny Coleman, who worked in the promotions department at the newspaper and Carl, the well-known sports writer, got married in Pittsburgh in 1955 and immediately headed to New York City, where he was assigned to cover the National Invitation Tournament at Madison Square Garden. "I took her along because I was on an expense account and New York City was a perfect place for our honeymoon, so it worked out well."

The Kennywood Days

The day after he accepted full time employment at Kennywood in 1956, Carl gave his editor a week's notice and was asked to cover one more event before he left, the Cumberland National Races, a sports car race in Cumberland, Maryland. "We were married then, so I took Anny along with me. I attended the races, came back to Pittsburgh, went down to the office, wrote my story, got out of there around 2 a.m. and went to work at Kennywood a few hours later."

Did he ever regret giving up his sports writing career? "I missed the journalism job for a short time, but there was never a reason to second guess my decision," Carl said. In 2005, five years after officially retiring from Kennywood, Carl said if he had remained a sports writer, he "would have retired much earlier" than he did as chairman of Kennywood. "I would have been relaxing much sooner and I wouldn't be here talking to you about the park business," he laughed.

As part of his new role in the assistant manager post, Carl was to take charge of sales, replacing Frank Danahey who had been with the company off and on since 1907. Danahey had been working with A.S. McSwigan and F.W. Henninger when they ran Duquesne Gardens for the Pittsburgh Railway Company. When the trolley company decided to get rid of the amusement park, it was turned over to McSwigan and Henninger, and Danahey came along.

For a span of nearly 50 years before Carl joined the staff, only members of the McSwigan and Henninger families had been in management positions at the park. That fact didn't appear to be a problem for the young sports writer, because he had little to no aspiration to work his way to the top or make the park business his career. "No, I was there for the money, that's all," recalls Carl.

Four years after Carl joined the team full time, park manager Carl Henninger had a heart attack a few days before opening day in 1960. Carl received an early morning call from McSwigan and was told to get to the park as early as he could "because we have to get this park open in a week and Carl (Henninger) just had a heart attack. He's in the hospital." Henninger ended up spending several weeks in the hospital and then several more at home recuperating before he was able to return to work.

Kennywood opened without a hitch the following week and for his first time ever, on the evening of opening day, Carl was invited to enter the inner sanctum of upper management. Each night after closing, the top executives would go up to a private lounge on the second floor of the park office for a drink before heading home. It was a tradition that Carl had only heard about. That night he was asked to join the group for a drink, even though he was only an assistant manager. His presence in that room was an up-to-then, unheard of event for someone in Carl's position. While up there with the big guys that night, he was told that he had been promoted to acting general manager until Henninger recuperated and returned. "I didn't get a pay raise but it was a big title and I got a free drink," he added.

When Carl Henninger returned to work in late June, McSwigan announced that Carl Hughes was being promoted to general manager, due to his splendid performance during Henninger's absence. Henninger remained VP and Carl as GM, reported directly to him.

When McSwigan died in 1964, Henninger became president and Carl, in addition to his park manager's position, became vice president, two positions he was to hold until 1976.

Many People, Similar Names – Follow This Closely!

Harry Henninger Jr., (whose father, Harry was treasurer and part owner of the park), had asked his uncle Carl Henninger to allow him to work for Carl Hughes in 1974. Henny, as Harry Henninger Jr. was called, became an assistant manager, reporting directly to Carl. In 1975 the board promoted Carl to the president's position and Henny became vice president. When Carl Henninger died in 1985 Carl Hughes was made president and chairman and in 1990 he handed over his presidency to Henny and remained chairman until he retired in 2000.

Carl was the first non-family member to reach the top management position at Kennywood. He began his career at the park during a time when there was a natural gap in the generations. He had proven himself by the time top management was needed and there were no family members ready for that responsibility. Brady McSwigan represented one side of the family and Carl Henninger and his two brothers - Bob who was in charge of refreshments and Harry, the treasurer - were from the other.

Following Carl, Bob and Harry, the next family members on the Henninger side of the family were Harry Henninger Jr. (Henny) who was Harry's son, and Bill, Bob's son. They were both in the military; both were young and neither ready to take over. Carl Hughes, who

Veal is Veal, Period.

"On one IAAPA trip to Italy, our group had been magnificently feasted for a week with sumptuous meals that always ended with a veal entree. When the time came for the final banquet of the trip, the group was so tired of veal that Carl's wife, Anny, told him that we absolutely could not feed them veal even one more time.

"Negotiations with the hotel to get a last minute change of entree were unsuccessful but the chef said he would roast the veal and nobody would know the difference. Carl reluctantly agreed but suggested, as an afterthought, that we double the amount of booze poured at the pre-dinner reception. 'By the time they get to the table, nobody will know the difference,' he supposed.

"It worked to the extent of getting everyone drunk but did not fool Anny. Taking the first bite of the meat, she roared across the ballroom, "Carl Hughes, you S.O.B., this is VEAL!"

JOHN GRAFF, FORMER IAAPA EXECUTIVE DIRECTOR AND PRESIDENT (PROFILED ON PAGE 155)

by then was thought of as an "honorary family member" was the natural choice to run the park. "I was lucky enough to be there at the right time."

Carl Hughes, 1982

Carl said he "never thought to question" why he was accepted or why he was the first to break the family barrier. "I was kind of adopted into the family, and it had never occurred to me to question," he said, noting that everything he learned about the industry was through on-the-job training from the Henninger and McSwigan families.

"My park experience amounted to what I learned from Brady and Carl and they were both children of the Depression, Brady especially.

He was very tight." Henny often joked that Carl was really the park's maintenance manager, even though Andy Vettel officially held that title. "I would walk every roller coaster to see if the wood the carpenters were taking out was truly rotten and needed to be replaced. I often complained to Andy that they were taking too much out and costing us too much money. I was on top of everything."

When Carl started full time in sales in 1956, McSwigan had wanted him to continue being responsible for PR. "He had to justify what he was paying me," said Carl. "After a couple of years Brady said we needed to have somebody else handle the publicity, someone who had more time for it than I did." Carl hired his wife Anny and she ended up handling Kennywood publicity for 31 years. She worked from home and had no office at the park, but "we did give her a shelf where she was allowed to put her stuff when she visited," laughed Carl. In 1993, the PR torch was passed to Mary Lou Rosemeyer, the Hughes' daughter.

Creating a Popular Park

The Kenny family had owned and farmed the land on which the park operated since the early 1800s. Kennywood Park had a long-term lease on the property which specified that once the lease ran out or was revoked, everything on the land reverted to the Kenny family if it wasn't portable and couldn't easily be moved. The company built several large wooden coasters in the 1920s, but thereafter, concentrated on buying rides that weren't anchored into the ground, which meant coasters and large dark rides were mostly out of the question.

In the years following the Depression, the park would usually add a small ride or attraction each season, but nothing very large or expensive. As a result, "the park had become somewhat stagnant by 1964. Our revenues weren't growing and we needed to do something," Carl recalls.

When Brady McSwigan died in 1964, Carl Henninger realized the need to build a signature ride if the park was to remain competitive with Pittsburgh's other parks. It had been 37 years since the last big ticket item had been built, The Racer wooden coaster, and management concurred that it was time to expand and to quit worrying about the lease stipulations. Carl Hughes was sent on the road to look at rides at other parks and to come back with ideas that would work at Kennywood.

At the Santa Cruz (Calif.) Beach Boardwalk, he saw and liked a car ride, patterned after the successful Autopia ride at Disneyland in

California. He brought back the idea and in 1966, The Turnpike ride, created by Arrow Development Company, was built in Kennywood. "We needed something that looked a little Disney in our park and this car ride was certainly something new for us," Carl said. "We tore down the old Laff In The Dark dark ride to make room for it."

In 1968, Carl Henninger decided to put in a major new roller coaster but couldn't find the space in the crowded and landlocked park to do so. One day, he and Andy Vettel, the park's maintenance man, came up with the idea that they could tear out the middle section of the Pippin wooden coaster, expand the ride dramatically, and in the process create an entirely new ride. They did so, and renamed the coaster the Thunderbolt, which is still in operation today. The Thunderbolt was a tremendous success and gave the park a big boost.

Straight Talker

"*Carl is a planner and a negotiator and has always understood his mission as an executive for Kennywood. He never leaves anyone wondering where they stand. After a meeting with Carl you know if you have the deal, have a chance for the deal, or if you are dead in the water. There are no gray areas with Carl.*"

BILL ALTER, LONG TIME INDUSTRY SUPPLIER OF GAMES AND TICKETS

Carl Buys the First Million Dollar Ride

Carl Henninger was able to purchase the land from the Kenny family in 1972, which "was probably the greatest thing he ever did for the park," according to Carl. Once the land was owned by the park company, there was no stopping them. The ideas began to roll and in 1975, Henny decided a log flume should be the next "big" ride. The ride was already a popular attraction in many other parks, but its million dollar plus price tag was a big deal for Kennywood, enough of a big deal that Carl and Henny had some trepidation going to the board for the money. The two made a good argument, the board OK'd the park's first-ever million dollar ride, and the Log Jammer was built by Arrow, and was an instant crowd pleaser.

Pete Knoebel, a good friend of Carl and at the time owner of Knoebels Amusement Resort in Elysburg, Pa. called following the installation of the Log Jammer and complimented him on adding the new ride. "Carl, Kennywood has just joined the ranks with the big guys." That was the initial big push that propelled Kennywood into the big leagues, Carl said. "People saw that we were serious and that we were dedicated to keeping the park an important leisure time activity in the Pittsburgh area."

Newer, bigger rides were added on a regular basis after that and the park continued to grow. Kennywood's biggest competition, West View Park closed in 1977, and Kennywood saw an immediate surge in attendance. "Our group sales efforts immediately went after their customers. They were a picnic park as well, and once they closed, the companies that had been having picnics there, needed somewhere to go, so I made sure they were very well acquainted with our park," Carl noted.

Kennywood Adds General Admission, Finally

Kennywood had always been a free-admission park, with everyone getting in free. Those who then wanted to ride could buy individual ride tickets or discounted tickets by the book or strip. By the late 1970s, most other parks in the country had added a small gate charge, more to keep the unsavory elements out than to make money. Carl, along with Henny, fought hard to create a general admission policy for Kennywood but Carl Henninger wouldn't hear of it at first.

Once Henninger agreed to try it, the biggest piece of advice Carl received from other park officials who had already gone to the general admission concept was, "don't charge too little, don't charge a quarter; charge a buck, because anybody can afford a quarter." They tried $1 and it worked well. Guests were entitled to watch all the shows and to enjoy the ambiance for the $1 gate charge. Several types of ride tickets were made available to those who wanted to ride. The general admission ticket was up to $8.50 when it was discontinued at the end of the 2004 season to make way for the pay-one-price ticket that includes park admission and unlimited rides on all the park's attractions. Kennywood was one of the last parks in North America to do away with a general admission ticket.

During his reign, Brady McSwigan had booked circus acts every two weeks during the season. Advertising for those acts was mostly in the form of colorful posters that were posted throughout town. A strong breed of advertising men known as billposters put them on fences, poles and buildings and could always seem to find a place to post them. When Carl Henninger became president, he kept the circus acts, but eliminated the billpostings.

"The moment Brady died I got word to get rid of the billposters," Carl recalls. "Carl (Henninger) had been talking with Ralph Wachs of Coney Island in Cincinnati, and they both agreed that bill posting was cluttering up the environment, much like graffiti. Those were the days when Lady Bird Johnson came out against billboards and wanted to eliminate them along the nation's highways."

When the park purchased the Skycoaster in 1994, it was installed where the circus stage had been, and "we stopped booking the acts," Carl noted. Kennywood was the first amusement park in the world to erect a Skycoaster. The daredevil ride had become popular as a stand-alone attraction, but no park had installed one, mostly because of its low capacity. In order to offer the Skycoaster experience and to avoid the problem of everyone wanting to ride it, officials came up with the idea to create an additional charge, an up-charge to those already in the park, of $14.95 to $24.95 per rider, depending on the number of riders.

It immediately became successful and even with the up-charge, a reservation system had to be developed. On most days all the available time slots for the entire day were booked by early afternoon. It was a huge success and the $250,000 ride was paid for in less than one season, paving the way for parks around the world to add Skycoasters as an up-charge attraction. "It far exceeded our expectations for the investment, plus the amount of publicity that it generated was astonishing," Carl said.

The Kennywood Family Expands

In 1983, Carl was on a trip to the Far East when Henny got the idea to buy another park and add it to the Kennywood family. "I came back and Henny asked me what I thought about us buying Idlewild Park and Storybook Forest, another old, traditional park complex about 60 miles from Kennywood in Ligonier."

Carl agreed that it was a good idea and took it to Carl Henninger,

As the chairman of the IAAPA Hall of Fame Committee, Carl presented the Hall of Fame Award to Charles Wood in 1992.

then chairman who took it to the board. "He said the only reason I wanted to buy Idlewild was to get rid of the competition. I said he was right, but I added that I felt we could make a few bucks along the way as well," Carl said. The board blessed the deal.

Several years later, talk between Carl and Henny centered on the city's need for a waterpark. There was no room in or adjacent to Kennywood and within a few days Henny had found what he thought was the perfect location, in nearby Homestead. It was an overgrown area of an abandoned steel mill, littered with trash, along the Monongahela River.

"The next thing I knew, he had me down there walking through the brush along a little path to the river," said Carl. "Standing

Taking Summer Vacations

"When I reached 70 I came up with a new policy for the company. I declared that when you reach 70, you can take a vacation in the summer."

CARL HUGHES

Carl with grandson Timmy Cauley in an advertisement photo promoting a senior citizen discount in 2005.

next to the river, looking back, we could see it was indeed a great location. He envisioned that we could start the slides at the top of the hill and let them run down to the river level." They went back to the office and started creating plans for Sandcastle, the area's first waterpark. "We were able to buy about 60-acres down there for a song." It opened in 1989.

Carl uses Sandcastle as the prime example of the relationship that he had with Henny through the years. "He was the thrust, the mastermind on most of our projects. We made a great team because somebody had to make his dreams a reality. That was my job."

Great Ideas Brought Big Crowds

Most anyone who knows the two readily agree that it was the combination of Henny's ideas and Carl's ability to make those ideas happen, that helped make Kennywood what it is today, a popular family park that brings in more than a million guests per year. "There were years that we were so popular and so successful that we had to cancel the advertising after a couple of weeks; we couldn't handle the crowds," notes Carl.

The next opportunity to expand came in 1995 when Henny received a call from Gasper Lococo, president of Funtime, a group that owned several parks. The company had a management contract to run Lake Compounce in Bristol, Conn. and was pulling out and asked if Kennywood would be interested in taking over. Lococo knew that the park, the oldest continuously operated amusement park in North America, having opened for the first time in 1846, would fit perfectly into the historic family of parks then owned by Kennywood Entertainment.

Carl told them that Kennywood wouldn't operate anything they didn't own, and a few days later, members of the Stephen Barberino Jr. Family, who owned the park, paid Carl and Henny a visit in Pittsburgh. As Kennywood chairman, Carl was definitely involved with the complex negotiations to buy the park, but he wasn't "out there" on the front line. "They kept me posted and I gave my suggestions and opinions," he said.

Another big opportunity found its way to Kennywood in the mid-90s. This time, it wasn't a call from someone who wanted to sell something. This time Kennywood was the object of interest and the suitor at the door had its checkbook in hand and a strong desire to buy the park. Carl and the others spent a great deal of time negotiating with Premier Parks, a company that had been buying up family-owned, traditional amusement parks throughout the country. Although he was personally against selling, the deal being presented was sufficient enough that Carl and the other officials felt they had the fiduciary responsibility to take the offer to the family-controlled board. In the end, the decision was made to turn down the lucrative offer and keep it a family-owned park.

Winding Down His Career

As anyone who has worked in management at an amusement park knows, summer vacations are usually not looked upon with favor and are quite a rarity. It's a tradition at most small to medium sized parks that owners and executives take vacations during the winter when the park is closed. Carl changed that policy, at least for himself, in 1991.

"When I reached 70 I came up with a new policy for the company. I declared that when you reach 70 you can take a vacation in the summer," Carl said, obviously not joking. It wasn't long after he initiated the policy that he and a long time friend were readying for a cruise to the north tip of Norway.

He discovered one thing while preparing to take the trip - it was easier to get away from the park than from his wife. "Anny asked if she was going. I said no, you have a job and you have to work, you can't go. She said well what about you? I said I'm covered by the new policy at Kennywood. When you're 70 you're allowed to take a summer vacation."

On every trip before that one, Anny had always packed his bags. The day he was to leave, he went out to the park in the morning and when he returned, his bags were nowhere to be seen.

"I said, where's my bag?"

Anny said. "What do you mean; I guess your bag is down in the basement wherever you keep it."

"I said didn't you pack it?"

Anny answered. "Why would I pack it, I'm not going anywhere. I'm working. That's my new policy."

"So I packed my bag. It was to be a black tie trip, very fancy, so I packed the tux and the shirts. It was only later that I discovered I had forgotten the tie and the only ties I could buy on the ship were red bow ties," said Carl. "I hate bow ties but I had to wear one almost every night." He also forgot to pack heavy clothing for his trip above the Artic Circle and had to go shopping for warmer clothing.

"By the way, I had to call a cab to take me to the airport that day. Anny was 'working and too busy' to take me," Carl notes, pointing out that was the first and last time that particular scenario played

Carl checking out the park in 1998
during Kennywood's 100th birthday.

out in the Hughes household. In fact, Carl thinks that event triggered Anny's idea to retire, which she did a couple years later. "At that point, she could go with me whenever I went, since she wasn't working any longer," he laughed.

In 2005, at 85 years of age, Carl treated himself to a new Corvette. "I started my love affair with Corvettes in 1976 and I've bought a new one every five years. This is my sixth one. I have always liked convertibles and sports cars."

Shortly after he purchased his new Corvette, a friend asked him how he could justify buying another expensive sports car at his age. "I told him that I figure I owed it to myself, a sort of payback for the 50 summers of my life that I gave up working at Kennywood. I figure I deserve it," he said proudly.

> ## Must Be Totally Rotten!
>
> *"I would walk every roller coaster to see if the wood the carpenters were taking out was truly rotten and needed to be replaced. I often complained that they were taking too much out and costing us too much money."*
>
> CARL HUGHES, ON COST CONTAINMENT

Despite his four open-heart surgeries, he proclaimed in mid-2006 that he was doing well. He also enjoys pointing out that the same doctor who performed all his surgeries was named the "best paid doctor" at the University of Pittsburgh Medical Center. Carl is proud that his procedures helped the good doctor win that distinction.

What's his secret to a long life? "A lot of bypass surgeries," he professes. "I've had a total of 14 bypasses and I've had two pacemakers. The first one lasted 13 years and I wore it out!"

"I don't consider myself old but I'm sure other people do."

Start of a 50 Year Love Affair

When Carl retired in 2000, he had been involved with the International Assn. of Amusement Parks & Attractions for 45 years, nearly his entire career in the park business.

He was the first non amusement park owner to hold a major office in the association and in 1974 he reached the IAAPA President's position before reaching the president's post at the park in which he worked.

When he first became acquainted with the association, Carl was in the inaugural year of his new career. "In November 1956, the same year I started full-time at Kennywood, Brady (McSwigan) asked me to go to the parks convention with him. It was held in Chicago, at the Sherman House Hotel and I quickly learned that as a rookie, one of my first jobs was to go down the street to a place called Zimmerman's, which sold discount booze, and buy enough to stock the suite."

Carl fondly remembers those early train trips from Pittsburgh to Chicago for the convention. "We could have flown, but the train was such an easy trip. We'd board in Pittsburgh, enjoy a few drinks, have dinner, party a little, and go to bed. The next morning we'd be in Chicago. Riding the train to the IAAPA convention was part of the experience for so many of us for many years."

He realized immediately that IAAPA leadership at the time was a tightly knit group of cronies. "It certainly was an association of good-ole-boys," Carl recalled. "The same people, representing the same family-owned parks showed up year after year. Very little fresh blood appeared and there were few, if any, true amusement park entrepreneurs in the crowd. It was all about family and I, as a non-family member, was really an outsider."

Carl Meets the Big Dogs

As a rookie, Carl benefited greatly from his networking opportunities at the conventions. During the Sherman House days, the nights usually ended upstairs in the Penthouse, with everyone "networking, sharing information, smoking, drinking, and telling tall tales." People sat in their own small groups, and if one was in good standing with his boss, he "might get invited to sit with him," or if one was really lucky, he'd be asked to join the table with one of the titans of the park industry. "When and if you were invited to sit down with one or more of the established old-timers, you were certainly honored."

In most cases, Carl not being an owner wasn't an issue during those early years. He was supported by most of the good-ole boys and ironically it wasn't long before he became a crony of most of the owners. "I was rubbing elbows with all these brilliant, important people, like Eddie Carroll Sr. of Riverside Park and Jack (John) Gurtler of Elitch Gardens. I have to admit that I was a bit intimidated at first, not because of anything they did, but by whom they were and what they represented."

One attribute that helped Carl cope through those years was his own attitude. "I've always had a big ego and felt I could handle anything. Looking back now, I realize that I really needed to act that way or they would have eaten me alive," he recalls. The likes of Carroll and Gurtler lovingly gave the five-foot, four-inch tall Carl the nickname of Little Lord Fauntleroy.

One of the earliest industry professionals who took Carl under his wings was Bob Freed from Lagoon Park in Farmington, Utah. "I was very impressed with him and for some reason he liked me. Bob and I talked about a lot of things and I took a great many new ideas back to Kennywood, thanks to him," he said. "He was one of the most innovative park people I have ever known."

Freed (whom Carl now considers one of his two mentors, with Carl Henninger being the other) had been on the IAAPA board and on many of its committees for years. Freed became the group's president in 1963, followed by a stint as chairman of the nominating committee. With the help of both Henninger and Freed, Carl was appointed to the IAAPA board in the late 1960s, and after several years, he was voted in as an officer. He went through the chairs and became president in 1974. During Carl's year as president, Bob Freed died and Carl had the honor to head up a committee that created an annual scholarship fund set up in his mentor's name.

Carl is widely recognized as the catalyst in changing the previous "Sherman House crony" management of the IAAPA into today's professionally run organization.

Carl at the Top

By the time Carl headed up the IAAPA in 1974, the corporate types from the emerging theme park industry were becoming more active and were soon challenging the way the association was run. "I would say the corporate theme parks, the ones that weren't owned and operated by families, brought a more professional type of person to the membership," he said. "That was good for not only the industry but for the association as well." Carl attended every annual convention for 48 years, missing his first in 2002.

One of Carl's goals as an officer was to put more "international" in the International Assn. of Amusement Parks & Attractions. Outside of a few Canadian parks and Blackpool (England) Pleasure Beach, there was not a great deal of international involvement. In late 1980, he and a small contingent of IAAPA officers and board members went to

Carl with daughter Mary Lou Rosemeyer in 1999.

Europe to help spread the IAAPA gospel. Today many single out that European trip as the first major effort to recruit non-North American members into the association.

Through the early 1980s, Carl was the unofficial organizer of European recruitment trips, believing that one-on-one visitation was the best recruiting method for the association.

The Trade Show, Another Hughes Influence

The decision to move the trade show out of Chicago for the first time and move it to Atlanta took place in 1973, during President Bob

Ott's watch. It's a move that Carl feels was the most significant single event to contribute to the growth of the IAAPA.

The first IAAPA parks convention held outside Chicago was in 1974, the year Carl held the gavel. Attendance for the trade show and convention that year was up, mostly because of the expanded exhibition space and expanded offerings such as educational seminars. On the last day of the convention, Carl noted that, "dozens of delegates attended for the first time from Europe, The Orient, Africa and South Africa."

During one of his last interviews as the IAAPA President, Carl pointed out that 1974 was a good year for the association, with overall membership growing by 18%. He also took the opportunity to caution park officials to "keep a vigilant eye on federal developments in Washington, particularly the ever possible climb in the minimum wage."

Under Carl's leadership the association retained Washington Attorney Albert McDermott to look after its legislative interests. Also during his reign, Carl helped change the bylaws, adding a 3rd VP to the officer's journey to the presidency.

Carl Helps Graff Take Over

As a member of the executive committee in 1984 and 1985, Carl was a part of the decision process that would forever change the face of the association; hiring John Graff as executive director and moving the offices from Chicago to Washington, D.C.

In 1984, Bob Blundred, then IAAPA executive secretary decided to retire. The executive committee voted to promote John Graff, who had been with the group since 1980 as Director of Government Relations and Legal Counsel in Washington, D.C., to the top post. Graff would go on to lead the association into becoming the largest and most powerful amusement industry group in the world.

The board felt Chicago was too limiting for an international association. They felt the Windy City was out of touch and not a relevant location for an association with members from all corners of the world. The committee agreed that the best thing for the association was to move its headquarters to Washington D.C., where international access was much easier. Plus, Graff had already established a lobbying office there in 1980 and had a home and family there. The office was officially moved in 1985 and Graff headed up the association until his retirement in December 2001.

Doing a little Monday morning quarterbacking, Carl looks back at those two decisions. "I'm very proud of what we accomplished during those years. It really set the foundation for a strong, worldwide association."

Carl, the Living Legend

One of Carl's biggest surprises of all time came in 1990 when he became the first living inductee into the IAAPA Hall of Fame. His response from the stage as he accepted the award brought the house down. "Being a living legend is great. It sure beats the other category (posthumous)!"

The year before this big honor, Carl had been appointed to the newly formed IAAPA Hall of Fame committee. He recalls the group's meeting when the first inductees were chosen. "We had been talking about dead people and I had been able to get a couple of my favorite candidates picked for the posthumous honor, including Bob Freed and John Allen, the roller coaster designer," Carl said.

Carl Hughes - On Stealing

"I have always admitted that I have never had an original idea. But I also have said I tried never to steal a bad one. So my advice is to only steal good ideas."

CARL HUGHES

"When we had finished talking about the dead guys and went on to the living nomination, I looked down and saw that my name was on the list. They had put it there at the last minute so I wouldn't see it before the meeting. I said well, I'm on this list and although I certainly do not deserve to be on it, I'll leave the meeting, which I did."

After the committee quietly and quickly voted him in, they brought him in from the hall and didn't say a word to him about the secret vote, and he didn't ask. "I honestly didn't know anything about it until the day they called my name from the stage during the convention. It really didn't occur to me. I was completely taken by surprise."

Prior to the knowledge that he himself would be voted into the Hall of Fame, Carl had written a short blurb about the Hall of Fame for the convention program: "It is my privilege and pleasure to announce the first inductees into the IAAPA's Amusement Industry

Hall of Fame. In this manner we will express our admiration and appreciation for those whose personal accomplishments and service to the industry have contributed in an extraordinary way to the success we all enjoy."

Little could he have known that he was referring to himself when those words were originally penned. Carl was inducted along with some of the best-known names in the amusement history. In addition to Carl as the only "living legend" inductee, that first Hall of Fame class consisted of: Walt Disney; coaster designer and builder John Allen; Carl's mentor Robert E. Freed; LaMarcus Thompson, creator of the first true roller coaster in the U.S.; Angus Wynne, founder and developer of the Six Flags park chain; and Kennywood's own Andrew S. McSwigan, who was not only the first president of Kennywood Park, but was also the founding father of IAAPA and served as its first president, 54 years before Carl did the same.

While he says the distinction of being inducted into the Hall of Fame didn't change his life, "it certainly is still pleasant nearly 20 years later to contemplate that my peers felt that way about me." When Carl retired in 2000, he stepped away from virtually all his IAAPA responsibilities, although he still tries to attend the annual trade show and convention.

By mid-2006, Carl claimed he had perfected retirement. "I have been married to Anny for 50 years and we only had one summer vacation together until I retired. "We changed that immediately. What do I do now? I'll tell you. I loaf. I think I have refined the art of loafing."

Living Is The Best

"Being a Living Legend is great.
It sure beats the other category."

CARL HUGHES, ON ACCEPTING THE HONOR IN 1990

CARL HUGHES

BIBLIOGRAPHY

ARTICLES & INTERVIEWS

Amusement Industry Oral History Project tape of Carl Hughes, a collaboration of the National Amusement Park Historical Assn. and the International Assn. of Amusement Parks & Attractions, interviewed by Jim Futrell, Oct. 12, 1998

IAAPA Hall of Fame Nomination Forms, 1990

Interviews with Carl Hughes, by Tim O'Brien: May 15, 2005; July 13 & 14, 2005; March 3, 2006; May 25, 2006

Keeping Kennywood Beautiful, Source of Pride for Hughes, *Amusement Business,* Sept. 7, 1974

Kennywood Press Releases, 1985 – 2000

Legends of the Industry, *Funworld,* by Jennifer Black, July 2000

Mighty Atom's In Army Now, *Pittsburgh Press,* by Carl Hughes, Feb. 10, 1946

The Chicago Days, *Funworld,* by Chuck Michio, November 1998

Tried-and-True: Step Right Up, *Funworld,* by Chuck Michio, July 1998

BOOKS:

Amusement Parks of Pennsylvania, Stackpole Books, 2002, by James Futrell

Kennywood: Roller Coaster Capital of the World, Vestal Press, 1982, by Charles Jacques Jr.

More Kennywood Memories, Amusement Park Journal, 1998, by Charles Jacques Jr.

The Amusement Park Guide, Globe Pequot Press, 2003, by Tim O'Brien

PHOTO: TIM O'BRIEN

Carl received a token of appreciation
from Bo Kinntorph following the
IAAPA Summer Meeting at Kennywood in 1992.

BO KINNTORPH

*"Miss Romeis had everything a singer
needs – as well as quite a decent voice."*

If only one theme park executive could be picked as the foremost
motivating force in uniting the vast global theme park industry, it would
have to be the charismatic Swede, Bo Kinntorph. In 1992, while holding
down the top executive post at Liseberg in Gothenburg, Sweden, Bo
also served as the first non-American president of the International
Assn. of Amusement Parks & Attractions.

He not only was a global cheerleader for the association, but a
major proponent of the concept of openly sharing knowledge in order
to create a stronger industry.

His gregarious personality, his keen business sense and his
ability to work with different cultures throughout the world truly
made him a pioneer in the international theme park field. His
language of choice, Swenglish, and his buffoonery have left straight-
laced park executives from Osaka to Orlando not only enlightened,
but doubled up in laughter.

Bo (pronounced Boo) is one of the rare park executives who made
his way to the top through the entertainment side of the business -
and he still sees himself as a showman. Whether it was writing plays
in high school, managing the entertainment program at the Swedish
FolkParks, being a nationally heard radio announcer and a nationally
seen TV talk show host for teens, working as an entertainment
journalist, being a theater critic or serving as the top executive at

a global record company, Bo had vast knowledge of what it took to entertain an audience.

As president of IAAPA, Bo's platform was to "get the word out worldwide" on how beneficial membership in IAAPA could be and to "guarantee that smaller parks and attractions around the world would receive the full benefit of membership." To Bo, who had discovered IAAPA shortly after joining Liseberg in 1973, the association was the

The KINNTORPH File

BO KINNTORPH *(Boo Chin•torp)*

Born: Oct. 2, 1928, at 7:28 p.m. in Arvika, Sweden

Married: Lotta Romeis, May 20, 1961

Children: Anna-Lena and Anders

Claim to fame: First non-U.S. president of the International Assn. of Amusement Parks & Attractions (1992); IAAPA Hall of Fame's Living Legend (1996); widely considered the individual most responsible for making IAAPA a true international organization.

First visit to an amusement park: Small local park in Arvika, 1945, then nine years later, he visited Gröna Lund Tivoli, Sweden's then largest park, in 1954.

Work experience: Always a showman and always able to entertain and please an audience. Through the years he was a nationally heard radio announcer and a nationally seen TV talk host for teens, worked as an entertainment journalist, served as a theatre critic and worked as the top executive of a global record company.

First job in an amusement park: In 1954 became head of bookings and production for the 240 FolkParks in Sweden. The live performance entertainment parks had no rides and he stayed with them for 14 years.

First job in a park with rides: When he joined Liseberg Park in Gothenburg, Sweden as CEO on Aug. 1, 1973.

Career: Remained with Liseberg for 20 years, always in the top position.

Legacy with IAAPA: Instrumental in the creation of the Institute for Industry Management school now held at The Institute at Wharton, at the University of Pennsylvania; helped create the On-Site Training Program. Both educational programs are still flourishing.

glue that was needed to bring all Earth's parks and attractions together, something that he felt would make everyone stronger, more competitive and eventually, more profitable.

Bo's First Time

Bo's first trip to an amusement park was in his hometown of Arvika, Sweden in 1945. Nine years later, he traveled to Stockholm and visited Gröna Lund Tivoli, at the time the country's largest visitor's attraction. It was in 1954 that Bo began a 14-year run as the head of bookings and production for the 240 FolkParks, scattered throughout the country. None of them had amusement rides but they all had plenty of entertainment, including outdoor theaters and stages, dance rinks, games, cafés and hordes of guests. Stage entertainment at the parks consisted of opera, operatic ballet, dramatic plays, comedies, revues, international variety acts, orchestras and soloists. Among others during those 14 years, Bo booked the likes of Frank Sinatra, Paul Anka, Quincy Jones, Count Basie and Duke Ellington. From 1959 through 1968, Bo also found time to produce or host 108 television and radio shows.

The FolkParks had first appeared in 1905 and were owned by trade unions and sports associations and were open from two to six days a week during the summer season. The long, light summer evenings in Sweden, which Bo calls the "land of the midnight sun and sin" were perfect for outdoor entertainment. They were most welcomed after five to six months of even longer dark and depressing winter days.

Bo was always able to deal with the best of them and was quite adept at handling politicians and union officials, but by the mid-1960s, politicians were getting on his nerves and were starting to meddle with the operations of the parks, something that Bo would not accept. He preferred to deal with the guests, not spend time trying to placate the political honchos who thought they ran the parks.

Bo - On the Record

In 1968, Bo already had 14 years experience in stage production, plus several years in radio and television, but he wanted more out of life. Only two areas were missing in his life plan at that time - experience in the record industry and the opportunity to operate a large amusement park or performance venue. He went searching first for his record industry experience and in 1969 was offered the top spot at a company in Sweden that owned several well-known record labels.

From 1969 to 1973, Bo served as CEO of Philips-Sonora (later Phonogram and PolyGram), which also owned several American,

British and European labels, and had its own production studios in Stockholm. Bo had previously learned the skills of producing entertainment on stage, in nightclubs, on radio and television, and now he was set to learn what it would take to sell entertainment and create new marketing tricks for his label.

Bo tinkling the ivories at home in Sweden.

During the years, Bo was twice offered the job of entertainment manager at Liseberg but turned it down both times. However, when he was offered the top position of the entire park in late fall 1972, he accepted. The final piece of his overall career puzzle was finally in place – he had his own park to rule and develop.

In 1973 he became the managing director of the park, a position he held until 1985 when he became president/CEO of the entire Liseberg Group, consisting of Liseberg Park and four subsidiaries: Liseberg Restaurants, Hotel Liseberg Heden, Liseberg Gäst AB (marina, cabin village, youth hostel, teenage hotel and camp site) and the Lisebergshallen arena (sports, musicals, shows). He retired in 1993.

Bo's Beginnings

Bo was born in the home of his maternal grandparents, near Arvika, in western Sweden, close to Norway on Tuesday, Oct. 2, 1928, at 7:28 p.m. He was the only child born of Ella and John Richard Kinntorph. "I was fortunate to see my mother and father live until they were 93 and 88 years old respectively, and they stayed healthy all their lives." He expects to do the same, he notes.

His early environment proved to be quite influential in his life's work. The resort town of Arvika had a population at the time of 8,000 and it had a theater, four cinemas, three hotels, two restaurants, five cafés, and the FolkPark. The little town was known for its high-quality amateur theater and its highly-regarded schools of music and general studies.

His biggest influences growing up were the professional revues, shows, comedies, drama and musicals that played each summer in the local FolkPark. "I got real pleasure from the witty responses, perfect timing and professional productions." Whenever he had enough money Bo would take the train to one of the bigger towns to see a performance that he had read about or heard about on the radio. "Excursions like that left me feeling good for several months!"

At 15, he was editor of his school's magazine and was soon writing short scripts for the nation's first teenage-specific program on Swedish Radio. He also wrote and produced stage shows at his school and created several ideas for musical revues for his local park. He directed a church play that toured through western Sweden.

He says he was a good child and was never precocious, but that he liked "dreaming, discussing, debating, planning and reviewing, and possibly questioned things a little too much at times." He did not go to the university, but briefly studied directing and technique under a Russian-Swedish drama teacher from Moscow who had a summer home near Arvika. Bo served briefly in the military in 1948, and was involved in helping create preliminary plans for a proposed glider airfield in his home town.

Bo De-Sprouts Potatoes and Meets Future Wife

Before heading out to pursue a professional career in Stockholm, Bo held many small jobs in Arvika. "During one warm, sunny summer I spent two months sitting in the basement of a grocery shop removing the sprouts from potatoes and I spent another summer rust-proofing military mess trailers, and for two summers I directed theater performances for summer courses at Ingesund Folk High School.

He first met two of his long time showbiz friends at Ingesund: Bengt Bernhag, who became one of the country's top record producers, and Stikkan Andersson, a composer, lyricist and music publisher who later discovered, produced and managed ABBA, the popular Swedish rock group.

In 1958, Bo was in the audience when Miss Lotta Romeis performed in a song competition in which she won. Several weeks later, she called Bo at the FolkParks, introduced herself and asked if she could audition. Already somewhat smitten by her, he replied enthusiastically that auditions were being held the very next day. It wasn't actually true, but he quickly arranged a tryout for Miss Romeis, "who was more beautiful than ever. I had seen and heard her on four previous occasions. She really had everything a singer needs – as well as quite a decent voice."

They soon began dating and in 1959 they traveled to the Riviera and rented a beachside house for a couple of weeks. He proposed to her in 1960, they married in 1961 and they produced Anna-Lena in 1962 and Anders in 1964.

When the two became married, Lotta decided to not continue her singing and acting career, instead she turned her attention to domestic duties and children. "Our children had the best mother in the world – someone who was always there for them and their many friends. And I got a considerate, sweet and happy wife, who was also a talented cook and fixer of lawnmowers, car engines and houses, as well as a green-fingered master gardener!"

Entering the Gates of Liseberg

While at the FolkParks he had created and sold entertainment to parks such as Liseberg for 14 years. During that time he worked with three different entertainment managers at Liseberg and knew that the park was less than what he considered spectacular. He was offered the entertainment managers job twice, but turned down all offers because he had seen how the park operated and felt it wasn't an organization in which he would fit. The park was the second-largest in the country at that time, and at its best could be described as "second rate," Bo says today.

Bo was working for the record label and living in Stockholm when he was offered Liseberg's top job along with promises that he had free reign to make the needed improvements. Officials wanted him to start within three months but that goal proved to be impossible when label executives informed him they wouldn't let him out of his contract until July, nearly nine months away. He accepted the job, worked out his contract, and started at Liseberg on Aug. 1, 1973.

The Gothenburg media were curious about the man. Heading up Liseberg was a big deal and they wanted to know who he was and what

During Bo's reign as CEO of a major record company, he presented singer Andy Williams with an award.

his plans were. Landing the job nine months before actually moving to town and taking over, made the media even more curious. He worked with them, but only gave them limited access to his personal life in Stockholm. He visited the park several times during those nine months, once being on opening day in April 1973. He was still working in the music business and didn't pay too much attention to what he wore, thinking he would be in the background of the day's events. He showed up in a pair of red jeans, not expecting to be noticed or photographed. On the front of the local paper the following morning was a photo of Bo, with the headline, "The New Boss in Red Jeans."

Bo was a little younger than his predecessor at Liseberg and his style was very different. The red jeans photo set the stage and told the world - "Hey, this guy, this new boss of yours, he's not like your previous boss."

Pop star Michael Jackson during a visit to Liseberg.

This Old Park of Mine

Liseberg was an old fashioned company when Bo first walked through the front gates. "I would walk through the park and the employees would all tip their hats to me. They were thinking, 'Oh, a very high person and boss so I must show respect and say hello.' It was a joke to me being treated that way and I was a bit embarrassed by it. They called me Mr. Kinntorph and at that time, they were all calling each other by mister and missus."

Almost immediately, Bo told everyone to "stop that" and proclaimed that from that moment on, people were to call each other by their first name, including himself. Right from the start he let everyone know that the era of the casual work place had begun.

People were impressed with his knowledge and his passion. He often heard from the employees that his predecessor "didn't know the business" and that he had landed his job only because of political clout.

Liseberg is owned by a private company, which is wholly owned by the city of Gothenburg.

For the first time at Liseberg, communication, planning and creative ideas started filtering down from the top. He held weekly meetings, a first for the management staff. "We talked about what we could do, about ideas, about planning. It was difficult for some to think that way because this was not the kind of management they were used to," Bo notes. "It was very interesting and we all learned a great deal. We were on track within a couple of months."

A few days before Bo took over, one of the historic buildings, which dated from the late 18th century, had burned down. A telegram was waiting for him on his first day in the office. It came from two comedy actor friends who observed, "We hear you're already under fire!" Shortly after the park closed following Bo's first season, the historic Concert Hall burned to the ground. During the park's grand opening festivities held in that building in 1923, Albert Einstein had discussed his Theory of Relativity in front of invited royalty and other guests of honor. "The telegram was right: I was under fire!"

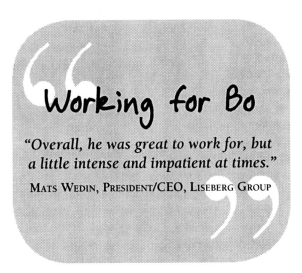

Working for Bo

"Overall, he was great to work for, but a little intense and impatient at times."

MATS WEDIN, PRESIDENT/CEO, LISEBERG GROUP

Bo – Was I a Difficult Boss?

During the course of his professional career prior to Liseberg, Bo had attended several management courses that had tried to teach him the importance of delegation. "I had listened with interest, but most of the time I wanted full control over what was happening. I never learned to be good at delegating," he freely admits.

He thinks he was "probably" difficult to work with at times. "I wanted to talk about my thoughts and visions, explain to all the staff what management expected and learn what they thought about our plans to grow. We were a very small team who worked well together, and we wanted to believe it was possible to become Sweden's top tourist destination, which had traditionally been in the capital, Stockholm."

Mats Wedin, who was hired as Bo's heir apparent for the top position and worked with him for many years before taking over, laughed when asked if Bo had been hard to work for. "I survived," Wedin chortled before becoming serious about his friend. "Overall, he was great to work for, but a little intense and impatient at times. He wanted to get things going and was meticulous and very detail oriented, which is absolutely necessary in a service industry such as ours. He bordered on being a micro-manager because he had a hard time delegating and a lot of people didn't quite understand his vision, but he was very good for Liseberg and was a fun boss."

Stimulating Creativity

To help formulate "far-out" ideas for Liseberg, and to provide a special creative environment, Bo built what he calls a playroom to which only he and three other executives had a key. There were no such things as a bad idea.

He had many ideas of what Liseberg was and what it could become, all of which were different than his predecessors. One of Bo's first ideas was to expand the length of the season in which guests could visit the park, a relatively new concept for any park at that time. "When we closed in September – six weeks after I started, I noticed we had a lot of prizes left over from lotteries and games, so we wrapped them in Christmas paper and sold them at a Christmas Market during December, a new event we created."

Bo's vision of Christmas at Liseberg ran for a few weekends in December for two winters, many years before other European parks,

PHOTO: TIM O'BRIEN

Bo gets a kiss from his wife Lotta.

including Liseberg, began holding successful annual holiday events. "Apart from the fact that it rained and we didn't have any indoor premises that were large enough, we did fine," Bo recalls. "Although the Christmas Market experiment was quite successful, we were ahead of our time, and it was not until 25 years later that Mats (Wedin, current CEO) and his friends committed themselves to the idea."

Bo Creates a Creative Playroom

To help formulate "far-out" ideas and to provide a special creative environment, Bo built what he calls a playroom to which only he and three other executives had a key. Inside were models, storyboards, sketches, photos and newspaper clippings pasted and stapled onto the walls. "It was private because we didn't want anyone criticizing our ideas or making fun of any of them. We had no visitors, no telephones and no calculators! We came up with a lot of crazy, funny and even practical ideas in the playroom. Luckily they didn't all become reality. At least not yet," he laughed.

Bo would try to build excitement within his staff, telling them there were fantastic and creative ideas everywhere. "Guys," he would say. "If you're interested in ideas, it's easy to come up with all sorts of them. Every morning when you read your paper before you come to the office, you'll see something that could help us. It could be a restaurant, it could be an advertisement, it could be anything." Some of his staff

It's a Natural!

"Our numbers were quickly multiplying in the park, so why not represent that with a rabbit."

BO KINNTORPH ON WHY HE CHOSE THE RABBIT
AS LISEBERG'S MASCOT

didn't understand this concept of free-thinking. "No, that's not very easy," they would proclaim.

Bo would retort, "You can read a paper and there is always something there. Maybe it's not something we can use now but maybe in two years or 15 years or whatever." They started bringing in clippings to Bo who would then post them on the wall and make it a point to discuss each one. It started the flow of the desired creative energy that he felt was necessary for the park to grow and flourish. The executives began to view things differently and when the rest of the staff perceived the changes, they too became excited and began to accept change. Bo said it was at that point that he began to see the differences, in both the attitude of the management and in the direction of the park.

Wedin, who was given a pair of small scissors by Bo to "cut out" everything that he found interesting, said the key to Bo's creativity and his personality is that he always maintained the curiosity of a child. "He was always learning and he was always the teacher. Curiosity opened many doors for Bo."

Inspired by Disney's training program, Bo quickly set up staff training, with annual awards given, along with Liseberg badges presented for notable milestones such as five-year and 10-year service. It was in creating awards for his own staff, that Bo visualized an awards program that would not only present Liseberg in a favorable light to the rest of the country, but would highlight "Someone Who Has Made Sweden Happier This Year."

During his years with the FolkParks he had been in contact with Evert Taube, a popular Swedish poet, composer, author and entertainer. While developing his idea for the new nationwide award, Bo contacted Taube's wife, a well-known sculptress. Astri Bergman Taube agreed to create a small sculpture – to be cast in bronze by a leading foundry in Paris – representing two hands clapping. After a year of discussion, Bo agreed on the design, and began awarding it during Liseberg's spring opening. The tradition is still carried on today, and has given the park some well-earned goodwill and publicity over the years.

Applause Goes Worldwide

In 1980, Bo introduced that same sculpture of two hands clapping to the amusement industry. He created the Applause Award, still presented every two years to "an amusement or theme park whose management, operations and creative accomplishments have inspired the industry with foresight, originality and sound business development." It is presented during IAAPA's fall trade show and convention.

For the first several awards, Bo picked out the winner himself. The first one went to the Walt Disney Company for Magic Kingdom in Anaheim, Calif. In 1982, Bo chose Opryland, in Nashville, Tenn., and in 1984, he went outside the parameters of the award and presented it to outgoing IAAPA executive director Bob Blundred. In 1986 the award received a boost when the now defunct trade magazine *Amusement Business* teamed up with Bo and Liseberg, formed a board of governors to pick the winners, and began soliciting nominees.

A Green & Pink Bunny Enters Bo's Life

In 1973, when Bo took over the park, he inherited not one, but three different logos, used simultaneously to market Liseberg. "It was very confusing and I think it confused the public," he recalls. "We finally came up with one specific design element and then we came up with the rabbit idea for a mascot."

He wanted the rabbit to be created in the park's official colors - green, pink and white. "My reasoning for a rabbit was simple: our numbers were quickly multiplying in the park, so why not represent that with a rabbit." Today there is an entire family of costumed rabbits for every conceivable occasion roaming the Liseberg streets. The rabbit is now a familiar figure to children, especially in Norway and Sweden, has its own stage show, and is featured in most of the park's TV and collateral advertising.

When the Gothenburg Highway Department put up new safety signals for pedestrians who cross the busy street to Liseberg's main entrance, it didn't use the usual "green man" to signal "Go." Instead, it used a green Liseberg bunny.

During the 1970s, Bo could usually be found on the front line, creating a friendlier and more comfortable environment for the park. Utilizing his extensive entertainment background, he tested various programming formats for the live stages and developed new ways to present artists and authors. He led experiments on new guest services, new ground surfaces, brighter color schemes, changes to garden layouts, and his landscaping crews soon started growing their own plant stock.

Bo and His Staff Attend Life School

Bo traveled a great deal and would usually turn his travels into best practice trips, learning as much as he could. In Anaheim at Disneyland for example, he learned how to make topiaries; in Branson, Mo., at Silver Dollar City, he learned the importance of a diverse attraction lineup; in Buena Park, Calif, at Knott's Berry Farm he learned how to create visually appealing retail shops; in Pennsylvania's Knoebels Amusement

Resort and Virginia's Busch Gardens Europe, he was taught how to care for the environment while expanding; in San Antonio at SeaWorld Texas, he observed the creation of a sculpture garden; in Pigeon Forge, Tenn., at Dollywood he learned how to present diverse entertainment options; and in Florida's Walt Disney World at Epcot, he learned how best to benefit from departmental centralization.

During IAAPA's 1993 Summer Meeting in Sweden, Bo hosted a Viking Party for the group.

"I have always enjoyed real-life lessons and demonstrations of quality," he recalls. "Every park I visited had something for me to study and a lesson to take home. Sometimes they were good ideas to implement, or sometimes they were bad ideas that I could avoid. There is always something to learn!"

It wasn't only Bo who learned from traveling. He organized trips for most of his senior directors and took members of the staff on journeys they never had been permitted to take in the past. For example, he found garden exhibitions in Germany to which he took his gardeners. "They loved the opportunity to see such things and they came home with great ideas." Bo said trips to trade shows and other parks were also beneficial. "The ideas our guys learned from others in their same line of work were valuable. They came back to work excited and eager to make things better."

Bo escorting Swedish King Carl XVI Gustaf through Liseberg.

The goal of all the training and all the education was to help the park become the "biggest and the best attraction" in the country, notes Bo. From the beginning the goal was to be number one. Bo's team initially asked him, "How long will it take us to be number one instead of Skansen in Stockholm?" Bo said it wouldn't take long. "No one here doubted we would soon be number one. In Stockholm, they laughed of course."

Bo can't pick one contribution that could be considered the best thing he ever did for Liseberg during his 20 years. "It wasn't just one thing, I think it was everything that we did and everything that all the people who worked with me did. It was totally a community effort. It was certainly not one person or one idea. Everyone contributed very much to our success."

Some Didn't Quite Get It

Several of Bo's ideas and decisions were not considered good ones, at least at the time. One of those was the addition of a 410-foot observation tower, built on top of the highest part of the tallest hill within the park. "I wanted a tower with a revolving restaurant right from the start. Everyone told me it would be a waste of money because we have so many foggy days here and on those days people wouldn't even be able to look down and see the park, let alone the entire city." He built it anyway and it remains a success to this day.

He felt it was wise to spend time and money on the environment - plant more flowers, add more water elements, create an environment where one can hear the birds among the screams from the thrill rides. He created more ticket booths, developed more programs and special pricing for retirees, continued the low general admission price while creating a larger selection of ticket and passport opportunities for those who wanted to ride the rides.

Bo uses his parents as an example of why he did certain things. "When my parents would visit, they were not interested in going on rides," Bo recalls. "They wanted to come in, look at the gardens, enjoy a show and sit down and enjoy a nice lunch or dinner. We've always known that we needed to have good restaurants, not just big rides. We don't want people to take their kids off the rides and leave the park to go find some place for dinner."

People Talked, Bo Listened

One way he learned what the people wanted was by listening to what park guests where saying. Sounds simple, but he always made sure he put himself in a position to interact with the guests. Bo thinks most people get into park management because it's fun. Then with the demands of everyday business, they soon forget they are in the fun industry and start spending all their time at the desk running the park as a very serious business. When they do that, they often forget about the needs of the guests and why they are in the business to start with.

"No, I never forgot. I always tried to spend a lot of time walking around the park. The first year, we didn't officially do surveys, but I met a lot of people. I would pick out guests at random, sometimes an entire family, sometimes a group of teenagers, and invite them to my office, offer them a cup of coffee or a soft drink, and ask them many questions. It was very interesting and I learned to look at the park through their eyes."

He also had the forethought to listen to the ever-important fourth estate – the journalists and photographers. "I had a good relationship with journalists here, and I would invite them up to my office and discuss many different things, all off the record. They are a perceptive group and were always able to provide me with valuable insight." Bo never forgot to ask for the thoughts of the park's employees. "A couple times every season, we would have staff meetings in the theater. Everyone who worked here was invited to talk with us about the new season, how they were doing, about our future plans and of course about their own ideas."

A New President Enters the Park

The Liseberg Group went through a big reorganization at the end of the 1980s and officials decided to hire a new park president, freeing up Bo so he could dedicate more time to the rest of the company and to long-term planning.

"I felt it was time to concentrate more on the future and appoint a president for Liseberg Park who would hopefully be the right man or woman to take over from me when I gave up the most enjoyable job in Sweden in a few years' time," he said. "He or she would also have to be able to work closely with me, accept and develop our policies, work with IAAPA and increasingly take over responsibility for our many wonderful contacts, mainly in the USA and Europe – as well as developing new ones. Later on he or she would presumably become CEO for the whole of the Liseberg Group."

Passing the Torch

"A candle loses nothing by lighting another candle."

BO KINNTORPH ON TEACHING
HIS REPLACEMENT, MATS WEDIN

Mats Wedin was hired as president and perfectly fit the job description that Bo had created. For six years they worked together and in 1993, when Bo decided to retire, "it was only right that I should leave the jewel in the eye of Gothenburg to Mats, who by then was mature enough to take over this beautiful park, a talented and enthusiastic workforce, and duties in an amusement park association (IAAPA) that had become international and included many good friends."

Bo, in the middle, enjoys a drink in Liseberg's
Ice Bar in 2005. Park executives Mats Wedin,
left, and Hansjorg Lechtaler join him.

When Bo retired at the end of 1993 the board of Liseberg set up the "Bo Kinntorph Scholarship," which is awarded annually to an employee of a small FolkPark, allowing he or she to spend the entire summer working in, and being trained in, different jobs in the Liseberg Group – from budget preparation to service duties. In November, the scholarship winner is part of the Liseberg entourage that travels to the U.S. for the IAAPA convention.

Two days after Wedin took over, Bo and his wife Lotta moved to Kuala Lumpur so Bo could work as one of the consultants on a project that involved building a large theme park at an altitude of 4,500 feet and a smaller historical theme park in Malacca. Wanting to stay active in the creative process in an industry in which he had a sterling reputation, Bo formed his own consulting firm, Vision House, upon his return from Malaysia a year later. Bo soon became involved with projects in

Spain, China, Portugal, Norway, Denmark and Sweden. He continues to serve as senior advisor to Liseberg, and says he would never consider working on a project that would compete with his old park. That's why he only accepts projects far from his homeland, he insists.

Getting Involved with IAAPA

IAAPA had no presence in Sweden in 1973 when Bo took over Liseberg, but once he found that such an association existed, it didn't take him long to become a major player in it. Within 20 years of first hearing of IAAPA, he had become its first non-American president.

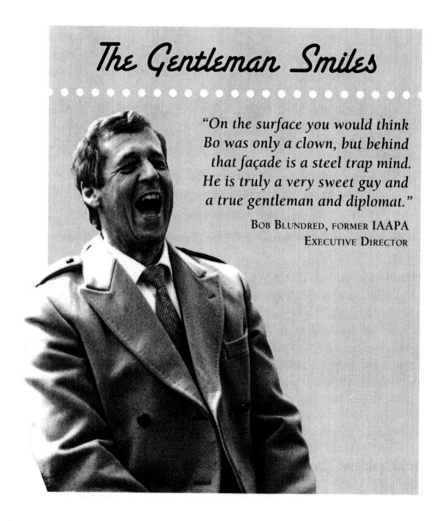

The Gentleman Smiles

"On the surface you would think Bo was only a clown, but behind that façade is a steel trap mind. He is truly a very sweet guy and a true gentleman and diplomat."

BOB BLUNDRED, FORMER IAAPA
EXECUTIVE DIRECTOR

"I'd heard talk about an American organization, of which few people in Europe were familiar. In 1975, I took my board chairman and head gardener to the U.S. and Canada to visit parks. We stopped by IAAPA headquarters in Chicago to find out exactly what they did and what they could do to help us. We met the director, Bob Blundred. It seemed like a good organization and we asked for membership straightaway." Blundred recalls that Bo was very interested in learning about the association and that he was a jovial person. "He was smiling and a happy sort of fellow and I was happy he got involved so quickly with IAAPA," Blundred noted.

Bo decided to take his financial manager along with him to his first convention in New Orleans in 1976. They toured the city and met the Batt family, owners of the local Pontchartrain Beach amusement park, which they toured. "My first visit to New Orleans was an important experience; lots of good, charming restaurants and bars, and of course music. I made lots of new friends, including Harry Batt, Stan Nelson, Bob Ott, Carl Hughes, Tom Spackman, Truman Woodworth and Bob Bell."

At the convention, it didn't take Bo long to find out how big of a park he really ran in Sweden. "We attended the first workshop on the first day, entitled Small Parks Operation. We sat at a round table and were encouraged to pick up the microphone and talk about our park and ask questions. When it was my turn, I spelled out Liseberg for clarity's sake and talked about our ticket system and ticket books, which we had been using since 1953, and I asked a few questions about how ticket books were used in the U.S. Then I talked proudly that we expected to grow and double our attendance in a few years' time."

An older gentleman in the room asked Bo how many guests they had that season. "When I said we had 1.5 million guests, they all had a good laugh, and someone reckoned that maybe we had come to the wrong workshop. We genuinely thought we were a small facility."

Putting the "I" in IAAPA

Bo was totally hooked on IAAPA after attending a few conventions. "It wasn't hard to see that we, in our magical showbiz world, needed an international platform where we could exchange professional experiences and build new types of partnerships across all sorts of boundaries." He notes that he was drawn to the association because it provided much needed and well-organized workshops, a big, wide-ranging tradeshow and the ability to act as spokesman for the business while at the same time, supply the world's media with news, tips and other information.

During the 1986 convention in Orlando, Bo was elected to the board for the first time. During a summer meeting two years later on the Queen Mary in Long Beach, Calif., he was asked to serve as IAAPA's third VP. He would then rise through the offices to become the group's first non-U.S. president in 1992. The day he was asked, Friday, Sept. 16, 1988, was an especially good one for Bo. His friend and Disney VP, Ted Crowell had taken Bo and his colleagues from Liseberg on an in-depth, behind the scenes tour of Disneyland. "It was an amazing morning, filled with much happiness and learning," he said.

Little did he know the day was going to get even better. He was resting in his cabin aboard the Queen Mary when former IAAPA president Jack Krantz knocked on the door, just before dinner. "He came into my cabin and asked if I would like to be third vice president. If so I would be voted in by the board at the convention in Dallas in two months' time." As a practical joker himself, Bo thought the entire scenario was a setup and went along with it. "Sure," he said. "What time should I start?" Krantz was able to convince Bo that he wasn't joking. "I had a week to think about it. After returning to Sweden, thinking it over and discussing it with my friends and the board of Liseberg, I said yes to the big adventure," he noted.

Putting the "I" in International

If only one theme park executive could be picked out as the largest motivating force in uniting the vast global theme park industry, it would have to be the charismatic Swede, Bo Kinntorph.

Shortly after joining the IAAPA Board, Bo made a point quite quickly. The topic of government and government relations have always been big issues for the IAAPA board and at one of his earlier meetings, when the subject of government relations was brought up,

Bo posed a question the board had never heard. "Do you mean the Swedish government or the American government?" He knew it was the American government being discussed, but he wanted everyone at the table to realize that IAAPA really was an international organization and that they had to consistently think beyond the borders.

In 1980, Bo presented the first Applause Award
to his "teacher and mentor," Dick Nunis,
President of Disneyland, Anaheim, Calif.

Bo also pointed out that the traditional summer meeting had never been held outside the United States. He invited them to Gothenburg, with Liseberg being host. The very memorable meeting, with its now-famous food fight during a Viking dinner in a castle on an archipelago, took place in September 1993. A record number for a summer meeting attended.

Bo – The Kid in the Candy Store

He recalls that he acted like a kid in a candy store during the first several November trade shows he attended. "There were many people who were really nice and helpful and they told me things I really needed to know. I learned not only from the seminars in which I attended, but from the people. We would go to workshops, then have dinner together and talk about the workshops and then get together for drinks after dinner and talk about our business long into the night. It was a very good way to become acquainted with the many ways people throughout the world do business."

Bo strongly believed in the global approach to business, a concept he embraced during his years in the music business. "From the beginning, I liked the idea of the IAAPA being a true international association. When they put me on the board, and then made me an officer, I realized that's what the membership wanted as well. I dedicated my time on the board and as an officer to two main areas: education and laying the groundwork for a wider international reach."

During his presidency, he was instrumental in creating two notable education programs, both of which are still flourishing. The first was the development of the annual weeklong Institute for Industry Management, originally held at Cornell University in Ithaca, N.Y. It has since moved to the Institute at Wharton at the University of Pennsylvania in Philadelphia. The second is the On-Site Training Program, where experts in various segments of the business take their expertise to individual parks for employee training.

Legend on a Legend

"Bo was indisputably the one individual most responsible for making IAAPA a truly international organization. He came in as president at a critical time in the organization's struggle to define itself. The force of his personality was such that once he committed himself to the internationalization process, it was all but inevitable that the organization would follow along - not reluctantly, but with enthusiasm."

JOHN GRAFF, FORMER IAAPA EXECUTIVE DIRECTOR AND PRESIDENT
(PROFILED ON PAGE 155)

As a non-American, it was easier for him to convince the rest of the people in the European parks and attractions business to join IAAPA and to show them that the association could provide benefits to non-American members as well. "It was easier for me because most park people in Germany or in France would say, 'Ah, this is not needed for us. This is not international. This is an American group. I was able to explain that while it started in America, it was a group that we all should join and be a part of as park owners and top management."

Bo Becomes a Living Legend

Bo said he was "very, very surprised and amazed" when his name was called as the Living Legend inductee during the 1996 Hall of Fame ceremony during the IAAPA Convention and Trade Show in New Orleans. "It was hard to believe that there would have been such a shortage of VIPs in 1996 that they had to choose me as a Living Legend! Living OK, but Legend?"

His acceptance speech surprised many. "It was undoubtedly short and somewhat confused," he now jokes. Few would disagree. He stood behind the podium in front of several thousand attendees and humbly told them. "We have much in common at this moment. None of us know what I'm going to say!" Once the laughter died down and the ice was broken, Bo was able to explain that he was (and still is) "very grateful, pleased and honored" to become a member of the Hall of Fame.

He also pointed out that his time in the industry and with IAAPA proved that entertainment is a true international language. In retrospect, he says the award didn't necessarily change his attitude about anything, but it did inspire him to keep working for IAAPA "for as long as they wanted me." Ten years after his retirement, he was an integral part of the international committee that worked on the IAAPA Strategic Plan in 2003 and 2004, and says it "was a very interesting and rewarding task."

In 2006, he continues to serve as senior advisor for Liseberg as well as a consultant for a number of hand-picked projects around the world. He still has an office at the park and he meets Liseberg's top executives every couple of weeks. While he hasn't slowed down much, he has been able to spend more time with Lotta, his wife of nearly 50 years.

"We now have the opportunity to spend some of those nice, summer days together here in Sweden, something we could never do when I was working full time at the park," he said.

BIBLIOGRAPHY

ARTICLES & INTERVIEWS

A Swedish Lead, *Funworld*, by Chuck Michio, October 1998

Bo Kinntorph: A Thoroughly Modern Man, *Funworld*, by J.D. Henderson, November 1991

Bo Who? Curriculum Vitae of Bo Kinntorph

Calls for Entries: 2006 Applause Award, *Amusement Business,* Dec. 22, 2005

Goodbye, Farewell, and Amen, *Funworld*, by Bo Kinntorph, November 1992

Interviews with Bo Kinntorph, by Tim O'Brien, June 23, 2005; Aug. 18, 2005; Nov. 1, 2005; Dec. 20, 2005; May 2, 2006; May 24, 2006

Interview with Bob Blundred, by Tim O'Brien, May 24, 2006

Interviews with Mats Wedin, by Tim O'Brien, Dec. 19, 2005; May 9, 2006

President's Letters, *Funworld*, by Bo Kinntorph, December 1991

Where are they Now? *Funworld*, by Tim O'Brien, September 2005

MARTIN SKLAR

"Walt always said whatever we did
would never be good enough again."

Marty Sklar began his half-century adventure with The Walt Disney Company at Disneyland four weeks before the park opened to the public on July 17, 1955. Since working at the opening of that park he has become the only Disney employee to have attended the openings of all 11 Disney parks worldwide.

Walt created and walked in only the original Disneyland, while Sklar has not only opened them all but has left his creative imprint on each one - from a dime newspaper printed for the opening of Disneyland to the names on the windows on Main Street at Hong Kong Disneyland, which opened in late 2005.

This is the story of a college journalist who went from creating *The Disneyland News* to be the king of the Disney creative team. His influence has helped make Disney the most creative parks group in the history of the industry. This needs to be a good story, an easy to follow and fun story, because for Marty, it has always been about the story.

For nearly 50 years Marty has been a Disney Imagineer. In 1961, he was moved into a different department and began working for WED Enterprises, Walt's personal creative brain trust, where he helped develop shows for the New York World's Fair. He became WED VP of concepts and planning in 1974, VP of creative development in 1979, executive VP in 1982, and president of the newly named Walt Disney Imagineering in 1987. In 1996, he was promoted to Vice Chairman and Principal Creative Executive, a position he held until he stepped

The SKLAR File

MARTIN ADRIAN SKLAR
Named for Adrian, regarded as one of the foremost costume designers during Hollywood's golden age.

Born: Feb. 6, 1934, in New Brunswick, N.J. Moved to Long Beach, Calif. when he was 12.

Married: Leah Gerber, May 12, 1957

Children: Howard, born in 1959, is a teacher, lives in Helsinki, Finland with two children. Daughter, Leslie, born in 1962, lives in Los Angeles and is married with two children. "Leslie is married to an Israeli and Howard is married to a Finn and when we all get together with their families, none of them speak English, and we don't speak their language. So, there's a lot of hugging."

Education: Long Beach Poly High School, 1952; UCLA with BS in political science, 1956.

Claim to fame: Learned the amusement and themed entertainment business at Disneyland from Walt Disney, then went on to become an Imagineer and eventually headed up Walt Disney Imagineering. If Walt needed anything written or communicated, chances are he called Marty. As the king of the Disney creative team, his influence has helped make Disney the most creative parks group in the history of the industry.

His Disney career: For nearly 50 years Marty has been a Disney Imagineer. In 1961, he began working for WED Enterprises, the predecessor of Walt Disney Imagineering. He became WED VP of concepts and planning in 1974, VP of creative development in 1979, executive VP in 1982, and president of the newly named Walt Disney Imagineering in 1987. In 1996, he was promoted to Vice Chairman and Principal Creative Executive, a position he held until he stepped aside in early 2006 to become Imagineering Ambassador for the Disney Parks and Resorts.

Mentors: "My dad, a teacher and school principal was a big influence. Both he and mom made sure we were brought up in an intellectually stimulating environment; Coach John Wooden at UCLA, who I covered for two years for the *Daily Bruin* newspaper, was an organized, dedicated man who knew how to motivate and I learned a lot on how to deal with people from him; John Hench was the most articulate and well-read person that I've ever worked with and he encouraged me in so many ways."

Continued on page 92...

aside in early 2006 to become Imagineering Ambassador for the Disney Parks and Resorts.

He was never an artist, he didn't invent things and he certainly never crawled under a ride to fix it. No, Marty's creative contribution for all these years has been the story and the creation of the vehicle to best tell that story along with his leadership of the Imagineering creative team. His creative writing and his story telling abilities have made him a star in the Disney universe. Before his death in 1966, Walt often called Marty if he needed a story told; from creating a newspaper to writing the script for a movie on Walt Disney World, Marty was one of Walt's key personal scribes for 10 years. It was Marty who wrote Walt's official obituary for the company.

As a writer and major creative force in a make-believe world where story directs nearly everything, Marty has been unsurpassed.

His First Walk Down Main Street

Johnny Jackson, executive director of the UCLA Alumni Association was working for Disney in publications in 1955, and when Walt said he wanted an 1890s tabloid style newspaper created to sell on Main Street, Jackson recommended Marty. "In early June 1955, I received a call from Card Walker, who was head of marketing at Disney at that time. He asked me to come in for an interview," Marty recalls. "He told me what they wanted, asked if I could do it and after my assurances that I could, they hired me for $75 a week. For me, it was a summer job because I still had a year of school to finish and I was about to become the editor of the UCLA *Daily Bruin*. I went to work in mid-June and two week later, I had to present my ideas for *The Disneyland News* to Walt. He liked it. This was two weeks before Disneyland opened and I was a 21-year-old who had never worked professionally. I was scared as hell." The paper sold 75,000 copies that first summer. In the fall, Marty went back to school, finished his last year at UCLA and returned to Disneyland. "I came back and never left," he jokes.

"Here it was two weeks before Disneyland was to open and everything was in chaos," Marty said. "What impressed me, in retrospect, was that Walt had time for this little thing I was working on which amounted to nothing in the big picture of things. But it was part of a story he was trying to tell. Main Street was a little town, and every little town at the turn of the century had its own newspaper. He felt a hometown newspaper needed to be part of his story."

The small detail, Marty learned immediately, is what makes the Disney story appealing. "Paying attention to small details like that helps create a more complete story about whatever you're talking about.

The SKLAR File

Continued from page 90...

Walt Disney as a mentor: Walt Disney was a "huge" influence. "When Walt Disney died, it hit me harder than when my own father died, because I never had to think like my father, but in order to write for Walt Disney, I had to think like he did and use the same words to communicate as he did."

Work philosophy: "For me it's always been about putting together people who are 1) talented, 2) creative, 3) want to work together, and then motivating them to do the best they can under the same philosophy that I learned from Walt Disney - if you believe in something, work hard, and do the best possible job, give the public more than they expect, and make sure that it's a great quality story."

Views on the media "I read non-fiction, I watch sports on TV. Whatever I watch, I'm also doing some kind of work while I watch. I also love movies."

Favorite Disney park: "Epcot, because that was my project, but you can't beat the original Disneyland. I always like to remember that this is the only park Walt ever walked in. It's also the park from which I started, where I grew up in the business, so its special to me."

Favorite Disney ride: "Space Mountain is my favorite ride I ever worked on. I've been on every attraction we've ever created for the parks except two. That's the Maliboomer in Disney's California Adventure. We didn't create it, so I wasn't pushed to ride it. There's no story or imagination to it." The other one is Raging Spirits, a loop coaster at Tokyo Disneyland. "I couldn't ride it when I was there because I just had knee surgery about a month before and I couldn't bend my knee enough to get in."

Favorite Non-Disney park: "I liked the old Knott's Berry Farm when it was a ghost town and had the early Western theme. I thought it was very well done and they had a theme and they really stuck to it. But, you know, none of the other parks I've been to really stand out to me."

Favorite Non-Disney ride: Spiderman at Universal Florida. "They did an excellent job. It's probably the best (non-Disney) ride ever built!"

First amusement ride ridden: The Cyclone Racer, a wooden coaster at the Pike in Long Beach.

Seeing how Walt felt about each little detail of the park taught me to pay attention to even the smallest details. The company still practices this approach today."

All for One, One for All

In addition to detail, Marty learned early on in his career that the Disney way was always about being a team player. John Hench, an original Imagineer with WED, told Marty, "When we get finished with a project, you or none of us can say, 'I did that, I did this,' because we all did it, so many hands touched it, changed it and made it better, that it's a we, it's never an I."

Marty said an individual's contribution can usually be found in the final product if one looks closely enough, but the Disney mind frame is to never point out "what I did" to anyone. "The best thing about Imagineering is that we have such varied talent. We have approximately 140 different disciplines and they all, in one way or another, have a role. There are so many things that go into the details of what makes up a park or an attraction that you have to have that kind of group mentality."

Marty professes that everybody who works as an Imagineer is a disciple of Walt. "Yes, we are because if you look, it's not our name on the front door, it's still Walt Disney." He notes that even today, most people don't know "who we are individually" at Imagineering and admits that there are some people who can't work that way. "Some have big egos and want their name in lights, and they soon leave. Some pretty talented people have left Disney to do their own thing, and, you know, I appreciate that and am alright with it. I'm still close to a lot of them. Some of them even come back and do consulting work for us."

Choosing Walt Over Academia

Marty graduated from Long Beach Poly High School in 1952 and went on to UCLA and graduated in 1956 with a political science major and history minor. He had wanted to pursue journalism, but UCLA didn't have a degree program for it and his family couldn't afford to send him off to college, so he stayed in Los Angeles. "I received an alumni scholarship to UCLA for $50 a semester, which practically was my entire tuition." He didn't let his studies in poly sci get in the way of his passion for the written word and he soon became sports editor, city editor and then editor of the *Daily Bruin* newspaper at UCLA.

Marty grew up in an intellectually stimulating environment. His dad was a teacher and a high school principal and wrote for several different education journals. "He was a big influence on me as was my mother because of the way they both approached life. We were living on a teacher's salary in the 40s and 50s, so we never had a lot of money. But, they always did things with my brother and me and we were always surrounded by my father's friends who were also teachers. He had one friend that he hired to help enrich our studies. She'd come over once or twice a month and we would talk about all kinds of things, just to enrich our intellectual experience. My brother Bob received scholarships to Yale, Princeton and Harvard and he's now a professor at New York University."

His parents were contesters, back in the days when you wrote 25 words or less and you could win a wide variety of stuff, based on your writing skills. They were very successful and among their winnings were a trip to Alaska and a car. "They were very creative writers," he adds.

His family moved to California from New Jersey when he was 12 and it's the Pike amusement park in Long Beach, Calif. that he remembers best. That was back in the days when "it was overrun by sailors." He recalls the Cyclone Racer, the wooden coaster that went out over the ocean, as a rough ride that once caused him to lose his glasses.

Visiting the Pike as often as he did was a good background for someone who would eventually go to work for Walt Disney. It was that whole run-down environment of the Pike and other similar parks that Walt reacted against in creating Disneyland.

Those Who Helped Shape Marty's Life

One of the biggest influences that helped shape Marty's future was UCLA basketball coach John Wooden, a person he would often write about as he was reporting sports for the *Daily Bruin*. "I got to know Coach Wooden quite well and I would go to practices and watch how he dealt with people. He was so well organized. I learned from watching him how to deal with people and how to motivate people and how to organize what you were doing. Those lessons have served me well through the years."

As could be expected, Walt Disney was also a huge influence on Marty, who notes that when Walt died in 1966, it hit him harder than when his own father died. He explains, "I never had to think like my father, but in order to write for Walt Disney, I had to think like he did, know what he wanted to communicate, and then use the same words that he would use. When writing for other people you always try to make it their personality. In addition, his values, his optimism, his continual motivation to do better the next time were all tremendous influences on me."

The hardest story Marty ever had to tell – in the form of an obituary - was the death of Walt Disney. He bitterly recalls that day. "I was in Imagineering and received a page to go to Card Walker's office. When I walked in, there was Card and Donn Tatum. They were the two top executives under Roy Disney at the time. Card told me to go into the next room and write the message for the company about Walt passing away," Marty said, adding that he couldn't believe that he had been put into such a position.

Marty Sklar, left, is joined around an early model of Epcot, by John Hench, Ray Bradbury and John DeCuir Jr. Bradbury developed the communication storyline for Spaceship Earth.

"First of all, that was the first news I had of his death. I also resent to this day and still can't believe that nobody had prepared a statement before his death. They knew he was dying and nobody had prepared anything on this man who had such an impact on the world. I had to sit there and in 30 or 40 minutes write two pages of stuff. What do you say? How do you remember all the things that you should say in those few minutes about somebody like this? I was really upset, but my deadline training for the *Daily Bruin* came into play, thank goodness!"

Marty's Story Behind Space Mountain

When the Disney team was planning Walt Disney World, RCA had the contract to provide the communications infrastructure. As part of

Marty wearing his famous "Travel Hat" which contains more than 100 pins representing Disney projects around the world. Marty's hat and his penchant for pins is said to be the catalyst behind the official Disney pin trading phenomenon.

the agreement, there was a quid pro quo that if the Imagineers could create an attraction at The Magic Kingdom for RCA to sponsor, there was $10 million set aside for the project. Designer John Hench had the assignment to create the attraction and Marty was to assist. The original concept they planned would take people inside a computer and tell them the computer story from the inside. It seemed like a natural since RCA was a pioneer in that business. The attraction was going to be put into the new Magic Kingdom at Walt Disney World in Florida in the

Flight to the Moon and Mission to Mars facility.

Hench and Marty worked on it for nine months and went through all the levels of RCA, all the way to the top and finally were told that it was time to present it to Robert Sarnoff, chairman of RCA. "We go in the night before and set up our presentation in their boardroom which was about as wide as a hallway and about two miles long," Marty recalls.

"There were nine storyboards, which were set up on one side of the room. When we finished setting it up, the RCA people said, 'You know, Mr. Sarnoff sits at the head of the table.' And, I said, wait a minute, we've got the storyboard sketches set up and they're way down there. How am I going to communicate with him? They said, 'Well, that's your problem. Mr. Sarnoff only sits at the head of the table.' So, the next day the presentation was made and I have never been in a more disastrous presentation."

When finished, Marty sat down at the table. Sarnoff writes out a note and hands it to the vice president next to him, who hands it to the vice president next to him, who hands it to the vice president next to him. He hands it to Marty. It reads, "Who are these people?" Marty shakes his head. "You can imagine how we felt. He didn't even know we were Disney people or why we were there. They hadn't briefed him."

CONSTANTLY RAISING THE LEVEL

"Working with Walt Disney was the greatest 'training by fire' anyone could ever experience. Walt was always pitching in with new ideas and improving everyone else's input, like a master chef brewing a new recipe. We were constantly breaking new ground to create unique projects never attempted before in this business. That, I'm proud to say, has never stopped in my more than 50 consecutive years at Disney."

MARTY SKLAR

Totally frustrated, Marty returned to the studio and reported back to his boss, Card Walker, then CEO of Disney. "I told him that I didn't care if he fired me, but I was not working with these people anymore.

Nine months of my life on this project and they don't even tell him what it was about." Walker stood up and said, "Marty, there's $10 million on the table. You can't walk away from it. You've got to find a way to get that money."

Marty went back to Hench and said that after thinking about it, the presentation was a huge mistake. Marty reported that, "We had a great show but we were doing what we thought they wanted us to do. What we should figure out is what we want to do. And then, let's see if we can sell them on doing that." The creative heads went to work.

This was in 1971 and the idea for Space Mountain had existed since 1964 when the ride couldn't be built because computer systems weren't sophisticated enough to control the vehicles speeding around in a dark place. By 1971, technology had been created that could make Space Mountain a reality. Hench and Marty went to work on preparing another pitch.

RCA was in the satellite communication business, "so we took this long entry corridor and installed several RCA satellites and at the exit of the ride, we put in a long moving ramp and took every consumer product RCA was making, including television sets and audio systems and made what we called the Home of Future Living, and gave it a very contemporary look."

It was time to go back to see Sarnoff again. "This time, I insisted that Card Walker go to the meeting because he knew Mr. Sarnoff. The night before, we went in as we did before and set up about nine storyboards. When we finished, a RCA person told us once again where Mr. Sarnoff will sit and I said, that's OK, except that I will have my back to Mr. Sarnoff the whole presentation because I am presenting it to whoever sits in this seat, as I pointed to a particular chair. He told me I couldn't do that and I told him that I didn't work for him and that I was indeed going to do that."

The next morning as people were filing into the room, they stationed somebody by that chair. They stopped Sarnoff when he came into the room and they said, "Mr. Sarnoff, the Disney people want you to sit here." He said, "Fine," and sat down. "You know, no one had ever asked him to change seats before. We made the presentation, we sold the project, we got the $10 million, and that's how we came to build the original Space Mountain. That $10 million is the equivalent to about $80 million in 2006."

Did Sarnoff and the RCA group intimidate Marty? "No, I was on the Anaheim City school board and when you have 500 parents at a meeting and they all want to lynch you, that's when you really get nervous. But, I never got nervous presenting to Mr. Sarnoff or Cliff

Marty in front of the California Screamin' coaster at Disney's
California Adventure theme park during construction in 2000.

Garvey, the Chairman of Exxon, or Roger Smith when he was the
CEO of General Motors. After stuff like that on the school board,
nothing fazed me."

The Story in the Park

It didn't take Marty long to realize that the story was what truly made
Disneyland unique. Walt took the failing amusement park concept and
breathed life back into it by adding the narrative. Many of the naysayers
in the industry at the time told Walt that his ideas wouldn't work. What
they didn't realize is that Walt was about to fundamentally change the
entire business, and story was to be at the heart of it all.

The original Disneyland was an anti-amusement park. Not seedy,
worn out and dangerous, but colorful, spic and span clean, and friendly.
The first time Walt told Mrs. Disney that he was going to create a park,

she said, "Why would you want to do that? The people who work in those places are awful, the places are dirty and they're not safe." Walt answered, "Well, mine's not going to be that way." The belief and optimism that he could do something different was very much in the heart and soul of Walt Disney and his disciples.

"Mickey's Ten Commandments"

BY MARTIN A. SKLAR

I. Know your audience.

II. Wear your guests' shoes.

III. Organize the flow of people and ideas.

IV. Create a "wienie" (visual magnet).

V. Communicate with visual literacy.

VI. Avoid overload - create turn-ons.

VII. Tell one story at a time.

VIII. Avoid contradictions - maintain identity.

IX. "Ounce of treatment - ton of treat."

X. Keep it up (maintain it).

"Mickey's 10 Commandments" is Marty's list of the do's and don'ts of Disney creativity and communications as he has understood and practiced them for more than 50 years. The list is now considered the "rules for success" of the themed entertainment industry.

Marty Becomes an Imagineer

When the work on the New York World's Fair began in 1961, Marty was loaned to WED Enterprises, the precursor to the Imagineers, and was assigned by Walt to work on John Hench's team to develop industry-sponsored shows and pavilions for General Electric, Ford, Pepsi-Cola/UNICEF and the State of Illinois. That work included storytelling and script writing for the Carousel of Progress and It's a Small World.

Marty's task while working with Hench's group was to help them come up with the basic idea of what they were going to present. "My assignment was to learn as much as I could about the Ford Motor Company and then work with John and the others on how to interpret that story in the pavilion. We probably spent a total of five or six weeks, traveling around to different parts of the Ford Motor Company. My duties were all about the story."

WED, the acronym for Walter Elias Disney, was Walt's privately-owned company. To protect anyone who switched back and forth between WED and Disneyland, as did Marty, there was an arrangement that one would never lose his seniority with the Walt Disney Company. After being "on loan" to the group for three years, Marty officially became a part of WED in 1964. After the World's Fair, the corporate lawyers became concerned that the appearance might be that Walt was diverting business from the Walt Disney Company to WED, his personal company, which Marty said Walt was always very careful not to do.

"Walt had an agreement with Roy Sr. (Roy O. Disney), his brother, that whenever somebody approached him about doing something on his own, like the World's Fair opportunity, he would take it to the company first, and say, 'Do you want to do this, or can I do it?' Disney (the company) had to turn it down before Walt would do it on his own." Because of that concern, WED Enterprises was sold to Walt Disney Productions and Dick Irvine, who was Marty's boss, stayed on as the head of the creative group, which kept the name WED for another 20-plus years before changing it to Walt Disney Imagineering.

Early Training at Disneyland

When Walt was starting work on the park, he went to his friend, architect Welton Beckett and asked him if he would "work with me on creating Disneyland?" Beckett replied, "Well, what is it? What do you want to do?" Marty speculates that this may be one of the first times Walt explained what he wanted to create to an outside person.

The advice Beckett gave him set the stage for how Disney park employees are trained to this day. "You know Walt, you're going to have to train your own people. To do something as different and special as you want to do, you have to have a cadre of people that understand you and how you work," Beckett advised.

People who understood Walt and his dreams, with most coming from his own studios, were the core of the original Disneyland team. Those he brought in were visually oriented and knew about creating the scene and a story. All the original designers at Disneyland came out of the motion pictures, including Dick Irvine, who ran WED and Bill Martin, who designed Frontierland and Fantasyland.

"I was the oddball, but was trained by all those brilliant people including Harper Goff, who originally created the Jungle Cruise," Marty notes, adding that he, in turn has done his share of teaching and training through the years. People once under Sklar's tutelage now work throughout the world.

Marty Fills a Gap

Marty cites his journalist skills in general and his storytelling ability in particular as the tools that led him to a successful and creative career. "As a journalist, I had a basic understanding about storytelling and I knew how to communicate a message in writing," he said. "For many years, I worked with all the big sponsors we have in the parks and it was essential that we were able to communicate their message for them. In Epcot for example, we didn't always have good information on what we should communicate, so we had to go get it and then create a story around that message. Our role was both designer and storyteller, and my background was quite useful. So much of what we do is about communicating, whether it's to an audience in a ride vehicle, on a stage, or in front of a garden, it's all about communication and storytelling."

He quickly learned how to work with the designers and soon found that most of them had no desire to be in an executive role. There was a gap on the executive level after Dick Irvine, who had headed up WED since 1952, became ill during the building of Walt Disney World. When Irvine had to step aside, Marty was poised to be the one to rise out of that gap and take over. He had personally worked with all the designers, understood their special quirkiness, knew how to organize them and perhaps most importantly, knew how to get the best out of them.

"You know, it's a people business number one, and if I have a legacy when I'm through with all of this, it's going to be the people who I have brought into the organization and mentored. I hired practically all the key designers, writers, and just about everybody in the creative division at Imagineering, including Tom Fitzgerald, who is now Senior Executive Vice President for Creative Development at Imagineering and runs the department on a day to day basis."

With his new job responsibilities and his growing work load, Sklar transitioned from writer to editor. "I haven't been a writer for a long time. I've been an editor for 30 years. Today, I don't do very much original writing except things for my own talks and Disney publications."

Marty watches as Herb Ryman adds the finishing touches to the illustration depicting the entrance of Epcot, in 1980.

He laughs when asked what he "really did" as the head Imagineer. "I worked with talent, primarily the project leaders, reviewing, giving advice, suggesting solutions, resolving conflicting needs, and standing for founding principles," Marty replied. "I met with the leaders and spent time selling their ideas to others within the company."

Bob Rogers, an early protégé of Marty's influence and now chairman and founder of BRC Imagination Arts, was one of those who nominated Marty for the IAAPA Hall of Fame in 2001. On the nomination form, Rogers wrote: "Marty Sklar has done for themed entertainment what Ed Murrow did for broadcast news. He helped invent it, then inspired,

Marty with John Hench at the 15th anniversary of Tokyo Disneyland in 1998. No one except Walt Disney influenced Marty's philosophy of creating for Disney Parks more than did Hench.

taught and trained a whole generation of people how to do it better and better. His leadership and encouragement have launched a thousand careers both inside and outside Disney, including mine."

Imagining an Imagineer

In 1986, Walter Elias Disney Enterprises (WED) officially became Walt Disney Imagineering (WDI). Even though the creative individuals at Disney had been known as Imagineers since the early days, the switch of the official name was made to honor the man who started it all. Harrison "Buzz" Price originally came up with the name, a combination of imagination and engineering, and Walt loved it, according to Marty. "The name change came about for two reasons," Marty explained. "First, we wanted explicitly to have Walt Disney in the name. When you said WED Enterprises, we knew who it was, but we wanted to be more out front."

The second reason for the name change, Marty points out is that it eliminated the phone calls "asking us to set up a wedding."

Being there in the beginning and being so vital in the group for so many years, it could be said that Marty defined what an Imagineer is supposed to be. "I like to think that I interpreted and reinforced Walt's creative approaches because it was really Walt Disney who set this whole thing up. I've worked hard to be the champion of Walt's philosophy and values over the years," Marty said. "John Hench was the king of design, but even being as smart as he was, he wasn't able to communicate easily down the line, so there was a role for me in helping to achieve what the great designers had developed."

One of Marty's beliefs is that no idea is a bad idea. "We say that because if you get in a meeting and somebody comes up with something and someone turns to him and says, 'That's a stupid idea!' you'll probably never get another idea from that person. So, we try

Socially Redeeming Ride

"The song will drive you bananas if you hear it often enough, but from a message standpoint, It's a Small World is an amazing, timeless attraction. I think it's one of the great things that Walt did."

There's just one moon and one golden sun and a smile means friendship to everyone.

"That message is as important in the world today as it was when we created the first It's a Small World for the New York World's Fair in 1964. The attraction's message is that we may be of different colors, we may have different beliefs, we may wear different kinds of clothes, but in the end, we're all together in one place on the earth. We're all in this together."

MARTY SKLAR

to create an open environment where people can say anything. Quite often, something that sounds dumb at the time will turn out to be just the little spark that sets everything off. Somebody will come in later and say, 'You know, I thought what so and so said was dumb, but I've been thinking about it and I think there's a little gem here.' It's amazing how many times that happens."

Marty said that he's been around so long and has discussed so many ideas that he has seen many resurface after many years. "When that happens, I know from experience that a lot of them won't work, but I don't say, 'Well, you know what? We tried that 20 years ago and it won't work,' because so much changes. If we went back through our archives, we'd probably find a lot of things that we could do today that we couldn't do at the time because the technology wasn't there."

The Evolution of Walt Disney World

In the mid-1960s, Marty wrote "Walt Disney's Epcot," a 25-minute film that was still in production when Walt died in December 1966. The film was devoted entirely to communicating Walt's visionary concepts for the Epcot project. Marty wrote two endings, one aimed for the Florida legislature in an effort to get the Reedy Creek Improvement District approved and the other customized to potential corporate partners, with the "thank you" message that none of this is possible "without your cooperation and participation."

"It wasn't clear at the time Walt died whether we would proceed with Walt Disney World and Epcot. Roy Disney had to belly up and make that decision to go ahead," Marty said. "None of the other executives of the company had much to do with WED because it was Walt's private laughing place, if you will. So, we had to convince them that we knew what we were doing in order to go ahead with the Walt Disney World project."

During 1967, the year following Walt's death, Marty, as well as the other Imagineers became frustrated that the Florida park project had been stalled. "It was clear pretty early that no one in the company knew how to get their arms around Walt's ideas about Epcot. We realized that only he could have pulled that off," Marty said. "However, we all knew how to build a theme park that would also be a resort destination."

The Magic Kingdom at Walt Disney World was put back on track and was built. It opened in 1971 and nearly eight million visitors came through its gates the first year. The Epcot concept that was to be the second phase of Walt Disney World was still being bantered

Marty and his wife of nearly 50 years, Leah,
had dinner at Lumiere's restaurant onboard the
Disney Magic during a cruise in June 2005.

around but "it was just too much a part of the heritage of the company to let it die. It was a responsibility we all felt to Walt. We all wanted to make something out of that concept and to keep Epcot a part of his legacy in Florida."

Marty had become VP of concepts/planning for WED in 1974 and a year later, four years after Walt Disney World first opened, Walt Disney President Card Walker approached Marty and said, "Now, we have to try to figure out what we're going to do about Walt's Epcot." "That's when we started having a series of meetings in Florida with energy people, healthcare people and people in transportation. We had probably eight or nine different meetings with people we invited from industry, government, and academia. We basically evolved the idea for Epcot, and we knew from the start that we couldn't build the whole covered community that Walt had been talking about. We evolved it into a theme park."

From the mid-60s into the 1990s, Marty was Imagineering's primary strategist in relations with American industry in the development of sponsored attractions for Disney parks, with an emphasis on Epcot. "We first convinced General Motors to be a part of Epcot, and then,

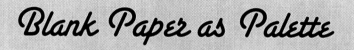

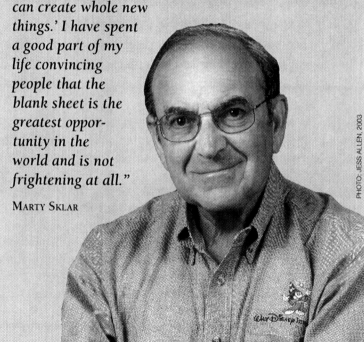

"I believe there are two ways to look at a blank sheet of paper. The first way is that the blank sheet is the most frightening thing in the world because you have to put down the first mark and figure out what to do with it. The other way, is to look at it and say, 'Wow, I've got another blank piece of paper. This is the greatest opportunity in the world because I can now let my imagination fly in any direction and I can create whole new things.' I have spent a good part of my life convincing people that the blank sheet is the greatest opportunity in the world and is not frightening at all."

MARTY SKLAR

PHOTO: JESS ALLEN, 2003

Exxon and Kraft. I was very involved in pitching the concept to these corporations to acquire partners that would help offset the cost and make it possible to build the new park."

Epcot, which opened on Oct. 1, 1982, was the last major project Marty headed up, "because after that one, there were just too many things going on." There were three Disney parks when Marty began his tenure as the leader of the Imagineers and by the time he stepped down as the group's creative head, he had directed the master planning and design of eight additional theme parks and resort amenities around the world. Walt didn't believe in sequels to movies, and he wouldn't have believed in sequels to theme parks either, according to Marty. "Our opportunity to go beyond what we did last time has always been an exciting challenge. Walt always said whatever we did would never be good enough again."

Championing Walt Disney

According to Marty, Dick Irvine, John Hench, Herb Ryman, Roger Broggie, and Claude Coats were among the key talents who championed the Disney concept and values after Walt died. "They all had grown up with Walt and believed in him," Marty said. "It was their loyalty and their respect for Walt and his ideas that carried the company after Walt died."

At the time of Walt's death, "we didn't have the single decision-maker who could say, 'yes' or 'no, I want to do it this way.' There were many conflicts. Personalities came out that had been modified by Walt's presence and now there was a lot of the 'who's in charge' kind of stuff. That was a hard period to get over, but you know, the problems and confusion finally coalesced in Walt Disney World once we got the go-ahead to continue. Dick Irvine really brought it all together."

The infighting went on for a couple of years, but it wasn't all negative. "Creative people generally have strong attitudes and if they didn't, it wouldn't be as good as it is. You've got to have strong person-alities who believe in what they're doing," Marty added.

Walt's Love of the Past

One thing Marty "really loved" about Walt was, that he had one foot in the past with a love for history and nostalgia, and one foot in the future with his love for new technology. "Those two things are pretty strong components of everything we do at Imagineering," he notes.

Walt believed that the background to any story, whether it be nostalgia, fantasy, or the future was as important as the story itself. If the environment wasn't believable, people wouldn't buy into the story. Marty recalls one afternoon in Disneyland when he and a photographer drove a car behind the scenes to Frontierland to take publicity photos. Walt saw what they were doing and was quite dismayed. "What are you doing with a car here in 1860?" Walt queried as he was making a very strong point to both Marty and the photographer. "Walt's point was that we had just destroyed the story. There was the Mark Twain (sternwheeler) with all these people aboard out in the wilderness and here we were with an automobile from another age. We had broken the continuity of the story. Visual intrusion is something we are constantly aware of today."

Marty notes that he learned a great deal about combining history and technology by observing Walt. As an example, he points out an incident that occurred as they were working on the Carousel of Progress for GE for the World's Fair. "GE had a vice president who was in charge of marketing, and he came out and we carefully described the show for him. When we were through, he said to Walt, 'Well, why would General Electric want to show all those products we don't make anymore?' Walt said, 'You know, I'm a storyteller, and one way you get through to people is to approach them with things they're familiar with and nostalgia is a part of that.' The GE executive said, 'Well, I don't care. We don't want to show those products.' Walt walked out of the room, went down the hall and into the lawyer's office at WED and told him, 'You get me out of this contract. I'm not working with that man, anymore!'"

The next week Gerald Phillipe, who was president of GE, had a previously scheduled visit with Walt and the first thing Walt said was, "I'm having trouble with one of your vice presidents." That was the end of the problem. The point, according to Marty, is that Walt felt as strongly as he did about how he approached the telling of stories. You just don't blast people with information. "No, you've got to sneak up on them. And, storytelling in the three-dimensional world is a lot about that. You don't just hit somebody with a pie in the face every time," he said.

Marty the Family Man

Marty was a Zeta Beta Tau man and Leah Gerber was an Alpha Epsilon Phi lady, both while attending UCLA. They met at a fraternity function in 1954 and began dating. On May 12, 1957, they were married. May 12 often falls on Mother's Day, a coincidence that has never escaped Marty. "In those years, I still get away with buying her only one present," he says with his wry sense of humor, obviously with tongue in cheek.

After the couple was married, they moved into a house less than a mile from Disneyland and he is quick to point out that the nearness of the park greatly influenced his kids, especially their son Howard, born in 1959.

Marty signs a book for a young fan during the 2005 IAAPA Convention and Trade Show in Atlanta.

"He wouldn't go to bed at night until the fireworks were over," laughed Marty. When daughter Leslie was born in 1962, she also was influenced in many ways by her nearness, both familial and geographical, to Disneyland. Both kids worked at the park on the Autopia attraction for a couple of summers, Marty adds.

"I found it interesting that at a certain age they wouldn't go to Disneyland with me any more," said Marty. One day they told him why. "Because you stop and pick up every piece of trash you see. It also takes so long to get down Main Street because every time there's somebody taking a picture of their family you stop and ask if they'd like you to take the picture with them in it," they explained.

"I'm sure I missed a lot of the kids' growing up," Marty waxes. "When I looked back at my travel schedule during the time we were selling Epcot to sponsors, I realized that one year I was gone for 26 weeks. When you think about that kind of travel schedule, it makes it hard on a family, but my kids are very solid. They grew up to be great people. Leah and I now have four grandchildren to take to the park."

IMAGINEER'S MISSION

"As long as there's a world left open to imagination, we will continue to dream and deliver amazing adventures, enchanting experiences and magical memories for families everywhere."

MARTY SKLAR

Even with his busy schedule, Marty never strayed far from community activities. He was elected to the school board in Anaheim in 1969 and served two terms on the board for a total of eight years. He also coached the Little League team. "Originally, it was because my son was involved, but when he went to the higher league, I continued to coach the younger kids. I enjoyed working with the kids and I coached along with a couple other parents who I liked working with. I found time for those kinds of things," he recalled.

He claims there's "no question that I've been a workaholic" and up until about 2004, "I can't remember a weekend when I didn't do something related to work. Still, almost every night, I'm doing some kind of paperwork or reading."

Marty's Community Activities

Through the years, both Leah and Marty have been involved in the community of Anaheim. He was not only involved in the school board, but also served on the Cultural Arts Commission and on the Parks and Recreation Commission. The two started the Michael L. Roston Creative Writing Awards, an annual creative writing competition in the Anaheim Public Library that was held for 20 years. In 1977 Marty was the recipient of the Community Service Award for Anaheim, presented by Cypress College.

He was honored in July 1995 as a Disney Legend by the National Fantasy Fan Club, and in September 1995, he became only the second person to be awarded the Lifetime Achievement Award, presented by the Themed Entertainment Assn. In 2001, Disney CEO Michael Eisner and Vice Chairman Roy E. Disney, officially named Marty a Disney Legend and in 2002, he was inducted into the IAAPA Hall of Fame.

When long-time Disney artist, designer and Imagineer Herb Ryman died in 1989, Marty and Leah together with Buzz and Anne Price, Lucille Ryman Carroll (Herb's sister), and Sharon Disney Lund (Walt's daughter), wanted to do something to honor his memory, highlighting his positive influence on the young people in Imagineering. Prior to creating the first visual depiction of Disneyland for Walt Disney in 1953, Ryman had graduated from the Chicago Institute of Art and was "hooked on teaching kids to draw in the classical traditional way, meaning that you can do your own thing, but learn how to draw properly first," Marty said.

In 1990, this group of Herb Ryman's friends founded the Ryman Program for Young Artists, now known simply as Ryman Arts. "That first year, we had one class and 15 kids in conjunction with the Children's Museum in Los Angeles," said Marty.

By 2006, there were nine different teachers, nine classes and 150 kids that Marty calls the "cream of the crop of talented high school artists" from across Southern California. The 14-18 year old students come from 60 different schools, and the diversity is enormous, according to Marty, who still serves as the president of the foundation. The classes are held on Saturday mornings on the campus of the University of Southern California, which donates the use of its fine arts classrooms to the program.

"It's tough to get into the program. It's competitive and with the dearth of art teachers and art programs in schools these days, this has become the premier program in California," Marty notes. "More than 90% of the kids in our program go on to college, and almost everywhere we go these days in Southern California - in graphics, design and animation - there's a kid that graduated from our program." In addition, Marty and Leah personally sponsor a scholarship for graduates of Ryman Arts to go on to the California Institute of the Arts.

Marty and Mickey at a presentation during an IAAPA seminar in 2005.

A Load of History

As can be imagined, Marty's long and illustrious career has garnered him boxes of memorabilia. "I never throw anything away, and my wife hates it. We moved from Anaheim to to Hollywood Hills in 1986 and I still have a couple storage facilities in Orange County filled to the top," Marty said.

If the bugs haven't gotten to it by now, Marty said he has "a treasure trove" of early Disneyland studies, writings he created for publications, and boxes of souvenir items. He jokes that he plans to fund his retirement selling on eBay.

He said he "honestly doesn't know" what he will do with his archives. Before making that decision, he knows he has to open those storage doors. "I'm kind of afraid to go in there, but, I'd love to know what I saved through the years and to know what condition it's all in."

But he is sure of one thing; nothing in good shape is going to ever be thrown away. "I hate the idea of throwing away. I remember when we moved from New Jersey to Long Beach when I was a kid, my mother threw away my Batman comic book collection. To this day I still resent that."

Following Another Fork in the Road

In March 2006, Marty took on yet another role within the Disney Parks & Resorts division of the Walt Disney Company. He announced the change to his Imagineering team in a memorandum on Feb. 15, 2006. "I knew that as my 72nd birthday and my 50th Disney anniversary approached, I would look for new challenges, knowing I am not ready for a lounge chair by the pool and the tennis court. So when Jay Rasulo (chairman of Walt Disney Parks and Resorts) asked me to talk about the future, I was all ears to a challenging proposal Jay made. It not only seems to be one of those ideas that is overdue, but it was clear to me that I am the perfect casting (perhaps the only candidate) capable of originating and organizing this assignment." He then notes as an aside. "I do have an ego, even if I hide it 99% of the time!"

Marty stepped down from his post as vice chairman and principal creative executive for Walt Disney Imagineering to assume his new role as Imagineering Ambassador for the Disney Parks and Resorts. His new job is to "communicate the Disney difference." He said he will be "representing the energy, passion and talent of the Disney Imagineers whom I have helped lead creatively and symbolically for so many of those 50 years."

The new role puts Marty in a unique position to tell the Imagineering story. "Imagineers are proven leaders in imagination, creativity, and innovation, but there are lots of audiences outside Disney – and inside as well – who aren't aware of the important role we play. That's the story I will tell."

He says this new opportunity to fill "another blank sheet of paper" with imagination and passion is an exciting challenge, and a familiar one. "After all, for nearly half a century, I've been doing that creatively, and as a creative leader of some of the most talented, committed and inspired people in the world: my fellow Imagineers. It's been great fun, and we have filled those blank pages with some of the most imaginative ideas, designs and experiences the world has ever seen."

Marty outlines two goals he wanted to achieve during his 50th year with the Disney organization. He wanted to see Hong Kong Disneyland open successfully, which it did in fall 2005, and to see a Disneyland 50th celebration take place. With Tom Fitzgerald leading the creative team on the Hong Kong project, Marty kept busy motivating Disney officials to start planning for the 50th anniversary of the park. "I kept saying this is really something, it's a one-timer, you guys. We need to do it and do it right and make sure that its something that stimulates our business. If we don't, people are going to come and there won't be anything going on and it'll affect business for the next 50 years."

He put his ideas in a booklet called 50 Nifty Ideas for Disneyland's

Hidden Mickey Phenomena

In the Disney world where team recognition, not individual acknowledgment reigns, Hidden Mickeys have become a way for individual Imagineers to put their own mark on a project. *"It's a way of getting around what we try to guard so strongly against. It's a way of saying ha, ha, we can play around with management. Even though management doesn't want us doing things like this, we can get away with it. It has now become a kind of a tradition."*

MARTY SKLAR, EXPLAINING THE SMALL IMAGES OF MICKEY MOUSE THAT APPEAR, PARTIALLY DISGUISED, THROUGHOUT THE WORLD OF DISNEY.

Fiftieth, and sent it to Paul Pressler in 2001. When Pressler stepped down in 2002, he sent it to Jay Rasulo, Pressler's successor. As it turned out, 35 of those 50 ideas became a part of the 50th celebration. Was he satisfied? "I asked what happened to the other 15?"

In the months immediately following the announcement of Marty's new role, the same question was heard repeatedly. "What are you going to do?" He laughs and tells everyone that he isn't totally sure but he would "figure it out" as he went along.

"I'm going to see if it works because I've been a hard charger all my life, and I wonder how much I can actually dial back. I'm planning to work less - maybe three or four days a week and see how that works." Marty promised Rasulo that he'd try it a year and then decide whether to keep going.

Marty explains that this transition is a way of easing out and slowing down while still being able to control his destiny. He moved out of the Imagineers building in Glendale into an office on the studio lot in Burbank, just down the hall from where Disneyland was originally designed. "I'm going to miss the people most of all, but I'm still going to maintain my friendships," he said.

"And I plan to go back over there just enough to annoy people."

BIBLIOGRAPHY

ARTICLES & INTERVIEWS

Disneyland and Walt Disney Imagineering Press Material, 1990-2006

Disney's Sklar Exits Imagineering Job for Parks Post, *Reuters,* by Sheigh Crabtree, Feb. 16, 2006

Imagineering a Dream, *Orange County Register,* by Michele Himmelberg, Dec. 18, 2002

Interview with Buzz Price, by Tim O'Brien, Feb. 10, 2006

Interviews with Marty Sklar, by Tim O'Brien, Oct. 11, 2005; Nov. 17, 2005; May 21, 2006; June 14, 2006

No Slowing Down for Dis Imagineer Sklar, *Amusement Business,* by Sheigh Crabtree, Feb. 22, 2006

Sklar Reflects on Imaginative Career, *Amusement Business,* by Tim O'Brien, Dec. 9, 2002

The Next Chapter, *Funworld,* by Marilyn Waters, June 2006

The Sorcerer's Apprentice: Marty Sklar, *Funworld,* by Bob Rogers, May 2002

Walt Disney Imagineering Memorandum, Change is Just Around the Corner, by Marty Sklar, Feb. 15, 2006

Walt Disney Imagineering's Marty Sklar, *The "E" Ticket,* Fall 1998

Welcome Marty, *Funworld,* January 2003

BOOKS

Building a Company: Roy O. Disney and the Creation of an Entertainment Empire, Hyperion, 1998, by Bob Thomas

Building a Dream: The Art of Disney Architecture, Harry N. Abrams, Inc.,
    Publishers, 1996, by Beth Dunlop
Disney A to Z: The Official Encyclopedia, Hyperion, 1996, by Dave Smith
Walt Disney Imagineering: A Behind the Dreams Look at Making the Magic Real,
    Disney Editions, 1996, by The Imagineers
Walt Disney's Disneyland, Walt Disney Productions, 1964, by Marty Sklar

HARRISON "BUZZ" PRICE

"Guessing is dysfunctional, ignoring prior experience is denial.
Using valid numbers to project performance is rational!"

Industry legend Harrison "Buzz" Price was an important soldier in the revolution – Walt's Revolution. He was there from the start, marching next to Walt Disney as the seed known as Disneyland was sowed. It was Buzz who showed Walt exactly where to plant that seed.

Buzz's ticket to legendary status was his pioneering use of numbers to foretell the potential success of a park. He first created, then introduced professional data analysis into the industry and was the first to prove his feasibility studies with the use of those numbers. Buzz calls his discipline of consulting - where the arts are combined with hard numbers - performance economics. In keeping with industry jargon, he also calls it roller coaster math.

His revolutionary studies have helped bankers and investors become familiar with and more trusting in the amusement park industry for more than half a century.

Starting with his first two studies for Walt Disney in 1953 and until Walt's death in 1966, Buzz personally worked on 160 of Walt's ideas. By the time he decided to hang it all up in 2005, Buzz had been involved in more than 5,000 studies for clients as varied as the Statue of Liberty, the Los Angeles Olympic Organizing Committee, New York World's Fair, Six Flags, SeaWorld, The Las Vegas Hilton, and the Catholic Church of Maracaibo, Venezuela.

Throughout his career, Buzz was a sought-after speaker, teacher and philosopher. He was the first recipient of the Themed Entertainment Assn.'s

The <u>PRICE</u> File

BUZZ PRICE

Born: Oregon City, Oregon, May 17, 1921

Education: CalTech, degree in engineering; MBA from Stanford

Married: Anne Shaw, April 29, 1944. "It was the happiest venture of my otherwise chaotic life."

Children: Two sons and two daughters, all work in the arts

Claim to fame: Pioneered the use of numbers to foretell the potential success of a park. He originally used numbers to justify his choice of location to build the original Disneyland in Anaheim, Calif. in 1955. Nearly 160 studies for Walt Disney later, he used the same economics model to pick out land in Central Florida for Walt Disney World.

First industry job: Hired as a consultant by Walt Disney in 1953 to conduct a site location plan and an economic plan for Disney's amusement park.

Favorite park: Disneyland. "I was the first to look at that site, so I'm partial."

Favorite non-Disney park: Busch Gardens Williamsburg (now Busch Gardens Europe) – "the landscaping and layout are beautiful."

Major influence on chosen career: C.V. Wood, "my boss at Stanford. He taught me dull wasn't all bad."

Personal business philosophy: "My big thing is *yes if* consulting, not the *no, because* variety. *Yes if* tells you what you can do with a project if you make changes, *no, because* just kills it."

Favorite park food: Martinis at the English Pub in Epcot at Walt Disney World in Florida.

First park memory: Oaks Park, Portland, Ore. "My biggest memory is that I fell into the monkey pond leaning over the edge and my father and mother had to fish me out."

Major awards: First recipient of the Themed Entertainment Association's Lifetime Achievement Award, 1994; Inducted as a Living Legend into the International Assn. of Amusement Parks & Attractions Hall of Fame, 1995; Became the first non-Disney employee to win the distinction of "Disney Legend" in 2005; Honorary Doctorate from California Institute of the Arts, 2005.

Lifetime Achievement Award in 1994 and was inducted into the IAAPA Hall of Fame as a Living Legend in 1995. In 2005, he became the first non-Disney employee to win the coveted Disney Legend distinction.

Following retirement in 2005, Buzz looked back upon his life journey in a novel way. "There are several negatives in my career that didn't happen; one of the most important is that I never went broke. As a matter of fact, I never had a losing month! I was only sued five times in professional arguments, and one of them, the 1984 Louisiana World Exposition in New Orleans, was very large and could have busted me," he recalls. "But I never lost a case. They were all thrown out of court."

More than anything else, it was the part he played in what he calls Walt's great revolution that stands out as the highlight of his life. "It was a revolution in new standards of performance and design and operation, storytelling and audience impact. I was happy to be part of that, even in a small way."

Buzz thinks it was the timing of Walt's great adventure that made it so remarkable.

"Walt taught the post-war world that there was a positive way to look at the imperfect society. Political life could be screwed up, wars and pestilence could occur, economies could get out of balance and we could be up to our ass in debt. But, there was a positive way to look at all of this and that was the message that Walt set out to put into his attractions."

Buzz Sits Down with Walt

Every project for Walt started with a conference on what it was that Buzz was to accomplish. "Sometimes, there was a lot of oohing and aahing, like Walt wasn't sure. But, he would start off with an idea like, 'I want to build the world's greatest winter resort' and we would have great discussion about it and he would say, 'What kind of research do we do?' It was my job to help him deal with all of this by creating a planning language that would test the feasibility and the viability."

Many of the 160 ideas Buzz and Walt worked on together took flight, helping Buzz build his niche in the amusement industry. Planning and feasibility studies were a revolutionary idea for this industry and the concept soon caught on, thanks to the work of Buzz. Before Walt's revolution, feasibility planning was nearly the last thing that would come to the mind of an attraction developer, Buzz notes.

One of Buzz's biggest surprises at the time was that he could present a quantitative discipline to a bunch of creative people who could understand it. Walt was most fascinated by the quantitative side of Buzz's crazy ideas. "In the 13 years I worked closely with him, he would call me every time he had a hot idea. We would talk it over, and most of the time he wanted me to put numbers around it. He knew the numbers could usually make a case for getting the capital."

Walt was always under pressure to get more money, and he was always battling with his brother Roy about the finances, according to Buzz. "Roy was very much a conservative, and if Walt had an idea that cost $100, Roy always tried to figure out how he could get it done for less. Walt would use my numbers as an argument to prove that his idea was right and that he should have the money to do it."

Walt's Dream of Artschoolland

In addition to Disneyland, one of Disney's passions was his concept for an arts school. Most of the artists working for him in his studio at the time were single disciplined people. He created an art school model that would produce artists that were well rounded renaissance people. His dream was to build a multi-disciplined art school of world-class status. The idea evolved out of his work with Chouinard Art School, from which he recruited many of his artists, "some of whom weren't very bright in other areas except their artistic skills," Buzz notes.

Walt asked Buzz to check out his art school concept and he ended up conducting more than a dozen studies, the first of which was an economic feasibility study in May 1959. The rest ranged from mission and purpose studies to facility programming and executive recruitment. The idea evolved into what became the California Institute of the Arts, or CalArts, to which Walt left half his estate, with ground breaking finally taking place three years after his death. Since opening, the school has sought to advance the practice of art and promote its understanding in a broad social, cultural and historical context. Buzz was the institution's second chairman and he has been a trustee of the world-class bastion of higher education for more than 40 years.

The Theme Park Business

Buzz was 32 when he entered the theme park business. He had worked for seven years as an engineer and had gone back to school to earn his MBA from Stanford. Upon his MBA graduation, he stayed there and went to work with the Stanford Research Institute (SRI). It was there that he was introduced to a new kind of consulting - data-based applied research.

He was in his second year with SRI when he received a call one Monday morning in July 1953 from Nat Winecoff, a movie executive who was helping Walt Disney with Disney's newest dream - an amusement park. Walt had asked Winecoff, on the urging of a couple

Buzz Price, right, looking over Herb Ryman's famous rendering of Disneyland in July 1953, with Walt Disney, left, and C.V. Wood who managed the construction of Walt's first park.

other movie-types who had prior dealings with SRI, to call and see if someone could help with the park concept. Winecoff invited Buzz to visit Walt the next day. He did, and Buzz walked away several hours later with two contracts, one for site location and one for economic planning, involving 12 weeks of work with a budget of $25,000, "a big fee for 1953," notes Buzz.

Walt's prelude to Buzz was, "I want to do this park, and I don't know where to put it, and I don't know how big it should be and I don't know how many people are going to come." Walt described the park he envisioned. It was to be 160 acres located in Southern California, was to have no roller coasters, no Ferris wheels, and have a berm around it to keep out the sights and sounds of the rest of the world. It would have only one main entrance in which all guests would pass, and he wanted everything to be a part of a storytelling environment. Custom rides would be created and would be subordinate to story and setting. He wanted it to open in 1955, a quick two-year turnaround.

Walt Disney highlights a point on the original model of Disneyland to C.V. Wood, left, and Buzz Price, right, in early 1955.

Buzz recalls sitting there, totally baffled, talking with Walt. "I asked him if he had any opinions of where he would like to see it located. He looked at me and said 'no, you tell me.' I created models and dove in, full of enthusiasm."

Buzz picked out a site in Anaheim, an agricultural town at the time. "We looked at the five southern California counties and computed the center of gravity from the census districts, and we did a growth analysis, which showed it was growing rapidly southeast toward Orange County. We needed 160 acres, so it couldn't be in downtown LA, but it had to be accessible to the freeway. There were three freeways in business at the time, so we had three spokes where we could go. We also looked at the climate, and the best climate was also in the direction of Orange County. We focused on an area we called the 'amoeba' because of its shape. We ranked 10 sites in the area, and Walt purchased our number one choice."

Conventional wisdom held that the concept - Disneyland - wouldn't work. However, for the first time in this industry, analysis was done through the use of numbers and the numbers said that it WOULD work. "Our numbers said the market was there, and that we should do big per caps and have a strong penetration," he said.

Buzz Ignores the Veterans

Buzz felt strongly that the numbers were right, but being that this was the first time for a study of this sort, and of this magnitude, he wanted to check it out further, if for no reason but his own edification. He packed up the renderings and created a dog and pony show to present to four long-time, well-respected park operators at the 1953 IAAPA convention at the Sherman House Hotel in Chicago. Present at that meeting were William Schmitt, owner of Chicago's Riverview Park; Harry Batt of Pontchartrain Beach in New Orleans; Ed Schott, of Cincinnati's Coney Island; and George Whitney of Playland at the Beach in San Francisco. Prior to the presentation, Buzz supplied the four with Chivas Regal and caviar in a private suite.

"I went through the ideas for the five distinctive areas and the story telling that would be used in each, and these guys were brutal. They said Walt should keep his money and leave this to people who knew the business. They said he had to have entry from all four sides and not just one main entrance in the front, that people didn't care about the landscaping, and none could understand the reason for the berm that Walt was building around the entire park that would hide it from the rest of the world." By the time Buzz returned with the report from the front lines, Walt had already purchased the land and was ready to get started. After hearing the sentiment of the four park veterans, Walt shook his head and said, "To hell with them."

What Buzz brought back from Chicago was a chilling evaluation from industry veterans of a new venture that was essentially already underway. Did Buzz himself like the idea of Disneyland? "I refused to pass judgment," he said. "I was not going to be like those guys who said it wouldn't work. I never once said, 'it won't work.' But on the other hand, I never once said it would be a slam dunk."

Buzz Creates New Methodologies

Buzz found himself in a new niche and admits that he was a bit awed by it all in the beginning. The concept of creating a data bank for an industry of which he had little knowledge was a bit daunting. Very quickly he was able to pull together some "bright guys" as his associates and together they began to build data and invent methodologies for analysis that were both new and effective. Many of those early methodologies have stood the test of time and are as valid today as they were more than 50 years ago.

One of the keys to the early studies, according to Buzz, was the realization that there was cyclic behavior that was basically predictable. Upon figuring out how to read those behaviors, a new method of analysis was determined. Once created, the methodologies could then be used for any attraction that drew large crowds of people.

Buzz was never an employee of the Disney organization. He was an outside source, essentially making him one of the first successful consultants in an industry now filled with a galaxy of well-trained brief case carrying change agents. Buzz claims he wasn't intimidated by Walt or by Walt's well-chronicled roughness. "No, I was absolutely enthralled. It was fun! I would often come late to meetings. I kind of assumed a pose that I'm not going to be overwhelmed by this guy. I'm not on his payroll, I can say anything I want, and I'll do my best for him, but I'm not going to be a minion."

He has wondered frequently if his tardiness was an unconscious shout of independence. "I would often come in 10 or 15 minutes late, and I really didn't mean to. But, I think it might have been the psychology of trying to show him that this stuff was not to be treated like the routine numbers found in the accounting department."

At first, there were many naysayers in the business who quickly proclaimed that these kinds of numbers studies were not needed "just to build an amusement park." Buzz noted proudly that it didn't take long before developers wouldn't even think about going to their banker or investors without having the right kind of numbers analysis in their hand.

His genre of studies and the resulting reports were soon considered essential business tools. "Guessing is dysfunctional, ignoring prior experience is denial. Using valid numbers to project performance is rational!"

Big Change for Buzz

For several years after Buzz's initial work with Walt, life was good and things were going well when he and his wife Anne lost their nine year old son Steven in an accident. One of Buzz's other SRI clients, Lawrence Harvey of Harvey Aluminum told him, "You need a change, man, get down here and work with me." Harvey had also lost his oldest son, and Buzz soon sought refuge in the world of integrated aluminum products. He worked with Harvey for three years. "I had a very good job, but Walt kept knocking at my door, and three years later, overwhelmed with all of his ideas, he twisted my arm to leave the aluminum business," Buzz noted.

To get him back, Walt set Buzz up in his own business which Buzz named Economics Research Associates (ERA), a company that Walt could use to supplement his own ideas as well as to by-pass corporate bureaucracy. He encouraged Buzz to accept other consulting jobs and to provide the new company a semblance of financial security. Walt promised Buzz that if necessary, he would pay ERA for three fourths of available time at per diem rates - a promise that Buzz never had the time to evoke.

"He knew damn well I'd learn a lot more and be much more helpful in the long run if I was not chained to him," Buzz recalls. This outsource approach would give Walt flexibility and an outside perspective in the complex business of evaluating the economic implications of his endless stream of ideas.

National Acclaim

"With his good looks and almost boundless exuberance, Harrison Price seems more like a recreation director than a sober business analyst."

NEWSWEEK, 1973

"Walt was not paranoid about ERA working for other park developers, which was critical for us as we were building an international company. In fact, he said his reason for wanting us to work for others was so we didn't become insular. It wasn't long before we had 40 people doing this stuff and it seemed we were working on everybody's park projects. We were doing all of Six Flags work, and then all the work for SeaWorld, and later, all the work for the Busch parks. In five years, we had a data bank that wouldn't quit."

By the late 1960s, if a new park was to be created or an old facility expanded, Buzz was the man to call. His reputation was above reproach and his contemporary style of economic study was in demand. Buzz said he had no idea of what a significant contribution he was making to

Buzz at Six Flags Over Texas in 1964.

the industry or that he was approaching legendary status. "No, I didn't," he laughs. "I was just too damn busy trying to keep my head up and the company afloat. We were a low overhead shop and within a short time, we were doing 150 proposals a year. We were crazy with work. I really didn't have time to ask what this was all adding up to or what historic impact we were making."

An amazing thing occurred during that period - no one cared if Buzz was working for their competition. "Today that couldn't happen," he said. "I was trusted to not cross over the line and I didn't. I very carefully didn't tell one company what another one was doing in a way that would be hurtful, so I got away with working for all of them."

In a 1994 speech honoring Buzz as the first recipient of the THEA (Themed Entertainment Assn.) Lifetime Achievement Award in Los Angeles, industry veteran Terry Van Gorder pointed out how amazing it was that the "major leaders and competitors within our entertainment industry knowingly and openly sought Buzz's wisdom and counsel simultaneously."

And his influence was not confined to the United States. By the time he shuttered his business in 2005, 35% of his work had been completed outside the country. "I was very big in Holland for awhile, and worked on 14 projects. I was really part of the scene there and we set up an office. We had a great project in France called Happy Land that didn't pan out, even though it was a great piece of land. It's where the Charles de Gaulle Airport is now," he recalls.

Buzz said that while his variety of economics was becoming widely accepted and was standing on its own, it was Walt's blessing and endorsement that made him the go-to man of the time. "Walt was the miracle man and people were keeping an eye on what he was doing and with whom he was working. Knowing that I was so deeply involved with his company, people hired me and I received a great deal of work. Maybe they were all searching for a piece of that Disney magic." The close relationship would continue until Walt's death.

Saving a Small World, After All

Through his own creative and design company, WED Enterprises, which changed its name to Walt Disney Imagineering in 1986, Walt became involved in the 1964 New York World's Fair. Of course that meant Buzz and his boys would also get involved and eventually work on seven different studies for the fair. Ford, General Motors, General Electric, and UNICEF/Pepsi-Cola all hired WED to produce shows for them. The UNICEF/Pepsi pavilion was to be a shared exhibit with joint financing with WED, a separate company than Disneyland owned wholly by Walt.

Buzz was called in to help save the deal with UNICEF/Pepsi for which WED had designed the internationally themed, It's a Small World ride. The deal was nearly dead when Buzz stepped in and created a deal package which clarified investor and financial organization of the project. It was accepted by both sides, and the planet's first It's a Small World was built and became a huge hit at the fair. Following the event, the ride was moved to Disneyland and has since been reproduced at other Disney parks worldwide. Millions of youngsters around the world can thank Buzz for the cheerful and colorful ride. Likewise, millions of adults who can't get the tune out of their heads now know exactly who to curse!

Finding a World in Florida

Late in 1963, as the company's role in the New York World's Fair was winding down, Walt asked Buzz and his ERA team to consider the idea of building a second park and to look seriously at potential sites in central Florida. They soon defined an area in the Orlando area as the number one choice in which to build a park. In 1964 the Walt Disney Company decided to go ahead with the project and within 12 months had purchased 27,000 acres for $150 an acre.

Buzz defined the location, picked out the land, and once Project X (what Disney insiders called the secretive project) was made public in 1965, Buzz created the economic master plan for all elements of land use around the park and the park itself. For several years, ERA and Buzz turned out many more studies for the project, including a planning manual for computerized cash flow analysis in 1966, and an impact study to be used to deal with state authorities in 1967.

Walt died in 1966, but his brother Roy kept the project alive and opened the Magic Kingdom at Walt Disney World in October 1971. "Both Disneyland and the Orlando park were created by a brilliant group of in-house and retained designers, engineers, planners and technicians," Buzz points out. "Walt had essentially blueprinted Disneyland. What happened in Orlando five years after his death was a tribute to the force and logic of Walt's conception and to Roy's determined implementation. Roy opened the $600 million Florida park without a penny of debt."

Buzz continued to work with the Disney group after Walt's death, but he had a substantially less central role, with the bulk of the strategic planning being carried out in-house. "That was appropriate," he notes. "My particular relationship with Walt and Roy was not easily transferable to a succeeding generation of corporate brass."

Walt's death in 1966 still haunts Buzz. "When he died, I was absolutely haunted by his absence for a long time in a particular way that I shall never experience again. I still dream about the man."

The Buzz Words

Buzz was bright, he was articulate and he was becoming well known. As a result, he was in demand as a speaker and it wasn't long before he also became a great orator. Buzz is unique in that he has combined a pioneering use of analytical numbers with one of the best vocabularies possessed by anyone in the industry. Seldom does one have the control that he possesses over both words and numbers. He can trace that dichotomy back to his parents. His Scottish mother was a word lady and loved the language, and his grandfather, according to Buzz, kept a Webster's Unabridged Dictionary in the outhouse. Buzz's father was a workaholic retailer with great number skills.

The influence of the two created a passion within him that he says "manifested itself as a love of numbers in a narrative framework." Buzz thinks numbers "are a drag" unless they tell a story.

He always looked for similar attributes when hiring employees. He searched for those who he refers to as "triangle people," those with one part verbal articulation, one part strong quantitative and numerical

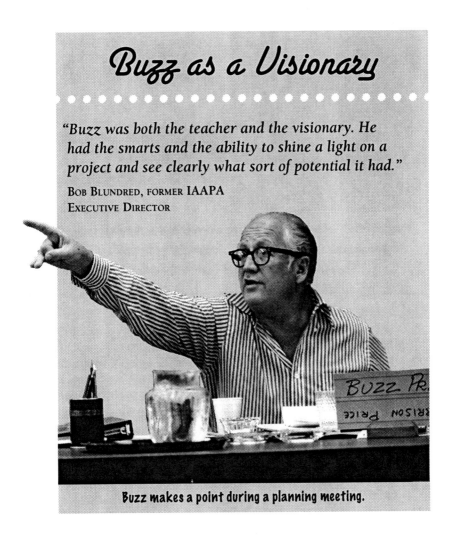

Buzz as a Visionary

"Buzz was both the teacher and the visionary. He had the smarts and the ability to shine a light on a project and see clearly what sort of potential it had."

BOB BLUNDRED, FORMER IAAPA EXECUTIVE DIRECTOR

Buzz makes a point during a planning meeting.

skills, and one part a love of humanity and a clear sensitivity to its foibles. "A triangle person can do anything. We didn't want a pure numbers geek, a pure computer nut. We wanted people that had all these polarities enmeshed."

Buzz, at the podium in 1968 during a travel research symposium, is accompanied by a stellar panel, from left: George Millay, Ed Ettinger, Doc Lemmon, and Charley Thompson.

Selling ERA; The End of an Era

In 1969, when he sold ERA to Planning Research Corporation (PRC) for $2 million in stock offerings, his company was involved in much more than parks and recreation. "We were stirring around in real estate and the economics of development. We were very profitable." He looks back now and says that while the deal sounded good, PRC was "one of those high flyers whose stock dived drastically, so I was screwed."

It didn't take long to realize that he had made a mistake by selling ERA. "We were doing well, had good momentum in the marketplace, and I had my independence," he recalls. "There was nobody at PRC, the biggest consultancy in the country at the time that knew the slightest or even had the foggiest idea of why ERA was important or what we were doing. I went to business school but I was very dumb about that transaction."

As part of the buyout deal, Buzz went to work for PRC as subsidiary president of ERA for four years. In 1973, when he couldn't endorse PRC's way of conducting business any longer, he led a revolution. "We called ourselves the Onward Sailing Club which consisted of the presidents of all the companies that had been acquired by PRC, and we organized a revolution and threw the founders out. At that time, I left ERA totally and went into the management of the parent company." He became a group vice president, then VP marketing, and then served briefly as chairman.

Buzz then experienced "a blindside attack" by a director of PRC who wanted his chairmanship. He was forced out and at age 56, the high-flying Buzz Price was unemployed and once again totally independent. When asked if getting fired from PRC was a low point of his life, Buzz answers from the heart. "The two low points in my life were the death of my son and my assassination by PRC. It's rather weird to put them in the same breath, but psychologically, they impacted me the same way. The result is that when you wake up, that's what you think about. When you eat dinner, that's what you think about. It's with you continually in a perverse and overpowering way."

New Venture for the Unemployed Price

In January 1978, he formed his own business, the Harrison Price Company (HPC) and brought in a team of seasoned professionals, including the likes of Nick Winslow and Sharon Dalrymple. It didn't take him long to get back on his feet. "I immediately pitched a big job to the American Management Assn., got it, and worked night and day on it for six months. I didn't have time to be bitter or feel sorry for myself or cry in my beer about losing my position with PRC." Other contracts followed and during the subsequent 12 years, HPC completed $27 million worth of work.

Ironically, when Buzz was dumped from PRC, the board told him he could have ERA back for free, but Buzz notes that he "didn't want to do that to those people. They had four years in which they were independent from my direct control and they didn't need me back." ERA got itself back, becoming an independent company that remains a successful and relevant entity today.

His new company, HPC went into "direct, friendly competition" against ERA, and many times through the years the two companies worked together on projects, supplementing each other's strengths. Buzz still wonders to this day why they treat him with such ceremonial dignity. "I took a lot of business from them over the years."

John Robinett, senior vice president of ERA, thinks highly of Buzz. "I think he's the father of all we do in terms of the analysis of the industry. He has indirectly contributed to the quality and success of attractions throughout the world."

Buzz, the Flexible Numbers Man

What Buzz did as a profession required mental flexibility and the ability to quickly get up to speed from one project to another. "Yes, that's exactly what I had to do, but in a way, that was the saving grace of this crazy business. You would burn yourself out on something and you'd work all night. Then you presented it to a client and most of the time you had the pleasure of pleasing them. Most often I had little if any time to enjoy the glow before whammo, I got a brand new challenge and was off and running again and staying awake all night again."

Buzz laughs at the widely believed concept that a consultant is only as good as his last job. "That's not really true because I've had some clunkers that didn't kill me. You can do a dumb job and it takes you a while to work your way out of it. But, we didn't have too many of those."

BUZZ'S LEXICON LEGACY

"Buzz Price came up with the term Imagineering. He suggested it way back in the early 50s and Walt really liked it, right from the beginning."

MARTY SKLAR, FORMER CREATIVE HEAD OF WALT DISNEY IMAGINEERING (PROFILED ON PAGE 89)

One job from which he did get fired was at SeaWorld of Texas in San Antonio which was being built by Harcourt Brace Jovanovich (HBJ). Buzz did the numbers and told William Jovanovich to expect between 1.2 million and 1.5 million at the park each year over the first three years. Jovanovich "summarily fired me for that projection, announcing to the media that he was building (a park) for five million visitors, three million at the start." While the park's first year of operation welcomed 2.8 million, Buzz said those numbers were pumped by deep discounts and promotions. They dropped drastically and ended up averaging 1.42 million a year during the 1990s, "right where we said they would be," added Buzz.

He was also fired a couple other times a bit more colorfully, for not bringing in the initial research numbers high enough to please the client. One such firing took place by Judge Roy Hofheinz when Buzz conducted a feasibility study for AstroWorld theme park in Houston, which was being built by Hofheinz, the Houston Astros baseball team owner and former Houston mayor. Buzz and his group estimated one million attendance for the first year and Hofheinz, wanting a higher number, "argued with me and called me a very dirty name and wouldn't pay the bill. In his first year, he got exactly what we said he would get."

One of the first and perhaps the greatest confrontation of Buzz's career was with NBC President Robert Sarnoff in 1959. Sarnoff was trying to get Walt Disney to partner with NBC to build what was to become Freedomland theme park in Bronx, N.Y. Sarnoff had his own set of studies, believed in the project and wanted Walt to build it.

"Walt came to me and asked that ERA do our own study on the project. We did and boy, how it differed from Sarnoff's big thick study saying how marvelous of an idea Freedomland was," he recalls. Buzz did a week of work on the project and all indicators said not to build the park. "I made my pitch and they made their pitch and Walt believed in mine." Sarnoff didn't trust the results of Buzz's study and there were quite a few words thrown between Buzz and Walt and Sarnoff and a group of NBC executives. Without Walt's money and expertise, Sarnoff didn't go forth on the park. However, developer Bill Zeckendorf picked up the concept and went ahead and built the $25 million park. Freedomland opened in June 1960 and barely made it through the 1964 season before the gates were permanently closed.

As these examples illustrate, Buzz was not afraid to dismiss a client's great idea as a potential money loser. "He has done much for our industry by setting high goals and standards," said retired Six Flags Theme Parks President Larry Cochran, who co-wrote Buzz's IAAPA Hall of Fame nomination in 1991. "But at the same time, he always told it like it was and never encouraged the development of a project, especially when his numbers and his experience lead him to believe it had limited chances of success."

The Famous Brain Storming Sessions

Buzz experienced his "best batting average" of satisfied clients during the time when he and his team offered specialized and highly organized brain storming sessions. Borrowing from the concept of an architect's design conference, Buzz called his special program a charrette. These were intensive one, two, or three day sessions that brought the client's group together with a diverse team of experienced outside consultants.

HPC conducted more than 150 charrettes and Buzz claims all but two clients were "very satisfied" with the results. "From our point, they were very exhausting, but they gave us the opportunity to eat, drink and socialize with our clients which was very beneficial," Buzz points out.

A charrette is at best a "quick and dirty" version of planning, he notes. "It can save a bucket of money because if a full design effort is started in the wrong direction, a million dollars can be wasted away in no time at all," he said. "A great number of projects with serious problems have been corrected or mercifully killed at conception by a relatively inexpensive charrette held during the beginning stages of planning."

Expo Work

Buzz's performance economics models not only work for parks, but also for any entertainment facility that attracts large crowds. Therefore, a natural evolution for his work was to expand into the world of fairs and expositions.

His involvement in the economic master planning and segment planning of international expositions spanned 34 years and covered 10 major projects that "were actually built," he adds. Those projects range from Seattle's Century 21 in 1962 to Portugal's celebration in Lisbon in 1998. The 1962 Seattle exposition was his first and was originally pitched to Walt Disney, who declined and recommended to the organizers that they hire ERA, which they did. Buzz projected an attendance of 9.2 million and it ended up attracting 9.6 million. Half of the expo projects that Buzz was involved with were carried out by ERA, the other half were during his HPC years.

The biggest and potentially the most dangerous lawsuit ever thrown at Buzz and his company was as a result of his analytical work for the Louisiana World Exposition, the 1984 World's Fair in New Orleans. The concessionaires were angered that the numbers he predicted weren't being realized and they sued while the event was still under way. Eventually the $12 million lawsuit was thrown out of court but it did scare Buzz into changing the way his personal finances were kept. While the lawsuit was active, Buzz transferred "everything we owned to my loyal wife. The process is called transmutation and with care it is legal. We went back to 50-50 after we won the case and I am now no longer economically dependent on her steadfast commitment to our six decade love affair," he noted.

Buzz accepting his IAAPA Hall of Fame Award, 1995.

Buzz as a Non-Parkie

His favorite park? "Well, you have to give a lot of credit to the first one – Disneyland. Maybe that's psychological. You know, I was the first guy who looked at that site and I have always been very fond of that one. From a regional point of view, I like Busch Gardens in Williamsburg a great deal. The landscaping there is beautiful."

Ironically, Buzz didn't spend a lot of time in parks and when he did visit one, he would go in, do his work and get out, claiming that he was too busy to stay around and have fun. "You can't write a report while you're goofing around in the park. I really didn't need to be familiar with what went on inside the park, I wasn't an operational consultant. In fact, I often completed my studies without going into the park at all. I wasn't into this park thing by virtue of some secret fascination. My passion was in the numbers."

However, when he did allow himself a few minutes of frolic while in a park, he'd make it a point to ride the coasters. "I loved them. If I went into a park and didn't ride the meanest ride, then in my own eyes, I was a sissy."

Buzz' Bizz Slows Down

In 2000, Buzz started getting the feeling that he had "been there, done that." His secretary of 25 years, Sue Utley, decided to leave and move back to Florida, and Buzz and Anne made the decision to move from Los Angeles to Palm Springs. It was a big transition, and it was his first legitimate attempt at slowing down.

Doing so allowed him the opportunity to pursue another challenge that many of his peers were pressuring him to face – to write his autobiography. "Walt's Revolution! By the Numbers," was published by Ripley Publishing in 2003 and completing the book was "a real

Buzz's View of the Future

"People will continue to go to parks, no matter what happens. Even with all of the trauma around them, do people stop wanting to eat, to love, to work, to play? No. It's as fundamental as that. If you aren't mired in some bloody battle for survival you're going to have time to play. If for $25 I can go play and give my kid a happy experience, I'm going to do it. The climate sucks. Things are all screwed up. Let's go play."

BUZZ PRICE

high" for Buzz. "During the process of organizing my notes and my thoughts while preparing to write that book, I began to understand what I'd been doing all my life, much more than I had ever had time to think about before. I really took my life apart and put it back together again on paper and finally said to myself, 'Hey shmuck,' this is what you've been doing."

After moving to Palm Springs, he intentionally allowed his work load to ebb. "As it started slowing down, I felt like I was treading water. I wasn't making the kind of money that was worth my effort," Buzz waxes. He finally thought, "Hey, I'm nearly 80, what the hell am I doing this for?"

On the other hand, (the one with warts, as Buzz is fond of saying) it was hard at first for him to turn away work, especially during those "semi-retirement days" when he had more time on his hands and needed less sleep. The one time workaholic discovered that the older he got, the less he could sleep. In his later years, it was not uncommon to get a note from Buzz that signed off, "Call at will, I have insomnia. Best, Buzz."

By the time he had reached 83, Buzz was turning most of the business leads over to two of the protégés he had trained, Sharon Dalrymple, who he calls the best report writer in the history of the business, and Fred Cochrane, who Buzz describes as a very creative financial analyst. In a transition starting in January 2005, he finally shut down the Harrison Price Company in October 2005, after 52 years in the business.

Buzz calculates that he flew "several million miles" during his career and through several periods was gone from home as much as 80% of the time. Anne didn't mind, because "we celebrated our reunions with great enthusiasm." Anne never took the back seat to Buzz from the day they first met, he points out. "She was a very active woman. She was on several boards, including the Pomona College Board of Trustees. She was a good mother to our four kids. She has also been a workaholic all her life."

He met Anne Shaw while he was a student at CalTech. "I was very unlucky in love and I finally asked my sister, who was attending Pomona College if she knew of a compassionate music major that she could fix me up with. She gave me Anne's number." On their first date they went to the movies and saw the Disney film *Fantasia*. Quite ironic, Buzz notes, considering his later dealings with Walt Disney. They courted for two and a half years and were married in 1944.

Anne became a successful musician and classical singer. She was a soloist with the L.A., New York, and San Diego symphonies and was a featured vocalist in Fred Waring's Pennsylvanians and the Roger

Wagner Chorale. Buzz said she was "a damn good singer, but unfortunately her voice pre-deceased her." Her brother, Robert Shaw was a world renowned conductor and musician.

He laughs when he recalls the difficulty his kids had understanding what he did for a living. "When they got older, I gave them copies of every speech I wrote and gradually they tuned in. I had two sons that could have worked out very well in our field but one went to Harvard and became an architect, and the other is a very successful heavy metal sculptor. Both daughters are also in the arts. One's a professional classical singer and voice instructor and the other is a folk artist who creates art with tapestries and abalone shells."

A Performing Artist in His Own Right

Bob Rogers, founder and chairman of BRC Imagination Arts said what Buzz practiced his entire career was an art form in itself. Buzz laughs at Roger's assessment of his work, but agrees with it. "Quite often, I was up there with a baton and a piece of chalk, putting together projects on a wall," Buzz notes. "I acquired the performance ability in the process of doing all that speechmaking. I had an absolute obligation not to bore people. I learned that if you didn't make them laugh in the first two minutes, you were dead."

As busy as he was with numbers work, Buzz points out that he always took time to enjoy music and the arts. "I like string quartets. I'm an amateur musicaholic and I've been a hi-fi nut ever since I was 10 years old." He's been known on many occasion to hang around a few days after a job to enjoy the local music scene. "We heard the symphony in Vienna and we heard the opera in Sydney."

Buzz's View of Old Age

In early 2006, when he was 85, Buzz lost vision in his right eye and the doctors quickly discovered that he had a plugged artery on his right side. The next day he had an angioplasty. He was amazed at the outcome. "My eye sight came back in about six minutes." The incident highlighted to Buzz that life and its functions, become more delicate as one ages. "You can't run around like a madman all your life, unless you want to hit the wall at full speed."

He said he never abused himself through the years. "No, I never smoked a lot, but I was what I call an aggressive social drinker," he laughed. "Plus I was a type-A personality all the way," noting that he is now busy working just as hard at enjoying life at a new, slower pace. "It's great and I have been surprised that I haven't had a harder time adjusting. I've got my fingers crossed that it will last a while."

In November 2005, Anne and Buzz downsized, sold their Palm Springs home and moved to Claremont, Calif., where Anne went to school and where she was on the board for 25 years at Pomona College. She remains an honorary board member. The upscale assisted living retirement home in which they moved was founded by the Congregational Church and is only six blocks from the university. Ever the numbers man, Buzz points out that out of the 400 people living there, 47 are from Pomona College and 10 are from CalTech, from which he graduated.

Buzz and an Australian friend celebrate Disneyland's 50th in 2005.

Proving that he still has his humor, shortly after the move he wrote, "Most of the people in this joint are well into old age and most are retired college profs. The vehicle of choice is a bright blue walker." In the announcement of the move, Buzz said the couple had "decamped" and were now "closer to the action, cooler in the summer" and because the center was originally run by the church, he was "taking a clean speech crash course, pray for me."

Buzz's Papers to Florida

One thing that made the move from Palm Springs to Claremont a little easier is that he had already dispersed 71 boxes and crates of his "professional memorabilia" including originals of all his studies, to the University of Central Florida's Rosen School of Hospitality Management. Following the publication of his book, he carefully categorized everything in those 71 boxes as to when the information in each could be released, with some of the boxes sealed until both Anne and Buzz are gone. "There are no real secrets in there but we think some people might be bothered by some of it," Buzz added. "Maybe 40% or 50% of it is restricted for 10 years. After that amount of time, nobody really should care. Plus, if anyone gets mad at something I wrote, who cares, I won't be around!"

He wasn't sure where his massive collection of papers and reports should go, but he wanted it to land someplace where it would be available for research and learning. "We did put a lot of thought into it and it was Dick Nunis, former Disney Parks President, who encouraged me to donate the stuff to the Rosen School. I originally offered it all to the University of Southern California and they acted like they didn't even know what tourism was."

The Teacher

"Buzz Price's companies have spawned most of the folks who today do the numbers crunching that is critical to the success of any amusement facility."

JOHN GRAFF,
FORMER IAAPA EXECUTIVE DIRECTOR AND PRESIDENT
(PROFILED ON PAGE 155)

Retirement Thoughts

"So far, it's been a lot of fun. I could have done it sooner but I don't think I lost out on anything by staying active. If I'm lucky, I'll live long enough to really experience this new phase, and I think I will." He said it wasn't the financial benefits of working that kept him active so long, it was the work itself. "There's nothing more exciting than when somebody calls up and says, 'I've got this project and it's this and that, and I need your help.' You feel like a damn missionary."

He claims to never have thought seriously about retiring before he actually decided to do it. However, he does admit that Anne "got on my tail" about two years before he actually hung up his hat.

She said, "You've got to quit and it's time to quit." In mid-2005, she took Buzz down to Disneyland and bought him the most expensive Mickey Mouse watch available. She handed it to him and said, "Now retire, damn it!"

Once he got his official gold watch, he surrendered.

He calls it the perfect parting gift.

BIBLIOGRAPHY

SOME OF WHAT APPEARS IN THIS CHAPTER ABOUT THE LEGENDARY BUZZ PRICE IS BASED ON HIS AUTOBIOGAPHY, *WALT'S REVOLUTION! BY THE NUMBERS*, PUBLISHED IN 2003 BY RIPLEY PUBLISHING. ADDITIONAL SOURCES ARE LISTED BELOW.

Articles & Interviews

A Pioneer's Pioneer, *Funworld*, by Keith Miller, November 2005

Amusement Industry Oral History Project tape of Harrison "Buzz" Price, a collaboration of the National Amusement Park Historical Assn. and the International Assn. of Amusement Parks & Attractions, interviewed by Holly Crawford

Anne Shaw Price Honored for Alumni Service, *Pomona College Magazine*, Summer 1997

Capex Management: Searching for Predictability, *At The Park*, by Harrison Price, Issue 48, 1999

Executive Profile: Harrison Price, *Orange County Register*, by Charles Siler, July 19, 1985

"He Was Framed: The Artistry of Herbert Dickens Ryman," a speech to the Economic Round Table of Los Angeles, by Harrison A. Price, March 22, 1990

Industry Veteran Buzz Price Releases Book of Fun, Numbers, *Amusement Business*, by Tim O'Brien, Nov. 17, 2003

IAAPA Hall of Fame nomination forms, 1991-1995

Interviews with Buzz Price, by Tim O'Brien, Sept. 14, 1995; Feb. 16, 2003; Jan. 9. 2006; Feb. 9, 2006; March 2 & 3, 2006; April 18, 2006; May 25, 2006; June 1, 2006

Legends of the Industry: Buzz Price, Making Meaning and Dreams Out of Numbers, *Funworld*, by Geoff Thatcher, June 2002

Location Vocation, *News-Pilot*, by Coll Metcalfe, April 22, 1996

Price Reflects on Career, Disney, *Amusement Business*, by Tim O'Brien, Feb. 24, 2003
Speech by Terry E. Van Gorder at the TEA Award Ceremony in Los Angeles,
    Oct. 15, 1994
The Fun Formula, *Newsweek*, July 23, 1973
The Numbers Man, *Orlando Sentinel*, by Todd Pack, Dec. 21, 2003
The State of the Gaming Industry, *Funworld*, by Harrison Price, November 1994
Will Parks Weather the Storm? *Funworld*, by Harrison Price, March 1991

BOOKS
Walt's Revolution! By the Numbers, Ripley Publishing, 2003, by Harrison "Buzz" Price

DR. ROBERTO ORTIZ

*"We are effective thanks to our mission
and the faith the country now has in us."*

This is the narrative of a caring, world-renown physician who built his country's first theme park. It's a story of how the profits generated by a successful park have helped save thousands of children's lives. It's a unique tale of how one man created an organization that not only utilizes amusement rides to entertain, but also to help create optimism and hope.

As a successful pediatric surgeon at the Hospital San Juan de Dios, in the Costa Rican capital of San Jose, Roberto Ortiz saw a need for a National Children's Hospital. Although it was not an easy task, he found initial funding for the hospital, had it built, and became its top physician, performing more than 27,000 surgeries on children, from its conception in 1964 through 1984 when he retired.

Once the hospital was built, finding consistent funding proved a challenge. During the 1970s, the good doctor was instrumental in creating the annual Flower Fair, and with its profits as seed money, began building the country's first modern, and still only, theme park.

In doing so, Dr. Roberto Brenes Ortiz developed a consistent revenue source for the country's National Children's Hospital. Since opening on Dec. 18, 1981 as the Parque Nacional de Diversiones, all profits have gone into the operating fund of the hospital. On average, $300,000 is deposited into the hospital's coffers each year from the park.

Believing that happiness is the best medicine, the doctor has improved the health and quality of life of millions of children –

through surgery and medicine as well as with roller coasters and costumed characters.

Attracting more than 800,000 visitors each year, the park's philanthropic mission not only provides funds for the hospital, but benefits thousands of the country's low income and disabled children. More than 200,000 free tickets are distributed annually to persons who cannot afford the elixir in which Dr. Ortiz so strongly recommends – fun and laughter. Inside the park, there are more than 40 rides and attractions, including roller coasters, family rides, water slides, and paddle boats on the serene lake.

The ORTIZ File

DR. ROBERTO BRENES ORTIZ

Born: San Jose, Costa Rica, May 8, 1923

Married: Ligia Volio Guardia

Children: Melania, Patricia, Roberto, Marco Antonio

Education: Universidad Nacional Autonoma de Mexico, medical degree, 1949; Children's Memorial Hospital, Chicago, Specialist in Children's Heart Surgery, 1954.

Claim to fame: Developed Costa Rica's first modern theme park to create a consistent funding source for the country's National Children's Hospital. Since Parque Nacional de Diversiones was founded in 1981, all profits, averaging $300,000 a year, have gone to help support the hospital which he founded in the mid-1960s. He has written five books and has received 80 honorary degrees and awards from universities and organizations throughout the world.

Industry kudos: Inducted into the IAAPA Hall of Fame, 2003.

Medical accomplishments: During the 24 years he served as the head of the surgery department of the National Children's Hospital, he performed 27,000 surgeries on children, including 2,000 heart operations.

Philosophy: Believing that happiness is the best medicine, Dr. Ortiz has improved the health and quality of life of millions of children through surgery and medicine as well as with roller coasters and costumed characters.

Little known fact about Dr. Ortiz: He owns a large dairy farm that has been in his family for nearly 170 years. He has participated in numerous local and international dairy cattle exhibitions and has been awarded several prizes for the quality of the milk produced on his farm.

Dr. Ortiz has entertained celebrities and public officials from around the world in his park. Former U.S. President Jimmy Carter visited in 2000.

More Than a Theme Park

The clean, well-managed park has become both an amusement and culture center for the country and provides guests an opportunity to become more familiar with Costa Rica's history and traditions. The park itself, while charming, safe and successful, would normally not be acknowledged beyond the country's borders. However, the man behind it, the man who pioneered a new, unique partnership to save lives, is quite noteworthy.

Dr. Ortiz, as the hands-on guiding light of both the hospital and the park, is proud of his service to the children of his country. When he came upon the idea of creating the park as a source of revenue for his hospital, he began to carefully study the global amusement industry. While traveling the world to learn the methods of integral administration systems of hospital medical services, the doctor attended many congresses and symposiums, both as a participant and as a speaker. The walls of his home office are lined with nearly 100 honorary degrees and other commendations from across the world. During those global treks, he would visit the local amusement and theme parks to get ideas and concepts for the facility he would eventually create.

The doctor enjoyed sharing a traditional dance in the Pueblo Antiguo section of the park.

"We studied construction and theming of other parks for many years, and we met with engineering and architecture professionals, as well as owners of private clubs and recreation centers, such as pools and public parks," Dr. Ortiz noted. "We also received much help from a great friend, Ken Davis, who owned Funtime U.S.A. in the United States."

The park's final plans were developed by a task force comprised of members of the National Children's Hospital Assn. and of architectural professionals. Ken Davis headed up the ride selection committee for the park's original arsenal of rides, which included: a Ferris wheel, carousel, an Octopus, a Spider, pedal boats, children's bumper boats, a small roller coaster, several small umbrella rides, a train, an inflatable castle, a Tilt-A-Whirl, adult bumper cars and 22 video games.

Successful Fund Raising

"*I never imagined I would achieve this (legendary) status in my country, but thanks to this credibility, I have been able to better raise funds to complete my projects.*"

DR. ROBERTO ORTIZ

Dr. Ortiz wasn't able to say how much it originally cost to start the park, but he did say it was built totally from the profits from the Flower Fair and private donations. Very little, if any of his own money or public funding was needed. Through the years, neither he, nor the board of directors ever received a salary. The land on which the park was built was originally leased, but in 1995 the hospital association succeeded in buying the 108 acres.

Some Concerned About the Money

He admits that while there was some initial concern among a few hospital officials about funding the construction of the park with money that could have otherwise gone directly into the hospital's account, there was no problem getting support for the project from the community.

"Thanks to our social mission which benefits the country's children, the park has always received important support from our friends in private business and institutions." He said his supporters were confident that he and his team would do a good job, just as they had done in the past, following through on the creation of the hospital and its programs. Dr. Ortiz was a proven commodity by that point.

From the beginning, the doctor was deeply involved in the park and personally directed its success by providing a "strong, but kind" hand to all the workers. "I demanded responsibility and honor," he adds. Those close to him say that while he often shows a fun loving personality, he is a disciplined, strict man. His daughter Melania has said in the past

Plenty of Support

"Thanks to our social mission which benefits the country's children, the park has always received important support from our friends in private business and institutions."

DR. ROBERTO ORTIZ

**Dr. Ortiz escorted Pope John Paul II
on his visit to Costa Rica in March 1983.**

that her father is "very demanding of himself and those who worked for him." He demanded the highest standards, she said, and he got the same from the people around him.

Before a series of strokes slowed him down in the late 1990s, Dr. Ortiz spent a great deal of time in his park interacting with visitors of all ages, as well as with the workers. He realized he needed to spend time on the front line to not only learn and better understand the business and his employees, but to make sure everything was being done that could be done to entertain his guests to the highest level of satisfaction.

His presence in the park has always been constant and active. When health issues forced him to retire from the hospital in 1984, he was able to spend even more time in the park and to be more active in the decision making process. While Dr. Ortiz has always been

considered the father of the park, he delegated the day-to-day administration and operations to a management team that reports directly
to the board of directors.

As could be expected of any park patriarch, the doctor knows and
loves every nook and cranny in his little kingdom, but he does admit
to being especially fond of Pueblo Antiguo, (the old town), built as the
second stage in 1994. The themed village is a combined re-creation of

A Personal Observation

*"The reputation of Dr. Ortiz among his colleagues
is that of a man who is brilliant, determined and
impatient - characteristics that made him successful
in the many causes to which he committed himself but
at times made him appear to be an autocrat. However,
the esteem with which he is held by the population-at-
large is evident. Here's an example. Kay and I spent
a few days with Roberto and his wife in a village on
the Pacific coast of Costa Rica. In every village in
which we stopped along the way he was immediately
recognized and greeted by people on the street. The
first night we were in our villa, someone in the village
was hosting a very loud and raucous party that ran
long into the night. Finally, a large group of villagers
descended on the reveling host and demanded he stop
his party because 'Dr. Ortiz (who by this time already
had the first of several strokes which have debilitated
him) is trying to sleep.'"*

JOHN GRAFF, FORMER IAAPA EXECUTIVE DIRECTOR AND PRESIDENT
(PROFILED ON PAGE 155)

San José the capital city, the nearby countryside and the Caribbean coast at the end of the 19th and the turn of the 20th centuries.

Authentic theming, colorful architecture, dancing shows, traditional cuisine and live folklore entertainment are all combined to present an entertainment package that can be found no where else in the country. In addition to being a part of the theme park, the buildings of "Old Town" are used as additional revenue sources, being marketed for conventions, corporate parties, weddings, and private meetings.

Never Quit his Day Job

To the doctor, the park, his social consciousness and his medical profession have gone "hand in hand" throughout his life. They have complemented each other and he has easily balanced them in his everyday life. Although he has deep passion for the park, the doctor said he was never tempted to leave the operating room and devote full time to the amusement industry. Nevertheless, the amusement industry gave him its highest honor by inducting him into the IAAPA Hall of Fame in 2003.

Dr. Ortiz's celebrity status, earned through his charitable acts and his reputation as a notable pediatric surgeon, has helped his fund raising efforts for both the park and the hospital. "I never imagined I would achieve this (legendary) status in my country, but thanks to this credibility, I have been able to better raise funds to complete my projects," he said. Using the park's motto, "The healthy child helping the healing child," he has been able to obtain major sponsors and donations to continue to expand the park and the programs at the hospital. "We are effective (fundraisers) thanks to our mission and the faith the country now has in us," he notes.

While fundraising is important to build and expand, the park's operating budget is not dependent on charity. The day-to-day operations of the park are self-funded. Forty-eight percent of the budget comes from admissions; events provide another 30%; merchandise sales provide 18%; and sponsorships provide 4%.

Today, due to the state of his health, it is impossible for him to be at the park as much as he would like. However, the park continues to be the center of his attention and he remains involved in current projects and is still busy soliciting support for the park.

Would he do it again? Yes, he says. "If it was necessary, I certainly would do it all over again, but this time around I would build a bigger hospital."

BIBLIOGRAPHY

ARTICLES & INTERVIEWS

Dr. Roberto Ortiz: A humanitarian devoted to children and his community makes a lasting impression, *Funworld,* by John Graff, July 2004

Interview with Dr. Roberto Ortiz, by Tim O'Brien, via email, Jan. 21, 2006

Interview with John Graff by Tim O'Brien, Nov. 17, 2005.

Parque Nacional de Diversiones, *Funworld,* September 1992

Parque Nacional de Diversiones press releases, 1990-2006

Travel.Yahoo.com

Dr. Ortiz and John Graff, former president of IAAPA, in the park in 2000.

JOHN GRAFF

"I wondered if my car was going to explode
when I turned the key."

To say that most amusement park owners and managers on the planet know John Graff or at least know of him, would be overstating the obvious. During his 20 year tenure with the International Assn. of Amusement Parks & Attractions (IAAPA), John visited more than 400 parks in 60 different countries during which time he wined and dined with the nobility, the rich, and the famous.

It's also safe to say that he personally knows more park people than anyone else in the world. No one individual, directly or indirectly, has had as much influence in the professional development of the industry's leading trade association as has John Graff. By transcending the barriers of language and culture to expand the influence of the association worldwide, John changed the global landscape of the industry.

While never directly working a day of his life in a theme park, John served as the catalyst that not only brought the worldwide industry together but helped change the face of the industry through his work within the association. It is said of John that as the head of IAAPA, he was the global ambassador, the face of IAAPA, who fostered a sense of fraternity among the association's membership. Through his work he helped create the framework that has protected the industry from government interference and has given new wings to the industry by understanding and developing structure and programming to meet its needs.

The GRAFF File

JOHN ROBERT GRAFF

Born: March 14, 1936 in Madison, South Dakota. He grew up in Clark, South Dakota, a village of 1,200 people.

Married: Kay Ellsworth, 1966

Children: Son, Chris, and daughter, Andrea.

Education: BA degree from the University of South Dakota in Government History; an MA from Indiana University in International Relations; and a Juris doctorate degree from Catholic University in Washington, D.C.

Claim to fame: No one individual has had as much influence in the professional development of the industry's leading trade association than John. By transcending the barriers of language and culture to expand the influence of the group worldwide, he changed the global landscape of the industry. Through his work he helped create the framework that has protected the industry from government interference and has given new wings to the industry by understanding and developing structure and programming to meet its needs.

Mentor: Truman Woodworth. "He was chairman of the association at the time I was hired. He taught me a great deal about both the industry and the IAAPA. He was a huge help to me."

Favorite theme park: Before it closed, Opryland in Nashville, Tenn. "I was always baffled why it closed because it was such a good park with great musical entertainment. Of the current parks, I love Busch Gardens, Williamsburg and I'm also very fond of Holiday World in Indiana."

Favorite ride of all time: The Octopus.

Coaster riding history: "I rode just about every coaster I ever saw because when you visit a park anywhere in the world, the park operators always wanted me to ride their coasters because that's the ride they were usually most proud of. I would ride it, maybe just once, but I rode them all."

The real truth about John's coaster riding: "I never really enjoyed a coaster ride. I was never afraid but it was just the kind of thing that got my stomach and equilibrium mixed up."

Hobbies: "I love gardening and I'm an avid reader. My favorite books are usually histories and biographies. I have two favorite reads: Les Misérables and Crime and Punishment."

TV habits: The History Channel is a favorite channel. "That's the only reason we subscribe to cable. Other than that, I have a couple of British comedies I love and I watch football games."

First amusement park: As a kid, the family would visit Excelsior Park once or twice a year.

His legendary 20 year run with IAAPA transformed the small, mostly U.S. park association of the early 1980s into the undisputable mothership of all industry related associations. Prior to that, his pioneering efforts as the first attorney hired by Marriott Corp. to specifically work in its theme park division in the mid-1970s, helped create many of the legal standards still used in parks today.

Born to Run for Office?

Born in Clark, South Dakota, John left home at 18 to attend the University of South Dakota, in Vermillion, where he received a BA in Government and History. He then headed to Indiana University in Bloomington, where he earned an MA in International Relations. He returned to his home state and went to work for the South Dakota Chamber of Commerce where he spent nearly four years. At age 26, he became the executive director of the Republican State Central Committee of South Dakota.

During that time, John expected politics to be his future. The state's senator, Karl Mundt, wanted John to run for congress and thought getting him into Washington D.C. for a little seasoning would be good. In 1970, Mundt landed John a job as counsel on the Senate Committee on Government Relations, where he worked for three years.

John says he went to Washington partly for the "political education," but also for the opportunity to pursue his doctorate degree in international relations. Nearly a year into his political career in Washington, he decided against a life in politics and chose instead to enter law school at Catholic University, where he earned a Juris doctorate degree. He worked all day on Capitol Hill, and attended law school at night.

First Attorney for New Park Company

As Mundt's term was running out in 1974, John went searching for work. A former congressman friend suggested that John look into working for Marriott Corporation because "it was a great company" and his son-in-law had done very well there. The company was looking for an attorney to do the legal work in its new parks division. John was hired and his long and illustrious career in the park industry had begun.

Marriott Corp. wasn't in the park business when John joined them but the company was in the process of laying groundwork to build several parks. Bill Marriott Jr. wanted to get into the business because someone had told him how lucrative foodservice could be at parks.

John Graff learns to drive in South Dakota.

Marriott was primarily a food and lodging company at the time, but officials saw theme parks as a bright new revenue stream.

The company initially wanted to build one park in the Washington area but as planning progressed, it seemed more efficient to build three at the same time. The company decided to build one in Santa Clara, Calif., one in Gurnee, Ill, north of Chicago, and the third in the Washington D.C. area near Manassas, Va., hoping to open all three during the bicentennial year 1976. The company easily received the necessary zoning and political go-aheads for Gurnee and Santa Clara, but Manassas proved difficult, and eventually, impossible.

"We really put a lot of expense and time in our efforts to get approval to build in Manassas," said John, noting that the situation there proved to be very political from the start. "There was one man on the County Board of Supervisors who really wanted us and as far as we could tell so did most of the community." There was however, a small but vocal and powerful group opposed due to the park's proximity to an historic battlefield.

To demonstrate the community support, the board of supervisors and Marriott decided to conduct a large public information rally. "We had the environmental engineers lined up to talk about pollution and water and how we were going to solve those problems and the road people were there to talk about the changes that were going to be made to facilitate traffic." Marriot's friend on the board was there, as was the press.

In front of the room, with cameras rolling, Marriott's "friend" on the Board of Supervisors said, "Mr. Marriott, don't you worry about water and sewer and all, we'll take care of all those problems. You'll get good access onto the site and won't have to worry about any of that."

Then, using an inappropriate and derogatory racial slur, this "friend" of the Marriott Corporation went on to say that in exchange for his support he wanted assurances that the company would not bring [a bunch of black people] into the area.

A deathly pall fell over the room.

Mr. Marriott rose to the occasion beautifully. "This will be a park for all Americans and we hope everyone will come. It will have a great American theme," he told the shocked crowd.

John said his heart sank and the entire project flashed before his eyes in a second when he saw the crowd's negative reaction to the man who was their key to getting the property. The approval never came for that location and after failed attempts at securing other sites in the area, Marriott decided to concentrate on its two existing parks that had already been in operation for nearly a year and abandoned its efforts in Virginia.

Ironically, in 1994, the Walt Disney Company wanted to build a major history-themed park nearly adjacent to where Marriott had wanted to build its Great America park. Disney's America, as it was to be called, also failed to get approval and was never built.

The Legal Eagle at the Planning Table

John was present at most of the planning meetings for the new parks, but didn't take an active role in either the creative or operations process. His hands were full of legal work.

As rides and attractions were being considered for the two new parks, David Brown an industry veteran who headed up the new park division mentioned to John that he had set up a meeting with a ride salesman and wanted John to sit in on the discussion. When John mentioned to Brown that he should prepare contracts, Brown informed John of the way things were done in the amusement business.

"We don't really work that way in this industry. There are no contracts," Brown said. "Everybody goes to this big trade show every year and if you see a ride you want, you tell the man and he tells you what it costs and you either shake hands on a deal and buy it or you don't. It's really just a shake of the hand business." John countered that, "We're talking millions of dollars and potentially three parks here. I don't think Sterling Colton (general counsel) is going to be content to put out millions of dollars on the strengths of nothing but some handshakes with people we've never met."

John set forth on the task of developing what he thinks is the first formal ride purchase contract, outside the Disney parks. "I was told there were no contracts on rides in the general industry," he notes. The first ride salesman to show up was the legendary Mack Duce, a highly regarded professional in the industry. Brown explained to Duce that Graff was the lawyer and since Marriott was a big corporate player, general counsel insisted there be a contract. The startled Duce said, "Well, we haven't been doing that."

Brown said, "I understand that, but we're immediately buying for two parks and there will be a lot of money involved. The company feels it needs contracts." Duce said, "Well, that's fine," and he proceeded to show the photos and the sales sheets for his rides. Every once in a while, John would throw some lawyer-ese toward Duce, like, "Well, we can cover it by this provision here," and he would read it to Duce. At one point, John suggested that they were going to need a few additional things in writing, such as a warranty on each purchase.

John, left and Dennis Speigel, right, with their
Brazilian buddies, Marcelo Gutglas and Alain Baldacci.

After the group played this little game for a while, Duce, in a very polite manner looked at Brown and said, "You know, I think it would probably be best if I keep my rides and you keep your contracts." He folded up his books, got up and left. Brown was apoplectic. However, John won out on his insistence that contracts be used for all ride purchases, and he recalls that drawing up that first standard contract wasn't as easy at it would seem. Duce eventually came back and through a process of negotiation with him and other vendors, John was able to create a contract form that was acceptable to all.

Through the years, John has been jokingly chided for introducing those demonic things into the industry. Ironically, in his 20 years with IAAPA, John was never offered an employment contract.

He was the attorney for the Marriott parks division for six years and during that time, his work on contracts, captive animal treatment and environmental issues were pioneering efforts and

John presents a Lifetime Achievement Award to Mrs. Lilian Thompson of Blackpool (England) Pleasure Beach in 1992.

among the first done on behalf of an emerging park phenomena at the time – the corporate theme park. One of the people John met during his years at Marriott who would eventually play a major role in his future career as an association executive was Truman Woodruff, a Marriott park executive. "He taught me a great deal about the industry and he was my mentor and friend, right up until the day he died," John recalls.

Noah Didn't Have These Problems

There were plans to build an animal area within the Gurnee Great America park and a group of animals had been purchased and were living on nearby farms. Their new park homes weren't ready when winter hit and since many were tropical, they wouldn't survive a typically cold and windy Chicago winter. Officials decided to ship them to the California park for safe keeping during the winter. As they were being prepared to be shipped and as a cold front was moving in, someone wondered aloud if a permit was needed to transport exotic animals across the country. They called John for the answer.

"I didn't know off hand, so I checked into it and sure enough, a permit was needed," he said. "When I went to get the permit, I found it was not a quick process. They would have to schedule a hearing and it became obvious very quickly that it was going to take more time than we had."

John said he could see it going on for weeks, all while the animals would be freezing to death in their temporary habitats. After three or four days of talking to officials about the permit, one of them looked at John and softly asked, "What would you have done if it hadn't occurred to somebody that you might need the permit?"

John said, "We would have loaded them on the truck and shipped them."

The Federal official smiled and said, "Why don't you do what you would have done?"

Some Truth to the Claim

John heard many times that IAAPA was an American association "with only a few" international members. That comment always rankled him, but he realized that in terms of significant international member participation in the organization and benefits bestowed to them, there was a measure of truth to the charge.

"We loaded them up and moved them to California, all without a permit, and no one got in trouble and all the animals survived," John noted. "The animals stayed in California when we decided not to build the animal component to the Gurnee park."

The Case of the Missing Coaster

While Marriott's California park was under construction, John received a call from the park manager in Santa Clara. It seems a roller coaster they had purchased from Europe was three weeks late in arriving, and nobody could figure out where it could be.

John asked, "What do you mean, nobody can find it?"

He said, "Well, we've been calling around and nobody knows where it is. You need to find it for us."

John said he had no idea where to start looking for the nine trucks of steel. He called Peter Schnabel, the sales agent for Intamin, the manufacturer of the misplaced coaster. The two decided that a personal visit to the trading company that had arranged the shipment would be a good place to start. John and Schnabel arrived in New York on a Friday and went directly to the trading company's headquarters located in the World Trade Center. They were invited to sit down at the table to discuss the matter.

"I need to find our roller coaster," John began.

"Well, we have no idea where it is," a representative responded.

"Well, how do we go about finding it? Did it arrive at the port?" queried John.

"Yes, it came into the port and we have the documents to show that. It was off loaded from the ship and was put on trucks and sent to California."

"It hasn't gotten to California. How do we find it?"

John recalls that it was an intriguing game of cat and mouse. It went back and forth for a while before someone suggested that a particular gentleman whom John prefers to call Mr. N, "just in case he is still alive," might be able to shed some light on the mystery.

Mr. N, who immediately appeared from somewhere down the hall, turned out to be the man who arranged for the trucks. "He was one of the most sinister people I'd seen in my life," John recalls. "He had a rat-like face, very neat, expensive clothes, and a chain watch fob across the chest, the whole thing. He even had his hair slicked back."

"I haven't a clue," Mr. N responded immediately to John's inquiry of where the coaster might be.

"These people tell me you arranged for the trucking."

"Yes I did, but I don't drive the truck." Mr. N explained that the trucking company also had no idea where the trucks were, because the shipment had been subcontracted.

It was nearly lunch and John was getting frustrated. "I don't know what to do now except call the FBI because this is obviously a case involving interstate commerce. I guess that's where we go next."

Everyone left the office to go to lunch and as John was standing at the elevator to leave, Mr. N came out and motioned for him to step aside. He then whispered, "Mr. Graff, I'm going to give you a little advice. I think this should be able to be worked out between us. It would be a great mistake for you to go to the FBI."

"Well, Mr. N, I don't know where else to go because you're not able to tell me where my ride is and I'm not going to go back and tell Mr. Marriott that we're just writing off this $9 million roller coaster."

John is surrounded by park executives
Nick Winslow, left, and Joe Meck during the
IAAPA President's Reception honoring Meck in 1994.

"Well, let's have lunch and think this over," Mr. N suggested. During lunch they came up with a couple of ideas, made several calls when they got back to the office, but by mid-afternoon, the mystery remained unsolved.

Toward the end of the day, John stood up and explained, "I'm going home, there's a birthday party for my daughter tonight and we're not

Roy Gillian presents the IAAPA Hall of Fame Award to John in 2001.

getting anywhere here." Then he told Mr. N, "I expect you to work on this over the weekend."

As John and Schnabel stood waiting at the elevator, John was once again taken aside by Mr. N. "You know, Mr. Graff, I've gotten to like you this afternoon. I think you're probably a fine young man with a career ahead of you," Mr. N softly noted. "You're going home for your daughter's birthday party. That's nice. Daughters are lovely things, aren't they? We just have to live and hope that nothing ever happens to them. I'm suggesting that you don't go to the FBI. That would not be smart."

John was told to think seriously about it over the weekend. "I was quite concerned," John said. "I wondered if my car was going to explode when I turned the key and I worried about it all weekend."

On Monday afternoon John received a call from the Santa Clara park telling him that the trucks had arrived. When John asked about the circumstances of their appearance, the only answer he could get was, "I don't know, they're just here." Three weeks late.

Marriott Bails Out of the Amusement Industry

Both of the Great America parks opened on the same day, May 29, 1976. They were spectacular and considered successful right from the start. The disappointment of not being able to build in Virginia, in Marriott's own backyard, coupled with park earnings from the two operating parks, that were good but not up to Marriott's overall corporate earnings growth projections, eventually caused the company to divest of the parks and focus on the hotel and food business.

John, however, had been smitten by the park industry. When it became evident that Marriott did not see it as a long-term growth area for the company, John began to think of moving into another line of work. "I decided I didn't want to spend the rest of my life drafting leases for fast food restaurants."

On a trip to Chicago in early 1980, John ran into his friend Truman Woodruff who was still working for Marriott as well as serving as the IAAPA president. He was in Chicago for an IAAPA Board of Directors meeting. He told John the board was meeting to discuss the hiring of a Director of Government Relations, who would open a lobbying office in Washington for the association. He added that the job would most likely lead in a short while to taking over as Executive Director of the IAAPA. He asked John if he might be interested.

While John had worked on Capitol Hill prior to joining Marriott and had a good grasp of government relations work, he was not particularly enamored with the idea of spending his life at it. On the other hand, an opportunity to manage the association was an appealing prospect. He said he would think it over.

Within a week, he called Woodworth and told him he was interested in the job.

What John was led to believe would be a quick decision on the part of IAAPA turned into something of an ordeal. While the board had approved the creation of the position, the selection committee became bogged down in a competition over who should be hired. Woodworth was, of course, urging John's hiring. Charlie Powell, a board member representing the Six Flags group, had his own candidate in mind and the committee was divided evenly between the two candidates. They haggled over this for weeks, with John occasionally calling Woodworth to see what was going on and always hearing the same message, "Don't worry, I'll get this through." Over a three month period John grew increasingly anxious but Woodworth remained confident.

Woodworth finally called to tell John that he had been chosen. It turned out that Woodworth had just kept calling meetings of the committee until he found a date when Powell could not be there. John won the job by a single vote. He and Powell became great friends after that and Powell became a key figure in the association's government relations program.

John Hangs Out the IAAPA Shingle

John began his new career as Director of Government Relations and Legal Counsel to the association in the summer of 1980. He opened an office in Washington and began to put together a government relations program designed to protect the industry's position on several key issues: retention of the amusement industry exemption from the federal Minimum Wage Law, preventing federal jurisdiction over the regulation of amusement rides, regulation of the keeping and display of wild animals and the move toward year round schools.

In 1984, the association's executive director Bob Blundred retired and John was elevated to the top, the fifth person in IAAPA history to ever hold that position and only the second since it had become a full time paid position in 1964. In 1997, through an organizational restructuring, the executive director's title was changed to president/ CEO and the title of the head of the IAAPA board changed from president to chairman.

John had been involved with association management earlier in his life and knew that the American Society of Assn. Executives urged its members to insist on employment contracts. He raised this possibility with Woodworth who explained in his typically gruff manner, "There won't be any contract. We will let you run the association until we don't like the way you are running it and then we will throw your ass out." That's the way it was for 20 years.

After a year of commuting between D.C. and the IAAPA office in Wood Dale, Ill., John and various members of the executive committee were able to convince the board to move the association's headquarters to Washington in 1985.

Shortly after taking over the association, the first of what would become a series of strategic plans was developed to chart the course for the organization. The first committee charged with this responsibility was chaired by Michael Jenkins of Leisure and Recreation Concepts (LARC). Jenkins had been involved with several projects outside the U.S. and his committee included a number of persons who had a strong interest in increasing the organization's international presence and influence.

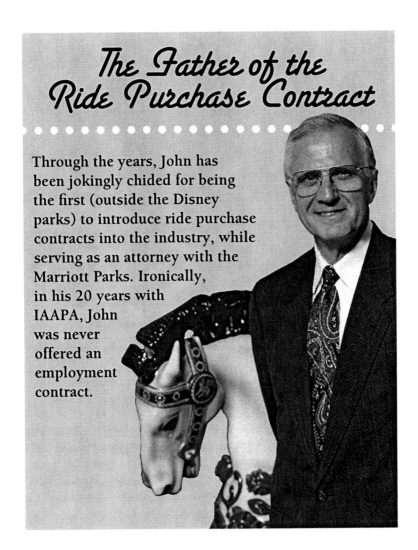

The Father of the Ride Purchase Contract

Through the years, John has been jokingly chided for being the first (outside the Disney parks) to introduce ride purchase contracts into the industry, while serving as an attorney with the Marriott Parks. Ironically, in his 20 years with IAAPA, John was never offered an employment contract.

Principal among them were Bo Kinntorph of Liseberg park in Gothenburg, Sweden, John Broome from Alton Towers in England, and Charles Wood of the Great Escape theme park near Lake George, New York. At the urging of these individuals, a plan was developed that would result, over time, in greatly expanded international membership and a much more active industry role for the IAAPA.

John playfully reenacts his confrontation with a tiger.

John Helps Put the "I" in International

As John was in the process of joining the IAAPA, there was a strong movement among the board and committees of the association to be more aggressive in recruiting international members. As counsel and heir apparent to the executive director's position, he was part of the first board tour of Europe in 1980 to spread the IAAPA word. That was the beginning of John's myriad travels on behalf of the association and the industry.

Trips would involve meeting with as many industry people as possible and extending to each a personal invitation to join the association. "We would visit various parks and get to know their ownership and management," John notes. "Today, we take it for granted that we all know each other from all over the world, but in 1980, that was definitely not the case. When I took over the association, there were less than 650 members worldwide, and nearly all of them were in the United States." By mid-2006, there were nearly 4,500 park and supplier members from 85 different countries, with nine of the 27 members of the board of directors (and officers) representing non-U.S. facilities.

John heard many times that IAAPA was an American association "with only a few" international members. That comment always rankled him, but he realized that in terms of significant international member participation in the organization and benefits bestowed to them, there was a measure of truth to the charge. One of the persons who persisted in that characterization was John's good friend, Geoffrey Thompson of Blackpool (England) Pleasure Beach, whose father and maternal grandfather were among the very first persons from Europe to become involved with the association as far back as the 1920s.

John was determined to change this perception by aggressively implementing the plan the board had adopted. The strategic plan called for greater representation of non-U.S. members on the boards and committees of the association. An international council was set up as a forum for those members and the council was assigned three seats on the IAAPA Board - one from each of three geographical regions.

Here Kitty, Kitty

"You get the damned thing off me and I'll quit hitting him."

JOHN GRAFF, IN RESPONSE TO A TIGER TRAINER TELLING HIM TO QUIT HITTING HIS TIGER, AS IT WAS PULLING JOHN OFF INTO THE WOODS.

These changes, reviewed and revised with a series of regular strategic plans over the years would result, over time, in IAAPA offering education and training programs on site for international members. In addition, John doggedly pursued the production of multi-lingual materials, participated in other trade exhibitions in Europe and Asia and eventually, won approval to open an IAAPA office in Europe in 2001.

John Calls Out, "The Russians are Coming"

Over the course of many years and many visits to Russia, John developed a genuine love for, and appreciation of the Russian people.

That relationship would provide him with many laughs and fond memories. The ties began when the chairman of the Russian association of parks, Arkady Gavrilenko, wanted to visit the IAAPA convention and trade show. The Russian ruble was not convertible so he had no way to pay for the trip. He proposed an exchange of visits with IAAPA picking up the tab for their trip to the U.S. and then they would pay for a return trip by an IAAPA delegation. Boyd Jensen, the president that year, quickly agreed that it would be a beneficial opportunity and he decided that he, John and Dennis Speigel, a past president, would make up the delegation when it was their turn to go to Russia.

The Russians came with a delegation of four people, all men. When it came time for the U.S. delegation to start its planning for the Russian trip, Jensen's wife Beverly expressed an interest in going along, as did the other wives, Donna Speigel and John's wife, Kay. Since the arrangement was to be a swap and the Russians had not brought wives, John wrote asking them if it would be OK to bring along their wives. Many weeks went by without a reply and John had about decided that the deal had soured and they would hear no more from the Russians. The reply finally came stating that the wives would indeed be most welcome.

The IAAPA delegation arrived in Russia after a long, tiring flight. They were not taken to their hotel as they had expected, but directly to the famous Moscow Circus where all six of them fell asleep in about five minutes, sleeping through the entire event. The next stop was the hotel, but again it was not destined for them to go to their rooms. The bags were sent up but the guests were taken to a banquet room where a delegation of hosts was awaiting them.

The head host was a deputy secretary of the Russian Culture Ministry, the government agency having jurisdiction over all the parks in the country. The secretary welcomed the Americans, expressed his pleasure that they had seen the circus and described the other national treasures the guests were to see during their trip. Then he said something in Russian that sent a wave of laughter through the room.

With the assistance of the interpreter John had employed, Tatiana Zhuschkova, the group had been able to follow what had been said, up to that last remark. The interpreter remained silent. Thinking it must have been some funny story he might want to respond to, John pressured her to explain the remark. With great reluctance she whispered, "The secretary said that they were originally going to arrange whores for you (the delegation) but you decided to bring your wives and we are most pleased to have them here!"

John and Disney's Ted Crowell,
sit and chat for a while in January 1987.

John Likes the Busts in Brazil

While the ties between the IAAPA and Russia were, and are still strong, John thinks in many ways the strongest friendships arising out of the IAAPA's strategies through the years were with the countries of South America. That's true for many reasons, he said. "The industry in those countries was not as far advanced as it was in Europe and language differences were not as hard to overcome as they were in the Pacific Asian nations." There were many trips to South America for the IAAPA delegation, and as could be imagined, many amusing stories.

News to Walt!

"No matter how hard I tried, I couldn't break my daughter, Andrea, from telling people that I owned Disney World."

JOHN GRAFF

On one such trip, John and IAAPA President, Dennis Speigel visited Brazil in 1989 to help establish a Brazilian parks association. The main event for the occasion was held in a building belonging to a Brazilian commercial organization and the main room of that building was a ceremonial hall. The perimeter of the room was lined with large bronze busts of all the former presidents of that organization. The image of the bust lined room planted the germ of a gag and it turned out to be one of the few times in the history of IAAPA that the board was totally fooled, at least for awhile.

Upon returning home, John and Speigel prepared a letter, with Speigel's signature, to each of IAAPA's past presidents. The letter described what the two had seen in Brazil and how impressed they were with the display of the busts of former leaders. They suggested that it would be a worthy thing for IAAPA to emulate. The presidents were told that a sculptor had been found who would make life-size bronze busts of all the IAAPA presidents to be placed in the IAAPA headquarters building for the "very reasonable" price of $5,000 each. He would work from plaster casts that would have to be provided by the presidents and there was an elaborate explanation of what kind of plaster to purchase and how to apply it. Each man was instructed to insert soda straws into their nostrils in order to breathe while the plaster cast was drying, a process which would "only take" four or five hours.

The response far exceeded anything Speigel or John had anticipated. Almost everyone took the bait. Some were excited about the project, with one past president asking if it would be possible to order two, one for the IAAPA office and one for his home. Others exploded with indignation that such a ridiculous and expensive project was even being considered. Telephone lines between board members and to the IAAPA office buzzed for several days before it dawned on everyone that the whole thing was too outlandish to be real and that it was indeed, a very good hoax.

John Meets a Real Tiger

Several years after the South American bust scheme, John was invited to be a part of the opening of a new wildlife area of Australia's Dreamworld, a park managed by IAAPA member Len Shaw. It was during that visit that he faced the most intimidating character he ever encountered in his travels, a not so affable tiger. John traveled to Australia via Hong Kong where he had attended to other association business. His wife Kay and his sister had gone directly to Australia and were to join him in Brisbane

Shaw met John at the airport in Brisbane and they headed directly to the park for a photo shoot. Following that event Shaw's plan was to take him to the hotel to check in. They arrived just as the trainer was leading a Bengal tiger to a small grove of trees where the photo was to be taken. The photographer was there and the tiger was sitting on a small platform. The trainer told John there would be no problem with the tiger and that he "could do anything" with it.

Assured that everything would be OK, John knelt down behind the tiger for the photo. "The tiger immediately made that hissing sound and it was quite clear that he was not happy having his photo taken with me," John laughed, noting that he "had the presence to stand up and slowly back away." However, he forgot that he was on the raised platform. He fell backward and as soon as he hit the ground, the tiger was all over him, grabbing his leg and pulling him off toward the woods.

Flailing his arms and beating the tiger as he was being dragged, John heard the trainer yelling, "Don't hit the tiger! Don't hit the tiger!" John complied noting, "Well, you get the damned thing off me and I'll quit hitting him." The tiger was pulled off and John was rushed to the hospital with a bad case of chewed up leg. He needed stitches but the doctors first had to treat him for any potential infection from the bite. A doctor wrapped John up and told him to come back for the stitches once it was known whether an infection had set in.

John's unexpected wildlife encounter kept him busy for a while at the hospital and he was unable to get to the airport, as planned, in time to pick up his wife and sister, who by then were getting worried. They had arrived and when John wasn't at the airport, they called the hotel only to find that, "We don't have any Mr. Graff here." Len Shaw went to the rescue and brought the American family together. Shaw went home that night and told his wife, "You'll never believe what happened today with the cameras rolling."

Once united, the Graff family headed out for a seven day drive around Australia. The doctors told him to come back in a week and if there was no infection, the wound would be stitched up. After the family's Australian tour, and before he departed Brisbane for the U.S., John checked back into the hospital for the stitching job on his leg. The anesthesiologist asked him what had happened and John explained that he had been bitten by a tiger. The doctor looked alarmed and said, "A tiger bite? That's the second one of those we've had in a week. They are going to have to shut that park down!" John calmly explained there had actually been only one attack and that this was his second visit.

A Few Domestic Challenges

One tenuous situation that faced the association in the early years of John's tenure was its relationship with the Outdoor Amusement Business Association (OABA), the trade group to which most carnivals and independent ride operators belong. The two organizations had lived in a love-hate relationship for years, but shared a common origin in the outdoor amusement business. Many IAAPA members had business dealings with carnival folk, but a level of distrust existed, basically involving amusement ride safety and perceived differences over the "quality" of the respective industries.

There was a view widely held by the public that carnivals were less safe than amusement parks. This was not necessarily supported by ride accident surveys and government reports, but the notion persisted.

During the 1996 IAAPA Convention and Trade Show, John congratulates industry veteran Peter Zwickau on becoming a U.S. citizen just days before the convention convened.

"Many carnival people felt, probably not without some justification, that many park people were all too eager to promote that belief," John recalls. "On the other hand, many park people looked at the carnivals as giving the amusement business a bad image."

The animosities had waxed and waned for years but during the period of the 1970s and 1980s the climate often became heated. John sat in on more than one meeting that could have easily broken out in physical combat. He vowed to do what he could through personal contacts and focusing on common problems, such as standards development, to try and bring the groups together. The

IAAPA trade show was also a bone of contention between the two organizations. While they never succeeded in reaching an agreement that would allow them to jointly produce a show, John conceived of several ways to make the annual IAAPA trade show more hospitable to OABA members.

There was another, more personal, thorn in John's side in those early years in the person of the legendary Harold Chance, one of the industry's most prominent and prolific amusement ride manufacturers. Chance was more involved with the carnival business than with parks but he sold to both and was widely known and liked by most in both industries.

A Lot Done in 20 Years

John's legendary 20 year run with IAAPA transformed the small, mostly U.S. park association of the early 1980s into the undisputable mothership of all industry related associations today.

John tried early to establish a good relationship with him. What he came to find out was that Chance hated attorneys. His experience with barristers suing ride manufacturers left him with an abiding dislike of anybody claiming to have a law degree. Chance told John, an attorney, of that hatred during their first meeting.

Whenever the two would meet, Chance would begin castigating lawyers. Similarly, but with what was probably inspired more by mischief than actual complaint, he would lay into the IAAPA for a multitude of sins, from overcharging its members to overlooking the interests of manufacturers. His favorite and most frequent complaint was that the drinks at the convention receptions were "cheap" booze. "I like good bourbon," Chance notes. "It seemed like all they would serve at any of the events was that cheap ass wine."

John took all this in good graces for some time but finally decided that he either had to stand up to Chance or forever be intimidated by him. One evening during a convention reception they got into such an animated exchange of insults that Chance's daughter-in-law Carol went to her husband Dick (Chance) and said she thought Harold and John were going to get physical and kill each other. Dick smiled and replied, "Let 'em go. Maybe they will."

John's coup de gras was accomplished during the president's reception at a convention in Atlanta. He hired a beautiful young woman clad in a most appealing and revealing outfit to stand at Chance's elbow all evening, moving with his every step, re-filling his glass with very expensive bourbon every time he took a sip. Chance enjoyed it immensely. The two continued to needle each other throughout the years but it was done in the spirit of fun and with great respect for each other. "I came to enjoy being with Harold but I have never been sure that Harold got over genuinely hating the lawyer in me," John says when telling this story.

Contacted at his winter home in the Islands in early 2006, Harold Chance was asked if he still carried a grudge against lawyers. "I never got over John being an attorney and I never will. I just don't like attorneys, period."

Travels with Kay

Kay was able to travel with John during his later years with IAAPA and over the years became nearly as well known as her husband. During the earlier days, she couldn't get away as often and stayed home with the couple's two children, who also had many opportunities to travel. "They loved it, especially when we were able to take them along to the parks," John said. "No matter how hard I tried, I couldn't break my daughter, Andrea, from telling people that I owned Disney World."

John met his future wife, Kay Ellsworth in 1964 while he was the executive director of South Dakota's Republican Party and she was a college student. Her cousin, a friend of John's, brought her along to a dinner party that John was hosting. They started dating, and were married in 1966. In 1969 they adopted their son, Chris, and in 1972, they added Andrea to the family.

Dear Board: "I'm out of Here."

On April 13, 2000, John wrote to the board of directors. "For some time we have had an understanding that I would give you two years advance notice of my intention to retire from the IAAPA. This letter is such notice. It is my desire to retire by April 15, 2002 or such earlier date after 12/31/01 as may be mutually convenient." His last day as IAAPA President was Dec. 31, 2001.

When John retired from his full time position with the association, he took on a volunteer post to work, in the name of IAAPA, with philanthropic organizations. He continues to work with Give Kids The World, the charity he had brought into the IAAPA fold in 1995. He has worked with several other organizations, in conjunction with the IAAPA, including the International Institute for Peace through Tourism, a volunteer group created to help the various segments of the travel industry develop programs that will help travelers recognize they are ambassadors for peace and understanding as they travel the world.

Through his work as chairman of the advisory committee for the Children's Hospital of Costa Rica, in San Jose, he is attempting to get theme parks and park suppliers and manufacturers throughout the world to donate used and surplus equipment to Parque de Diversiones,

Spreading the IAAPA Word

"*John was the perfect person to take IAAPA into the worldwide marketplace. Early in his tenure at IAAPA the first strategic plan was presented and approved by the board. That plan called for IAAPA to truly become an international association, covering the entire world with members and programs. The leaders of the association who hired John soon found they had the proper person in place to carry out that mission.*"

BILL ALTER, LONGTIME INDUSTRY SUPPLIER OF TICKETS AND GAMES

which is owned and operated by the hospital as a revenue source. (See pages 145-154.)

"Retirement is great, I really am enjoying it, but I would be unhappy if I didn't have this charity link to the organization," John notes. He still serves on the IAAPA Hall of Fame Committee, something he has done since 1990, and the Applause Award committee. "I really am grateful for these opportunities to stay in with the crowd."

"I'm not unhappy at all with my decision to leave," John notes. "There comes a time for everybody to do that and it was my time." He was inducted into the Hall of Fame in 2001, the year he retired.

John's Retirement Years

A letter from an unknown prison inmate in the late 1990s has led John to pursue another passion during his retirement years – the revision of the criminal justice system. He has been a volunteer with the group, Justice Fellowship, whose mission is to reform the criminal justice system, and provides free legislative help to the group.

John's busy retirement which includes his law reform work, his philanthropy work with the IAAPA and spending time with his family also includes his lifelong pursuit of education. He is a big fan of The Great Courses, a home studies program by The Teaching Company. "It's all in my effort to keep myself educated," he said. His completed courses include one on "Saint Augustine: Philosopher and Saint," and one on "Understanding Existentialism." Perhaps the one that he most enjoyed (and that he was most surprised that he did) was entitled "Einstein's Relativity Theory and the Quantum Revolution."

As John studies Einstein, the industry he helped bring into the 21st century is thriving and continues to change. In 1974 when John went to work for Marriott, most of the amusement parks were family-owned, "mom and pop" operations, but by 2000, the number of viable family-owned parks had diminished greatly and barely existed. IAAPA, under John's leadership, transitioned as well to reflect those drastic changes within the industry.

"Something I have always welcomed through the years was change," he notes. "Toward the end of the century, a new generation started stepping into the management of parks and along with them, came new ideas and new approaches. To stay viable, the association and its members, had to openly embrace them, which we did."

BIBLIOGRAPHY

ARTICLES & INTERVIEWS

General Managers' and Owners Luncheon, *Funworld*, January 2002

Graff: IAAPA is a Long Way From Being Too Big, *Amusement Business*, by James Zoltak, Sept. 14, 1998

Graff to Speak at GM and Owners' Luncheon in Orlando, *Funworld*, October 2001

Graff Named to Congressional Tourism Board, *Funworld*, August 1988

Graff to Retire as IAAPA President in 2002, *Amusement Today*, June 2000

Graff's Career Path in Politics Takes Turn into Parks Biz, *Amusement Business*, by Julie Fingersh, March 22, 1993

IAAPA 75th Anniversary Booklet, 1993

IAAPA Press Releases, 1986-2001

Industry Change: A Global Vision, *Australian Leisure Management,* April/May 1998

Interview with Harold Chance by Tim O'Brien, April 26, 2006

Interviews with John Graff by Tim O'Brien: Nov. 16, 2005; Jan. 18, 2006; March 7, 2006; May 6, 2006

John Graff, Difference Maker, *Amusement Business,* by Tim O'Brien, Dec. 24, 2001

John Graff Tribute Video, September 2001

HAROLD CHANCE

"It was all about the nuts and bolts."

As a pioneering mid-20th century amusement ride builder, Harold Chance's influence has been felt across all segments of the amusement industry. Chance-built rides can be found today throughout the world in carnivals and zoos, family entertainment centers and small as well as large amusement and theme parks.

The reach of his influence has been so wide that he's the only person who has been installed into three major Hall of Fames – the International Assn. of Amusement Parks & Attractions (IAAPA), 1991; the Outdoor Amusement Business Assn. (OABA), 2003, and the Showman's League of America (SLA), 2005. He was also inducted into the Carnival Heritage Museum Hall of Fame in Kinsley, Kans. in 2000.

Harold is the most prolific amusement ride builder in U.S. history. He introduced at least one new ride a year for more than two decades and was the first manufacturer to mass produce rides. He was among the first ride builders in the U.S. to trailer mount portable rides for the carnival industry and through his own experiences as a carnival owner, understood how important it was to create a ride that could easily be set up and taken down. That understanding would not only put Harold on the road to riches, but would change ride manufacturing forever.

A trailer mounted ride has its base built into the trailer on which it is transported. The ride stays on its trailer and is erected by means of hydraulic power. Harold wasn't the first to do it, but he took the art of trailer mounting to a new level and in doing so, revolutionized the portable ride industry.

The CHANCE File

RICHARD HAROLD CHANCE

Born: Sept. 25, 1921 in Wichita, Kans.

Married: Marge Westwood, Oct. 4, 1946

Children: Dick, Susie, Judy, Katy, and Nancy

Claim to fame: Prolific ride manufacturer for both carnivals and parks; revolutionized trailer mounting for portable rides; started what was to become the world's largest and most influential maintenance and safety seminar.

Education: One year at Wichita State University only to please his father.

Mentors: "My dad was a wonderful mechanic and he taught me more than most people ever learn. He let me change oil, and hang with him when I was very young." Herb Ottaway was another mentor. He was the man who originally started the company that would become Chance Manufacturing. "Herb was also an excellent mechanic and he taught me what I needed to know that my dad hadn't already taught me."

Business philosophy: The "same philosophy that everyone should have - Treat everybody like you want to be treated and try to make as many friends as you can. Most of my customers wound up being good friends of mine."

Hobbies: "I always played golf on Wednesday afternoons. I didn't care who was coming to town, I played golf on Wednesday afternoon, period."

Thoughts on books: "I've read practically no books, but I have written one. My family urged me to write down my life history, so I finally did and only a few were printed, mostly for family and friends."

Thoughts on movies: "I took Marge to a movie; it must have been in the mid-1960s. I tend to go to sleep in a movie and that night I kept snoring. She kept jabbing me with her elbow and finally I said, 'One more jab and I'm through with the movies.'" She jabbed him one more time and Harold hasn't been to a movie since.

Thoughts on TV: "Sports are all I ever watch on TV. I watch all sports."

Major awards: Only person to have been inducted into the top three amusement industry Hall of Fames – IAAPA, OABA, and SLA. He has also been inducted into the Carnival Heritage Museum Hall of Fame in Kinsley, Kans.

He was the catalyst behind the creation of the industry's first amusement ride safety seminar taught by ride manufacturers, state and insurance ride inspectors and risk managers. Since that first class in 1972, the seminar has graduated more than 8,000 students and is the largest and most proactive annual safety and maintenance school in the world.

Growing Up Just Like Dad

Harold Chance grew up playing with nuts and bolts and tinkering around in a commercial garage owned by his father Gerald, a mechanic. He could take the motor out of a Ford truck in about 45 minutes by the time he was 12 years old. "My father was very patient with me and would show me how to do the things I was interested in," Harold said, noting that he still has his father's tools and he "always thinks of him when using them."

School was boring for Harold and by the time he was in high school, he was so far ahead of his classmates in shop class, that he practically became a teaching assistant. He was dependable beyond his age and did what he said he would do. Although he did get into his share of what he calls "minor violations" during his youth, he took his responsibilities quite seriously. He was told by his parents that he had to stay in school, and that he did, not being tardy or missing one day - from kindergarten through 12th grade.

Harold was told he needed to go to college and went only to satisfy his father. "I told him I wanted to be just like him, a grease monkey, but he talked me into going for at least one year. I didn't do well because I didn't like being there but I tolerated it just because he wanted me to go," Harold said, adding that he had wished many times during his business career that he would have made more of an effort to learn more and perhaps stay in college. "I have done business with many very educated and smart people and at times that bothered me, but I was always honest with them and was usually able to hold my own."

With the help of his equally talented brother-in-law Herb Ottaway, Harold's father built a set of four miniature gasoline race cars and during the summer took them from town to town as a concession. He would set them up in a vacant lot and charge a dime a person for a ride. Harold would usually be invited to go along to help. Ottaway then built a miniature steam train that soon joined the race cars on the circuit.

Race Cars and Trains – All Summer Long

In the early 1930s, the race cars and miniature steam train found a summer home in Manitou, Colo., where the family rented a roadside lot and operated the rides from Memorial Day to Labor Day for several years. Harold, his two sisters and his mother would stay on site throughout the summer selling the tickets and providing the rides. His father would set everything up, and then go back to Wichita to work in his garage.

Harold recalls the summer-long event did quite well, for the times. "I remember one summer when we brought back $1,000 cash and in those days, those were big bucks. We stayed out there all summer, paid all of our expenses and brought that much cash home. Dad thought it was very successful," he said, noting how much he enjoyed those summer months. "I would not have traded them for anything, as I felt like I was helping the family. Our summer home was a tent and after those years I never wanted to go camping again!"

The summer operation lasted until Harold graduated from high school in 1939. After his one year of college, he tried to enlist in the Navy, but was turned down because he was colorblind, something that he was surprised to hear. "I thought they were very picky, but nevertheless, I did my thing, I tried," he said.

He landed a job as a welder's helper for 40-cents an hour at Alexander Aircraft in Colorado Springs, Colo. where he ended up spending two years building aircraft motor mounts and landing gears for Douglas Aircraft. He then went back to Wichita, took a job at Beechcraft and soon passed the test to become a government certified welder.

A Member of the College Bored

"I told my father that I wanted to be just like him, a grease monkey, but he talked me into going to college for at least one year. I didn't do well because I didn't like being there but I tolerated it just because he wanted me to go."

HAROLD CHANCE

Harold and Marge on their wedding day, 1946.

Harold and Marge on their 50th anniversary, 1996.

Harold soon became bored as a welder and went to work for a small shop making tool and dies for the defense industry. He became proficient in that line of work and took a job at a larger tool shop in Neodesha, Kans. and within six months was promoted to foreman. While he wasn't allowed to enlist earlier, Uncle Sam soon came knocking, but his employer kept getting Harold deferments, claiming that he was needed in Wichita because the work he was doing was directly related to military efforts. Finally, the Army quit giving deferments and in 1944, Harold joined the U.S. Army. Thirteen weeks later, at age 23, he was on a ship headed to the South Pacific.

He was assigned to the infantry and instead of working as a mechanic as he had hoped, he ended up working out of a foxhole in Okinawa and Guam, where he fought in three separate battles. He recalls the day he got word that he would be heading home. "We were in the South Pacific sitting on the ship getting ready to invade Japan when we heard that the war was over. That was a happy day."

Back Home and Back in Business

Soon after returning to Wichita in 1946, Harold ran into Herb Ottaway, who by then had a successful business manufacturing small trains. Ottaway asked, "When can you come to work?" Harold quickly replied, "I'll be there in the morning." Harold was put in charge of running the shop. It was a small operation with less than 10 employees, turning out 10 to 15 trains a year. That little shop became the genesis of possibly the most successful U.S. ride manufacturing company in history.

It was the summer of 1946 when he met his future wife Marge, who had just graduated from nurses training. After six months of courting and driving around town in Harold's new Ford sedan, the two were married on Oct. 4, 1946. Within a decade, the couple had five children.

Brothers Herb and Harold Ottaway, along with their father Lester, built Joyland Park in Wichita in 1949. It was a major park for the time and had a large wooden roller coaster. As Ottaway became more and more involved in the park, he left Harold to run the train shop. One day Ottaway came into the shop and said, "Harold, why don't you continue to run the (train) shop and also put one of the trains in Joyland as a concession, and I'll give you a five year lease on it. At the end of five years, the park will take over the train and you can take over ownership of the shop." It didn't take Harold long to accept the offer.

Five years later, Harold turned over the train and its operation to Ottaway and in turn took over the manufacturing business. He said it provided him a good way to get into his own business, "but there weren't enough people wanting trains" at the time.

The train operation at the park had been successful for Harold and he had made good money, causing him to be "scared to death" when he walked away from it after those five years. The train manufacturing plant wasn't doing much business and without the money from his train concession, his income was cut considerably.

Harold Plans to Get Rich Quick

In 1954, as a way to survive, and "get rich quick," Harold entered the carnival business. He had no route, no rides - just the desire. It didn't take him long to discover that carnival life was not going to be the means to easy money. "But it did turn out to be a sure way to get old quick," he laughed. "Luckily I continued to keep the train manufacturing company going and it was from this shop that I was able to build and rebuild some of the rides that we used on our carnival."

Harold purchased a few kiddie rides, a merry-go-round, several games, and a few "very used" trucks from a friend who had retired from the carnival business. He picked up a few more attractions and was able to put together a 10-ride show. He opened in Alamogordo, N.M. for a six week run, and made money. The next spot was Ada, Okla. and he made money there as well.

But from there on, it was downhill for R.H. Chance Amusements, the traveling show. For the rest of his first season he was able to book only poor and mediocre spots because the good ones were already booked by older, more established shows. The only thing that consistently made money, according to Harold, was Marge's cotton candy wagon.

The carnival stayed together for two seasons, but by early 1956, Harold figured he could do better if he parked all the rides, added a train and created an amusement park. He leased a vacant lot on the banks of Lake Tanacoma in Rockaway Beach, Mo., and opened his first park in spring 1956. Business was sluggish from day one. "The people weren't interested in amusement rides; they were there for the water, the boating and swimming." By mid-July, he was broke and realized it didn't make any sense to remain there. He packed up his rides and found a lot near Muckogee, Okla., where he moved the rides and set up another park, a location which ended up being successful for two seasons.

"I was still running the manufacturing plant and I had enough cash flow to keep my one employee busy and keep my own finger in it," he said. By late 1957, the manufacturing business had grown to a point that demanded his full time attention. He came in off the road, closed his park, sold his rides and according to Harold, "never looked back."

"My years as a carny were not profitable or necessarily pleasant ones, but I did learn a great deal. I experienced first hand that carnival operators have a tough life on the road. It's very hard out there and I think having lived that life even for a short time established my view of the way I did business with them for the rest of my life," he said. "I learned to respect them. They certainly earn every penny they make."

New Home for His Business

The manufacturing company had been operating out of a "modest" 2,400 square foot building and there was no room to park trucks or to expand. During the summer of 1960, Harold found an 8,000 square foot building with plenty of storage space and outdoor parking. "The building already had been financed, so I was able to purchase it by taking over the note. We had a new home!"

At the time, he still called his manufacturing business Ottaway Amusements. "In the beginning, I didn't change the name because I would have had to put up a new sign on the building, and that would have cost too much money," he notes, adding that when he bought the new building and moved the business, his wife Marge insisted that, "You're now going to change the name of the company and go by Chance." In 1960, Chance Manufacturing was officially founded.

The Chance Booth at the 1970 IAAPA Trade Show in Chicago.

Harold had the opportunity to purchase two adjacent acres for $9,500 an acre, but decided against it because he thought at the time he would "never ever" desire to expand. "I felt if I couldn't make a living out of this size of a building, forget it. I didn't want any more property." He laments about the price he had to pay for that extra acreage later on, when he expanded the plant.

With the new factory, the new name, and with the complete attention and dedication of Harold, the company continued to create miniature trains and soon added a new ride, the Pump-It handcar, to its line-up. "Business was lean at that time and we developed the Pump-It out of desperation," he said. "We had observed what Hodges had accomplished with his handcar ride and thought perhaps he had not come close to saturating the market." Harold and his lone employee at the time, Harold Phillips, developed the ride and put it into production. They took it to the parks convention and trade show that fall and sold several. During the next 25 years, Chance Manufacturing would sell 186 units, "all at a nice profit," Harold adds proudly.

To this day, Harold credits the Pump-It with saving the company. "Times were lean and that little handcar brought in some much-needed cash flow," he said. "Our version was a little different than the one Hodges built, but it was based on the same idea. They were very popular and profitable."

Harold receives an IAAPA Exhibitor's Award from Patricia Bennett, while his son Dick looks on.

New Line of Rides, by Chance

Harold continued building the miniature Ottaway Steam Train introduced by Herb Ottaway in 1946. In 1955, Harold introduced the B-14 Miniature Streamline Train, of which 14 were eventually sold, and in 1958, he premiered the B-20 Aerotrain, modeled after the General Motors "train of the future." He was able to get enough information and enough drawings from General Motors to scale it down and create an accurate miniature version of the modernistic train. It was built in a 20 to 24-inch gauge, large enough that adults could easily ride it along with the children. It was equipped with a four-cylinder gasoline engine, the first non-steam driven train created by Harold.

"Everything about the Aerotrain was perfect," he recalls. "That is except for the volume of sales. We could only sell six. It was one of the prettiest trains I ever built and I had high expectations, but for some reason it didn't sell."

While the Aerotrain didn't sell as had hoped, it turned out to be a valuable project in research and development that laid the groundwork for future successes. Much of what was learned during the creation of the Aerotrain is still used in the company's train production today.

The Ride Nobody Wanted

"I am not too sure to this day where we went wrong. Thank goodness we didn't lay too many of those eggs."

HAROLD CHANCE, ON THE PIXIE PLAZA,
THE KIDDIELAND ON WHEELS THAT NOBODY SEEMED TO WANT.

After losing in his gamble with a futuristic model, Harold decided he needed to go back to concentrating on the frontier-themed locomotives that had previously done so well for him.

A new style train was built as a result of that decision and it turned out to be the most successful miniature train model any company anywhere has ever built - the C.P. Huntington. It first hit the market in 1961 and the first was sold to Wichita's Joyland and was still in use there 45 years later. The C.P. Huntington used the gasoline power train developed for the Aerotrain. Harold calls it a "fake steamer." During his 25 years (1960-1985) at the helm of

Chance Manufacturing, he sold 316 of them, and through 2006, the company had sold more than 400.

Harold Starts Building Bigger Rides

The first major non-train ride Harold built was the Trabant. It came about when international ride salesman Mack Duce imported a Trabant to the U.S. from Germany in 1963. Showman Carl Sedlmayr of the Royal American Shows had purchased the ride with the understanding that he would receive royalty on each Trabant manufactured and sold in the U.S. Duce owned the rights to the ride and after touring the Chance Manufacturing plant (to make sure Harold and his team could build it), he asked Harold if he would like to buy the rights to "a great new ride."

He said he would like to take a look at it and off he and Duce went to visit Sedlmayr while the show was playing the Wisconsin State Fair. Harold liked what he saw, agreed to build it, and gave Duce the exclusive sales rights. Sedlmayr asked for no up-front money, but wanted a royalty on each ride sold. They agreed on the deal, shook hands and no contract was ever written.

Harold recalls the day he first saw the Trabant. "I watched them set it up and I instantly saw the possibilities of trailer mounting it on one trailer. I felt confident in this ride and knew our company could make it a winner." By the time Harold retired in 1985, he had sold 230 of them. The first few sold for $29,750 each. Duce ended up having exclusive sales rights to not only the Trabant, but to all of Chance Manufacturing rides. It was another handshake deal that lasted until Harold retired and the company's new owner, Harold's son Dick, took the sales duties in-house.

Harold Designs His First Major Ride

The first major ride Harold and his team designed and built from the ground-up was the Skydiver in 1965. Along with inventor Joe Brown, Harold set out to build a trailer-mounted Ferris wheel from scratch. During the design stages, he started thinking outside the box and ended up with the Skydiver, a one-of-a-kind portable thrill ride, not the Ferris wheel that he had set out to design. "We priced them at $65,000 and they sold like hotcakes for several years," he said, noting that 64 were sold by 1985. The following year, Chance Manufacturing acquired the rights to build a portable Rotor from the Velare Brothers, a Canadian carnival family. Again he got a ride with no money down and royalty only due when one was sold. Twenty-five eventually were sold, mostly to carnivals.

In 1967, the first Starliner Tram Train was built. It was a rubber tired passenger train that quickly became popular for parking lot operations and sight seeing tours at zoos and historic locations.

No honest biography can be written about a great man without pointing out his failures as well as his victories. One of Harold's biggest mistakes was agreeing to build an Olympic Bobs ride in 1968. One of his regular customers asked him to build it in time for the HemisFair, set to open six months hence in San Antonio. He agreed, bought a used German-built Bobs for reference and went to work. It opened on time but there had not been time to complete all tests before the fair began. When the first problems with the ride occurred during the fair, they were fixed on the spot. However, "the more we worked on it the worse it got," claims Harold. "The fair soon asked us to remove the ride. We refunded the customer's money and called it a bad deal. Thank goodness we only built that one."

It should be pointed out that following the fiasco at the HemisFair, Harold hit a home run that same year with the Zipper which eventually sold more than 200 units by 1985.

Another "misjudgment" came in 1976 when Harold came up with the idea to combine six kiddie rides onto one trailer - a one-stop kiddieland. He called it the Pixie Plaza. A kiddie wheel was mounted on one end of the 40-foot trailer, and a kiddie chair swing at the other

Easier Up – Easier Down

A trailer mounted ride has its base built into the trailer on which it is transported. The ride stays on its trailer and is erected by means of hydraulic power, making it easier and quicker to set up and take down. Harold Chance wasn't the first to do it, but he took the art of trailer mounting to a new level and in doing so, revolutionized the portable ride industry.

**Harold, right, closes the deal to purchase the
Allan Herschell Company from Lynn Wilson in 1970.**

end. A kiddie Scrambler and a small merry-go-round were built on one
side, with a Tubs of Fun and a flying boat ride on the opposite side. The
rides folded up for easy transporting.

Excited about the Pixie Plaza, the sales team, along with the
prototype, headed to Gibsonton, Fla. for the annual carnival trade show.
Not a single order was written and the company wasn't able to sell the
prototype, even at a discounted price, from the trade show floor. "I am

not too sure to this day where we went wrong. Thank goodness we did not lay too many of those eggs," Harold waxes. The ride eventually ended up at Coney Island, in Cincinnati.

Harold had learned an expensive lesson with the Olympic Bobs - never market a ride until it is tested, retested and tested some more. However, his resolve never to do that again lasted less than one year when he became excited about a new ride called the Toboggan and agreed to build it. He announced its creation and had it for sale before the first one was ever built and tested.

Walter House of Amarillo, Texas had invented the Toboggan, and Harold loved it the minute he saw it. A deal was immediately struck with House for all manufacturing and sales rights. By this time, Chance Manufacturing had a good reputation within the industry and ride operators knew they could trust the quality of a Chance-built ride. Before the first Toboggan was ever built in the Wichita factory, he had a dozen firm orders. It initially sold as a one-trailer ride for $35,000.

The ride was built and worked well from the start, but it was the trailer that caused the problems this time around. Only after trailer mounting the very first Toboggan off the production line did Harold realize the trailer axle weight exceeded allowable highway restrictions. He had not figured a second trailer into the price, but to make it a legal load, it had to be transported on two trailers. It could have been an expensive miscalculation if Harold would have had to eat the price of that second trailer. He tried to buy back the original contracts for $5,000 each but there were no takers as everyone wanted the new ride. Finally, he offered to sell the showmen the second trailer for $7,500, below his cost, and all who had already ordered the ride, agreed on those terms. Once the Toboggan problems were solved in 1970, the company turned its attention to manufacturing two more new rides, the Turbo and the Radar, eventually selling 22 and 1, respectively.

The Company with Moxie

What distinguished Chance Manufacturing from other companies in the early 1970s, according to Harold was that, "We were brassy, we were progressive, and we were coming up with new stuff all the time." At the carnival trade show, Harold's son Dick would sit in the lobby with photos and sales sheets of the company's newest products. The carnival owners would walk by, look at the material and many would end up buying a ride before the show opened. The showmen consistently needed new rides to help them acquire better fairs and locations and with Chance Manufacturing's reputation, they knew they had better buy quickly before production was sold out.

Ride manufacturing in the U.S. was a "very sleepy industry" during the early years of Chance Manufacturing. Eli Bridge was building the Scrambler and the Big Eli Ferris wheel, Sellner had the Tilt-A-Whirl and there were a few rides being built by Jack Eyerly and by Frank Hrubetz. However, no one could match Harold's output. "I created a lot of attention when I brought out at least one new ride each year. There is no question about it, our ability to come out with new rides is what propelled us to the top," said Harold.

Adding Allan Herschell

Harold was attending the parks convention at the old Sherman House in Chicago in the late 1960s when he ran into Lynn Wilson who then owned the Allan Herschell Company. It turned out he wanted to get out of the business for many reasons, but mostly because of the liability issues that were becoming prevalent. It was too much for him to worry about, he explained to Harold. Within a year of that chance meeting, Harold had finalized the purchase of the company.

BUILD THEM & THEY WILL SELL

"We were brassy, we were progressive, and we were coming up with new stuff all the time."

HAROLD CHANCE, ON WHAT DISTINGUISHED HIS COMPANY FROM OTHER MANUFACTURERS DURING THE EARLY 1970s.

Allan Herschell (AH) was founded in 1883 and by 1970 when Harold took over, it was the largest amusement ride manufacturing company in the world, having built thousands of rides over the years. Chance Manufacturing was founded in 1960 and was one of the smallest.

"It was a pretty big deal at that time to buy that big of a company with such a famous name and it stretched me out pretty good. I paid cash for the inventory and the payment for the drawings, tooling and manufacturing rights was determined by a percentage of the selling price of any Allan Herschell ride that we built and sold over a 10 year

PHOTO: TIM O'BRIEN

Legendary carnival owner Pat Reithoffer, left,
with Harold during an IAAPA Trade Show.

period. It didn't take an awful lot of cash but it wound up being a several million dollar deal by the time it was all over," Harold said. Dick Chance sold the assets of AH to the Allan Herschell Museum in North Tonawanda, N.Y. in December 1997.

The AH company had been producing The Iron Horse miniature train and it "really was a piece of junk," Harold recalls. "I knew my train was a lot better than his, so the first thing I did after I bought the company was take that train off the market and out of the catalog."

Prior to 1971, Chance Manufacturing had never built a carousel because Harold felt the market was being well served by AH and a hand full of other manufacturers. When he purchased AH, he took the company's 36-foot machine and immediately redesigned it. "Their merry-go-rounds were too modern. We changed the scenery to the old, ornate style; we replaced the florescent lights with hundreds of incandescent bulbs, and replaced the wood floors with aluminum flooring. In all, we made a more beautiful carousel." The market loved the new look of the carousel and Chance Manufacturing sold more in 1971, the first year of production, than AH had the previous five.

Harold continued to introduce new rides through the 1970s, including the Flying Bobs, 1971; the Music Fest, 1974; the Zumur, 1975; an 80-foot Giant Wheel, 1975; and the Casino, 1976. By 1976, the production facilities had grown to 110,000 square feet on 10-acres of land, and the number of employees had grown to 170.

Showman Larry Davis and Harold on the links in Palm Springs, Calif. in 1991.

In 1977, Harold diversified his product line by purchasing the manufacturing rights to the product line of Minibus Inc. of California, then owned by MCA Inc., the parent company of Universal Studios. They were ready to get out of the manufacturing business and "we gained a new product in the Minibus." The acquisition led to the formation of the Chance Coach division. Later, the Alamo City Streetcar line was added to the coach division. "We found it to be a tough business in which to make a profit," Harold said.

During the late 1970s through 1985 when he retired, several more rides were created by Harold and his team, including the Sea Dragon, 1979; Space Shuttle, 1981; Star Fighter, 1982; Wagon Wheeler, 1983; Falling Star, 1984; a 50-foot Carousel, 1985; and finally, the Thunderbolt in 1985.

Passing on the Torch

Dick Chance was made president in 1978 and Harold became chairman. In 1985, at age 65, on the company's 25th anniversary, Harold retired, selling 100% of Chance Manufacturing and Chance Coach to Dick on March 1. Harold is quick to point out that he "did not make a gift of the business" to his son. "We had all the assets priced by outside appraisers to reach a fair selling price," and Dick was able to arrange the necessary financing through a local bank.

"In a way I hated to relinquish control of the business that I had spent a lifetime building," Harold noted, adding that had he sold to anyone else, he would have feared for the security of his long-time, loyal employees, those Dick was already familiar with and whose jobs he would protect. "I made the right decision," he proclaims.

Harold took Chance Manufacturing from a one-person shop to a $12 million business employing 200 persons when he retired in 1985, and the momentum continued. Ten years later, the company employed 400 and was grossing nearly $40 million.

Life as a ride manufacturer is "not all that great," Harold was heard to say many times during his career. In addition to the major financial risk involved in continually needing to introduce new product, the safety and liability issues were an overriding concern that was with him 24/7. "I am proud to state, that in my 25 years there was never a ride accident on a Chance-built ride that was caused by mechanical error," he said, explaining that any accidents that did occur were proven to be caused by patron or operator error.

Harold, the Safety Pioneer

Harold lived his commitment to safety. Through his personal financial assistance, his participation, and his influence, the first of what is now the world's largest annual safety seminar began in his plant in 1972.

"I wanted to start a safety seminar and I took the idea to the AREA (American Recreation Equipment Assn., a group of ride manufacturers and operators) meeting and announced that I was going to develop a safety seminar and I would be very pleased if you guys would get involved. It's going to be a week-long school and I would like to see each one of you send at least one person to help teach about the safety and the maintenance of the rides you're manufacturing."

The support was large and the first safety seminar was held in Wichita at the Chance Manufacturing plant, where it was held annually through 1975. Since then, it has been held in a different location each year and has revisited Wichita on many occasions. In 1972, 32 students attended, along with 50 instructors representing every U.S. ride manufacturer. By the time it left Wichita, the seminar was averaging more than 130 students per year.

In 1995, AIMS (Amusement Industry Manufacturing & Suppliers International) was formed and took over the seminar, opening the school to students and manufacturers worldwide. Through 2006 more than 8,000 people had received amusement ride safety training, thanks to this week-long seminar.

Harold Becomes Mr. Fix-it

"I'm the fix-it man. There are a lot of widowed people living there and none of them have any mechanical ability. You can't get the natives to do anything, so I'm sure I've fixed more toilets since I went down there than most people do in a lifetime."

HAROLD CHANCE, ON BEING RETIRED AND LIVING IN THE BAHAMAS.

By creating greater awareness of safety and the need to be proactive on safety issues and legislation, Harold pioneered the concept of self-regulated safety. "By teaching ride operations, maintenance and safety programs to the ride operators, it was my thought that if an accident did occur, we could show the courts that we were making every effort to operate and maintain our equipment properly," he said.

John Hinde, seminar director of AIMS, attended the first safety seminar in 1972 as a ride mechanic and he thinks Harold's vision of the need for industry self-regulation was far ahead of its time. "The safety and maintenance manuals he created for his rides, right from the beginning, set the standards for all others to follow," Hinde said. "He was the first manufacturer to readily and unselfishly share his manuals and his expertise with others, in the name of safety."

In the mid-1990s, an award was created by AIMS that is given each year to an instructor who gives the "best presentation" at the AIMS Safety Seminar. It was named the Harold Chance Award.

Retirement Days

Harold maintained an office when he retired and he continued to come in on most mornings, have coffee with Dick and discuss the business. Dick said his father never made a nuisance of himself or got in the way. "No, once all the financing was in place and the company was mine, he pretty much told me it was my baby and I had to make it a success," Dick said. "I've got to hand it to him, when he decided to retire from ride manufacturing, he really retired."

AREA's Board of Directors, 1964-65, from left were Watson Bray, Allan Herschell Company; John Allen, Philadelphia Toboggan Company; Harold Chance; Lee Sullivan, Eli Bridge Company; and Art Sellner, Sellner Manufacturing.

"Heading into retirement, I knew I wasn't going to be one of those guys who relied on golf, travel or the rocking chair to keep busy," Harold notes. "I wanted to do something and to stay busy, but not get into something that would tie me down." One of the first things he did was to start a small company that he operated out of his home workshop. Chance Chariots Ltd. specialized in customizing golf carts for golfers and carnival operators. He worked alone, never advertised and never had one sold before it was finished. He customized nearly 50 carts, closing down the business when it "started feeling like work."

Harold has also been buying back some of the old steam trains that he built 50 to 60 years ago and is in the process of restoring them. He plays "a little golf," but notes that he still isn't very good, although he and Marge have lived in a house next to a golf course for nearly 40 years.

Meanwhile, Chance Manufacturing, now known as Chance Morgan (following the acquisition of Morgan Manufacturing in the early 2000s), is being run by Dick's son Michael Chance. Dick's other son John is also involved, as is his daughter Amie. The fact that his grandchildren are now involved with the company pleases

The Great Carny Lessons

"My years as a carny were not profitable or necessarily pleasant ones, but I did learn a great deal. I experienced first hand that carnival operators have a tough life on the road. It's very hard out there and I think having lived that life even for a short time established my view of the way I did business with them for the rest of my life."

HAROLD CHANCE

Harold. "I am tickled to death and very proud of my son and my grandchildren for keeping the company going," Harold said. "It's hard to believe it has been around that long. It certainly has been in good hands since I left."

In the mid-1970s, a friend invited Harold and Marge to visit them at their retirement home in Treasure Cay, a small resort on the island of Abaco in the Bahamas. Marge loved the area and according to Harold, she couldn't get it out of her system, "so we bought one."

That's where they now spend their winters, heading back to Wichita each spring.

Having the desire to stay busy, and loving to tinker with things, has made Harold quite the popular handyman hero in Treasure Cay. "I'm the fix-it man. There are a lot of widowed people living there and none of them have any mechanical ability. You can't get the natives to do anything, so I'm sure I've fixed more toilets since I went down there than most people do in a lifetime. They miss me when I'm gone, and I'll tell you, I get lots of treats."

When there are no toilets to fix? "Sometimes I fix things that are not even broken, just to keep busy," he laughs.

BIBLIOGRAPHY

ARTICLES & INTERVIEWS

Associated Press Wire Story, by Paul Stevens, April 9, 1979

Chance Acquires Rights to Bradley & Kaye, *Funworld,* April 1987

Chance Manufacturing Co., *Amusement Park Journal,* by Charles Jacques, Jr., March 1985

Chance Mixes New Ideas, Old Principles to Keep Ride Company Moving Forward, *Amusement Business,* by Tim O'Brien, Feb. 27, 1995

Chance Rides Press Releases, 1965-2005

Chance Rides Top the Trashpile Market, *Wichita,* by Phillis Spade, March-April, 1973

Chance Sells Allan Herschell Assets at Auction; Purchased by Museum, *Amusement Business,* by Tim O'Brien, Dec. 22, 1997

Fun on the Move, *Wichita Trends,* Sept. 23, 1965

Herb Ottaway, Founder of Joyland Amusement Park, Dies at Age 91, *Amusement Business,* by James Zoltak, Feb. 16, 2004

Interview with David Norton, Norton Auctioneers, by Tim O'Brien, Sept. 15, 2005

Interviews with Dick Chance, by Tim O'Brien Sept. 15, 2005; Jan. 13, 2006

Interviews with Harold Chance by Tim O'Brien, Oct. 25, 2005; March 21, 2006

Interview with John Hinde, AIMS Seminar Director, by Tim O'Brien, Jan. 12, 2006

Interviews with Michael Chance, Sept. 16, 2005; Jan. 9, 2006

Lot's of Fun We all Profit From, *Funworld,* February 1992

SLA Picks First Hall of Famers, *Amusement Business,* by Tom Powell, Jan. 7, 2005

The Chance Zipper, *Amusement Today,* by Scott Rutherford, June 2005

The Thrill Ride Builder, *Kansas City Star Magazine,* by Susan Stoffle, Nov. 27, 1977

24-Year-Old Chance Firm Optimistic About Future, *Amusement Business,* by Steve
    Rogers, July 28, 1984
Wichitan Harold Chance Builds Most of U.S. Amusement Rides, *The Wichita
    Beacon,* 1968

BOOKS
*The Book of Chance: A Pictorial Review of the Life of Harold Chance, His Family and His
    Friends,* Chance Industries, 2003, by Harold Chance

RON TOOMER

"I'm not sure if I ever really invented anything."

The first roller coaster ride that legendary ride designer and rocket scientist Ron Toomer ever experienced was aboard the very first roller coaster he designed - the Runaway Mine Train at Six Flags Over Texas, in Arlington.

That was in 1966 when he was 36 years old. He started designing coasters following a short career in aerospace in which he worked on America's first satellite, and later as part of the team that created the solid fuel boosters for the Minuteman rocket program.

Ron, using his ingenuity and engineering experience revolutionized the design and the building of steel roller coasters. In his 33 years in the business, he is credited with the basic design of 80 coasters, many of which were record breakers, in more than a dozen countries. His design contributions range from the relatively simple Runaway Mine Train and Corkscrew coasters to complex machines, including the Magnum XL-200, the first coaster to top 200 feet tall.

When Ron entered the amusement industry, deals were consummated with hand shakes, and few, if any contracts were ever signed. He points out that "back then," the industry was a people's business. He retired when the emphasis on big business overtook the emphasis on the people, focusing instead on well-written contracts and bottom line results. He left the industry when the rules of daily business nearly prohibited him from dealing as he always had with his friends and peers.

Ron visited amusement parks as a teen but ironically, was never much of a rider. "When we were kids, we used to go down to Long

The TOOMER File

RONALD VALENTINE TOOMER

Born: Pasadena, Calif., May 31, 1930 as William Valentine Toomer. He was named after his father's brother who was killed during WWI. "My mom realized she didn't like the name William, so it was changed to Ronald Valentine Toomer within a couple weeks."

Married: Betty Boughey, June 15, 1957

Children: Greg, Carol, Gary, and Christopher

Education: Bachelor of Science in Mechanical Engineering, University of Nevada at Reno, 1961

Claim to fame: Using his ingenuity and engineering experience, Ron revolutionized the design and the building of steel roller coasters. In his 33 years in the business, he is credited with the basic design of 80 steel coasters, many of which were record breakers, in more than a dozen countries.

Design contributions: They range from the relatively simple Runaway Mine Train and Corkscrew coasters to complex machines, including the Magnum XL-200, the first coaster to ever top 200 feet tall.

First job in the amusement industry: Arrow Development Company, 1965 as the company's first engineer.

First task with Arrow: Wading around in the Pirates of the Caribbean ride at Disneyland determining water flow.

Mentor: Karl Bacon, one of the founders of Arrow. "We worked together from the start and he taught me to be patient and not rush into something. I would spend a great deal of time designing some mechanism, and he'd say, 'Well, that really looks good, but let's think about something different.'"

Business philosophy: "Honesty, it's the major thing that has helped me through life."

Greatest professional accomplishment: Building of the first Corkscrew coaster. "In my mind, it changed the amusement industry."

Most gratifying moment in career: "I had a gratifying moment every time I saw a ride operate for the first time."

Continued on page 210...

Beach (California) where they had the big amusement piers and parks. I remember standing in front of the Cyclone Racer, the big wooden coaster at the Pike and watching the thing, but I never did get on. No one in my family ever rode the big rides so I guess that's why I never did."

The Man with the Queasy Stomach

He did partake in a few of the minor rides, but soon learned he had a major problem.

"I'd get motion sick real easy. The whole industry now knows about that and I don't ride a lot of stuff, even today. I can go on a coaster maybe once, maybe twice, but that's about it," he notes. "Carousels don't bother me too much but I still get sick in a car when somebody else is driving."

The irony that he gets motion sickness on his own rides is not lost on the media. "Ron Toomer's job makes him sick to his stomach," proclaims the opening sentence in a *Financial Post* story. "Roller Coaster King Ron Toomer Has a Job He Can't Stomach," is the headline over a *People* magazine article. *Forbes* magazine noted that "Toomer suffers from chronic motion sickness and prefers raising bonsai trees to riding roller coasters."

What does he say in response? Maybe the best comeback in all of recorded history came when the *People* magazine reporter questioned the fact that he didn't ride his own designs. "Hey, the inventor of the electric chair didn't try out his creation either," Ron answered back.

Who Makes These Things?

His eventual career path even surprised Ron, who can't recall that he ever wondered where amusement rides came from. "It never entered my mind that I would ever be involved in the creation of rides," he said. "Amusement rides are sort of just there, few people actually stop and think that somebody had to design and build them."

He recalls the difficulty of getting his four children familiar with "what daddy did for a living." Daughter Carol once told her dad that she stopped telling her friends what he did. "They never believed me anyway," she reported.

As a young man Ron, first and foremost, wanted to be an auto mechanic and during high school, took several vocational auto mechanic classes. He graduated in 1948 and spent two years at Pasadena Junior College, concentrating on auto mechanic vocational classes. Following junior college he went to work as a mechanic for a Ford dealership.

He was drafted into the Army in 1952 and went to infantry basic training at Camp Roberts in California for 16 weeks and spent another eight weeks in Leadership School. The Army wanted him to go on to officer candidate school, but he refused, knowing he would have to sign up for an additional three years, something in which he wasn't interested. Two years would be enough, he reasoned.

Ron was put on a ship headed to Germany. In a casual conversation with another German-bound soldier, the topic of snow skiing came up and his new friend suggested that Ron, with the snow skiing skills he had learned as a teenager, should join the Division Ski Team, which he did during his two months in Berchtesgaden. He skied every day and competed in several inter-military championships, an experience he still recalls as "fantastic."

Done My Time, Looking for a Life

When he came home from the Army in 1954, he "poked around, looking for employment" and went to work for the Southern California Gas Company as a serviceman. He had no desire to go back to college until one day he had an epiphany.

The TOOMER File

Continued from page 208...

Proudest moment in career: "The day I was inducted into the IAAPA Hall of Fame. It's something you get from the people that know you and have worked with you. It's a pretty high point in my entire life. It meant that my peers thought I'd done something right and well. It did a lot for me to get that."

Favorite coasters created: The Magnum XL-200 at Cedar Point in Sandusky, Ohio "stands out as one of the best rides I ever created."

Hobbies: "I did the bonsai thing while in California, but when I moved to Utah, it was too cold for them, so I picked up woodworking. Today, I do a lot of woodworking, and I carve waterfowl and pheasants."

Favorite amusement park: Cedar Point. "They have a lot of great rides there, and I think it's the greatest park ever. They aren't afraid to do new things and they are always improving what they do. They get it."

Favorite movies: "*Field of Dreams. The Music Man* has to be right up there as well."

On *Roller Coaster*, the movie: "It really didn't have much going for it. It was interesting, but you know, that's not reality."

Worst kept secret about Ron Toomer: The legendary coaster designer easily gets motion sickness and while he rides each of his designs once, that's it.

"I had a friend who worked all day at one job and all evening at a gas station. I would go down to the gas station and chat with him and one night as I was leaving, I thought to myself, my God, this guy is married with a couple of kids, and he's working two jobs. I thought that could be me some day," Ron said. "Right then I decided I was going back to college and get a degree in mechanical engineering."

Since he hadn't planned to pursue a four-year degree, Ron had not taken college preparatory classes in high school. When he decided to pursue an engineering degree, he returned to Pasadena City College to obtain the credits he needed to matriculate into a four year program.

While studying at Pasadena City College, he worked part-time at the Jet Propulsion Laboratory as a draftsman and became involved in designing "tiny little vectoring motors that were used on the first satellite to get it into and to keep it in orbit." The work interested him and as a result, he started thinking a career in aerospace might be in his future.

As did most youngsters of the time, Ron became interested in the space program, but unlike many of the others, never wanted to be an astronaut, partially because of his propensity toward motion sickness. It was also due, he admits, to the fact that he never considered himself "a daredevil type of person." Even during the period when he rode his coaster creations, he never raised his arms or enjoyed the "airtime" provided.

"No, I just sit there when I ride a coaster. I rode enough of them in the beginning to get to the point that I could at least figure out what it was all about." Figure it out he did. "It's kind of funny because after I rode a few, I would sit at the drawing board, and I could actually internalize what it was going to feel like riding that particular element."

Betty, I Do, Now Let's Go to Reno!

Following his prerequisite courses at the city college, he and Betty were married and the newlyweds headed to Reno in 1957 where he had been accepted into the University of Nevada. "I had to work while taking classes, so it took me another four years to finish college," he explained.

One activity that Ron became involved with while attending the university was the local junior ski program, where he taught youngsters to snow ski. "After that, the skiing thing just got lost in the shuffle of school, family and then work," he noted. "I also worked part-time during college as a waiter in a casino in Reno. I made a lot of money doing that!"

With a college degree stuck under one arm and limited experience in solid rocket fuel from his days at the Jet Propulsion Laboratory, Ron landed a job as a mechanical engineer at Hercules Powder Company in Salt Lake City in June 1961. There, he worked as part of the team on the solid fuel booster for the second stage of the Minuteman missile.

He left Hercules and joined Thermastest Laboratories in Sunnyvale, Calif. in March 1962 as a mechanical engineer. He was responsible for research and testing of high temperature materials for use in the aerospace industry and he managed a program to design, develop and manufacture heat shield char sensors for the NASA Apollo program.

Thermatest went bankrupt in May 1965 and Ron was soon to be out of a job. A welder he worked with had previously been with Karl Bacon and Ed Morgan at a firm called Arrow Development Company. He told Ron that they were looking for a mechanical engineer.

Ron Follows the Arrow

Ron was introduced to Bacon and it wasn't too long after that meeting, that he was knee-deep in the waters of the Pirates of the Caribbean ride at Disneyland measuring water flow. "That was the first thing I did for Arrow," he recalls.

He jokes that within a few months he went from designing heat shields for Apollo spacecraft to working on the Pirates of the Caribbean ride at Disneyland. "Talk about a career change," he laughed. His next assignment was to design a roller coaster, a type of amusement ride of which he had never ridden.

Ron doesn't think any one thing better prepared him for his professional life as the world's pioneering designer of steel coasters. "I think it has more to do with my whole life experience, everything I had done up to that point - the experience I had in science, in aerospace, in cars and everything mechanical."

While all those factors prepared him for his professional career as an engineer, it was his relationship with his parents that prepared him to be the businessman that he became. "Both my parents were from England and my mom played a major role in what I became," he waxes. "She was always very honest and straightforward and I ended up pretty much the same way. I just don't believe in lying and cheating, no matter what it's about or for what reason. While that background didn't necessarily direct me toward designing roller coasters, it certainly had a lot to do with the way I looked at life and ran the company."

Ron Becomes First Engineer at Arrow

He didn't realize it at the time Bacon and Morgan hired him, but he would be the company's first and only engineer. His main job, nearly right from the start, would be to design roller coasters. The first series of coasters were the Runaway Mine Trains, named so because of their rustic resemblance to the trains used in mining operations.

Ron Toomer sits behind his desk at Arrow shortly after taking over as president in 1986.

Randall Duell, a pioneer in theme park design, was one of only a few in those days who worked exclusively on amusement park and ride design. Duell had created Six Flags Over Texas, in Arlington, the first Six Flags park for Angus Wynne in 1961. He had ordered a "runaway mine train type of coaster" from Arrow in 1965 before Ron began his tenure there. Arrow already had built the world's first log flume for that park in 1963.

"I was charged with trying to figure out how to do all the calculations and all the layout design and the geometry. Karl (Bacon) and I worked closely together on it and we just learned nearly everything as we went," he said. "At that time we didn't know anything about friction or the numbers that we should use. We did a lot of rolling tests and pulling the cars along the track to see exactly how much it took to allow them to keep moving because friction is, of course, the big thing there." No one had done that kind of engineering work before. Those were truly pioneering studies.

While there had only been one tubular steel coaster built to date, Duell specified to Arrow that was the tracking system he desired for

Ron Toomer working the ski lift at California's Mt. Baldy in 1956.

his mine train coaster. Arrow had built the Matterhorn at Disneyland, which was the first true tubular steel coaster, and Duell had his mind made up that was the style of coaster he wanted. There was never any talk about building anything else.

Million Dollar Mine Train Becomes a Reality

Ron and Bacon proceeded to develop a coaster that would fit into the theme that Duell had proposed. That first Runaway Mine Train opened in spring 1966 and was a "very wild ride that had several bumps and forces that we didn't like from the start, but park officials at Six Flags didn't want us to change a thing because the people who rode it loved it and they didn't want it changed," Ron admits. The Six Flags coaster was the first million dollar ride built outside of Disneyland.

"One of the things the tubular pipe rail does is to allow us to create sharper turns and other elements that you can't do on a wooden coaster. We can bend the pipe in any direction and do unique and crazy things," notes Ron. Because of that flexibility, Arrow's pioneering efforts with tubular steel became the basis for an entire new approach to coaster technology, in which virtually every steel coaster built since has at its genesis.

The Sky is the Limit

"Given enough time, space, and money I can design and we can build just about anything the park can dream up. Pushing it to the limits is what a thrill ride is all about."

RON TOOMER

Six Flags Over Georgia received the second mine train coaster in 1967, followed by Cedar Point in 1969, and Six Flags Magic Mountain and Six Flags Over Mid-America (now Six Flags St. Louis) in 1971. "We had a winner and the sales just kept coming. New amusement parks were popping up all over the place during those years and many wanted our Runaway Mine Train."

Corkscrews Aren't Just for Wine Anymore
While the mine trains were very popular, Arrow officials felt more could be done with the pipe coaster concept. In the early 1970s, they started thinking about an idea for a ride that turned out to be the ever-popular and revolutionary Corkscrew coaster. Ron recalls the day Bacon returned from Disneyland with the idea.

"Do you think we could do something like this?" Bacon asked Ron, as he waved his arm around in the air.

Ron responded: "You mean, like a corkscrew?

"Yes, that's it," Bacon said. "Like a corkscrew."

"Heck, yes, we can do that," said Ron, adding that he never saw anything that he didn't believe the company could build.

Ron thinks the Corkscrew was his greatest design accomplishment, and that its revolutionary design changed the amusement ride industry forever. When Ron and his team began work on the ride, "we first became concerned over G-forces and the affect they had on the riders," he notes. They first conducted G-force tests on the Giant Dipper, Santa Cruz Beach Boardwalk's legendary wood coaster. He said that was the only time that he ever used a wooden coaster to test technology for a steel coaster.

"To begin with, we worked with models and little two-inch cars. We made a corkscrew track that the cars would run through and we would put things in those little cars to show that they wouldn't fall out. We had park people come by and almost all of them thought it was a good idea." However, the Corkscrew idea was set aside at the time as the company worked to fill its orders for flume rides, of which the company built 22 between 1970 and 1975.

One day in 1974, Bacon revisited the need for the development of a new, major ride and told Ron, "We've got to get something new going, a new type of ride. Let's get back to this Corkscrew thing."

"After he told me that, we built a one-fourth scale model, this one with a chain lift and one spiral," Ron recalled. "After working with this model, we decided it wasn't enough of a ride, so we added another spiral, made it go upside down two times and kept tweaking it until we liked the way it looked. We were then confident enough to build

TOOMER: THE CAREER

Ron Toomer started out at Arrow in 1965 as a mechanical engineer. Six years later he was promoted to manager of engineering; in 1981 he became manager and VP of engineering; in 1986 he became president; and in 1993 he became chairman of the board. He retired in 1998.

During the 1993 IAAPA convention, Ron Toomer greets
Geoffrey Thompson, left, then head of
Blackpool (England) Pleasure Beach at the Pepsi booth.
The Arrow-built Pepsi Max Big One hyper coaster
premiered in Blackpool the following spring.

a full-scale ride in the back yard of our shop." It consisted of a double corkscrew, and a straight section. A ramp was built with a 45-degree drop from which the car would be released to go through the corkscrew element. It was enough to test g-forces and to develop other essential numbers.

After numerous successful test runs, Ron decided the Corkscrew was safe for people. A couple Arrow employees volunteered to be the first to ride it, which they did successfully. "Once we worked out a few additional problems, we were hell-bent to get the thing into production," Ron said. "We built the entire, full size ride in our yard and ran it day and night for 5,000 complete turns. Several park people came by to look at it, but it was Marion Anderson of Knott's Berry Farm who stepped up to the plate first to put in an order." The world's first

So You Want to Design Coasters?

"Through the years, I received a lot of letters from kids wanting to know how to get into the coaster design business. I would tell them as gently as possible that they stood a better chance of becoming an astronaut and walking on the moon than they did breaking into this industry. I always pointed out that you could count the number of us doing this ride design thing virtually on one hand."

RON TOOMER

PHOTO: PAUL RUBEN, APRIL 1988

Corkscrew premiered at Knott's in 1975 and closed in 1989. The ride was sold to Silverwood in Athol, Idaho for $250,000 and reopened in that park in 1990 as the Gravity Defying Corkscrew.

The Corkscrew was the first steel coaster to turn people successfully upside down. While the notorious Flip Flap, the wooden looping coaster of 1895 and the more advanced Loop-the-Loop woodie of 1901 both inverted riders, they had brief histories and not too much is known about them. It was the Corkscrew that set the standards for modern day inversion. The first Corkscrews sold for $700,000 each, plus installation.

Thinking Big Without Loops

In 1989, Arrow was the first to break the 200-foot barrier when it built the 205 foot tall Magnum XL-200 (Magnum for powerful, XL for extra large and 200 for feet) for Cedar Point. Some called the ride a hypercoaster, a name that would catch on, mostly with coaster aficionados for any coaster over 200-feet tall that did not contain loops or inversions.

The Magnum didn't start off as a 200-footer. "Cedar Point executives came to us and wanted us to build a big steel coaster on that piece of land right next to Lake Erie," Ron recalls. "We had it designed to be 180-feet, but Cedar Point's Dick Collingwood came to me and asked if we could make it 200-feet and I said of course." Ron always believed that anything could be built if there was enough land and enough money available. Magnum's final bill was in the neighborhood of $8 million.

While the Magnum is plainly the crown jewel in Ron's life work, he is also proud of the Steel Phantom he created at Kennywood, West Mifflin, Pa., in 1991, and the 209-foot Desperado, built in Primm, Nev., in 1994. "I love the placement of the Desperado because it's so tall and the surrounding land is so flat. You can see it a good 10 miles before you get there. It's quite a landmark."

During his years with Arrow, Ron worked on nearly every ride created that needed mechanical engineering, from the antique car family attractions to the behemoth coasters. He engineered many of the people moving systems that Arrow manufactured as well, including the Hershey Chocolate Tour, the two dark ride transportation systems for the ill-fated Six Flags Autoworld in Flint, Mich., the Goldmine Ride at Blackpool (England) Pleasure Beach, and the Living Island Dark Ride at another ill-fated theme park attempt, the $14 million World of Sid & Marty Krofft, in the Omni International in downtown Atlanta, Ga. The latter may have experienced the quickest demise of any theme park anywhere. It remained open for only five months and 17 days.

What Have I Done?

Ron enjoyed the art of creating amusement rides and has been outwardly proud to be a part of the industry. "It was always fun for me, that's for sure. There are not many things you can do where you can start out with a big blank piece of paper and end up standing out there watching thousands of people having fun on what you created. I would stand on the unloading platform and listen to the comments that riders were making as they got off the ride. It gave me a tremendous boost that people really had fun on my creations. That's very satisfying." During the early 80s, Ron calculated that nearly 200 million people a year were riding on the coasters that he and Arrow had created.

He said he always took the safety of those millions of people very seriously. "Everything we did, we carefully and thoroughly analyzed its safety," he notes, adding that many of the first safety-oriented devices and controls that are now common, were created out of necessity. "When we first started thinking about the Corkscrew, there were a lot of issues, including the most obvious of how to keep people from falling out. To fix that problem, we created the over-the-shoulder harness. We figured out how to build the harness by creating a seat that we could rotate upside down and had people sit in it to see how it felt. We tested all sizes, and my kids were used for the small ones."

He laughs when he thinks about the design and engineering work he completed during those first several years in the business. "We relied on a now nearly extinct tool," he recalls. "Karl and I would sit there for days going over all the calculations, one at a time on a slide rule. Most of the engineers of today have never seen a slide rule and they can't believe we didn't have a computer when we first started building these things."

Ron doesn't think the computer has made the process any quicker. "I still don't understand this, but we spent less engineering hours doing it the old way than they do now with the computers. I think it's because they calculate reams of information today that's not really necessary, just because the computer can easily do it."

Ron says while he is known for his early engineering and design work, he never considered himself an inventor. "No, I would simply take ideas and make them work. I'm not sure if I ever really invented anything," he said.

Ron Toomer in front of Valleyfair's Excalibur in August 1989.

PHOTO: PAUL RUBEN

Ron Holds Coaster Riders in Suspense

"Karl Bacon and I would sit around and talk about ideas while we were working. One day, we wondered out loud if we could create a coaster that would swing under the track, instead of ride on top like everything else that was being built. I looked at him and said, sure, we can make something like that, and of course, everyone knows the first one turned out to be a disaster." That first one, Bat, was built at Kings Island, near Cincinnati, in 1981.

Ron thinks Bat was a good idea, but it experienced a great deal of downtime due to engineering problems. He blames most of the problems on the fact the company was in a bit of internal turmoil at the time, having just been sold to Rio Grande Industries. "They hired new people and I was never too happy with the way the thing (Bat) looked and I knew even before it was built that it would need reworking, but they (Rio Grande) needed to get it built." Bat was taken down in 1983 and scrapped.

All was not lost however. Arrow engineers learned a great deal from their pioneering work on Bat. With a better understanding of what was needed to build a successful suspended coaster, the company built and premiered two in 1984, the XLR8 at AstroWorld in Houston, and the Big Bad Wolf at Busch Gardens, Williamsburg, Va. The latter is Ron's favorite suspended ride he ever built. "It really is a fantastic thing. You swing down over that lake, and back up the hill. It's a great location."

Anton Schwarzkopf's company started work on the Big Bad Wolf, but when financial problems forced bankruptcy, the company had to pull out of the project. "Busch officials came to me and wanted to know

Classic Comeback!

"Hey, the inventor of the electric chair didn't try out his creation either."

RON TOOMER, RESPONDING TO AN ENQUIRY ON WHY HE DIDN'T ALWAYS RIDE THE COASTERS HE DESIGNED.

if I could make a ride that would fit the existing footings and layout, and that's what we did," Ron said.

Arrow Development, Arrow-Huss, Arrow Dynamics

Karl Bacon, Ed Morgan and Walter Schulze opened up a small machine shop in Mountain View, Calif. in 1946, not to build amusement rides and go down in history as the longest running steel roller coaster manufacturer in the world, but to tackle "difficult and unusual mechanical engineering tasks," as Bacon would note on several occasions. The three men took nearly any work they could get in those days and eventually ended up working on various amusement industry projects, including the creation of playground equipment for the San Jose (Calif.) school district. They built several small rides for Alum Rock park in San Jose, including a small merry-go-round, and in 1952 built a small paddle wheel boat they called Lil' Belle for Lake Merritt, owned by the city of Oakland, Calif.

Morgan read that Walt Disney was getting ready to build an amusement park and tried to sell a paddle wheel boat similar to the Lil' Belle to Disney. In late 1952, Disney officials visited the shop, decided against the boat, but were impressed enough with the men and their capabilities to give them several jobs for the original Disneyland. It was the start of a relationship that lasted nearly 20 years. Arrow was given contracts to build The Mad Hatter's Tea Party, Snow White's Adventure, Mr. Toad's Wild Ride and to modify a circa 1922 Dentzel carousel, all to be finished in time for Disneyland's opening in July 1955.

By the end of 1959, they had added the Casey Jr. Circus Train, Dumbo the Flying Elephants, Midget Autopia, Alice in Wonderland, and the historic Matterhorn Bobsleds to the Disney lineup. Arrow would eventually provide a great deal of work for Walt Disney World in Florida as well.

In 1959, the company entered the world of coasters with the creation of the Matterhorn Bobsleds, the first coaster built with tubular steel. Prior to the Matterhorn, the small steel coasters that existed ran on flat iron rails, not on the tubular pipe tracking system. Using tubular steel track and polyurethane wheels created a revolutionary and unique system that beckoned in the new age of the roller coaster.

Arrow had a part in nearly every ride Disneyland installed through and including the opening of Walt Disney World in Florida in 1971. Walt strongly depended on the company and when it looked like Arrow was having financial problems and needed an infusion of new money to continue, Walt Disney stepped in and purchased a third of the company. Although the partnership lasted for only a few years, it kept the company viable so it could keep building rides for Walt's parks. In the early 1970s, several years after Walt died, Bacon and Morgan, who by then owned 100% of the company, decided it was time to retire, and they put the company up for sale.

Ron and Betty Toomer with a replica of a 1920s Dentzel carousel horse presented to them by the staff of Arrow Dynamics during a 1991 company outing at Lagoon Amusement Park in Farmington, Utah.

Ron Stranded as Bacon, Morgan Sell Out

Arrow was sold outright in 1972 to Rio Grande Industries, which ran the Rio Grande Railroad. It was an odd period for big business as it was a time when most were trying to decentralize. By the time they found Arrow, Rio Grande had already purchased an oil pipeline company, a computer company and a trucking company. The railroaders also had plans at the time to create several theme parks in addition to buying the ride company. Coincidentally, Six Flags was also owned by a railroad company during this period – Penn Central.

Ron and the others at Arrow were apprehensive about the original owners selling but were excited about the possibilities of a cash infusion from a big corporation. However, Ron said it didn't take long for him to realize that Arrow was in for trouble.

He recalls the day when one of Rio Grande's top officials, Max Erlich, visited the factory, looked at the original Corkscrew under development and asked, "What makes you guys think anybody would want to ride this thing?" Then Gus Aydelot, president of Rio Grande, visited and made the comment that, "I don't know why the hell anybody ever wants to go to an amusement park." George Denton, who Rio Grande brought in to run Arrow had been running a muffler plant for the Ford Motor Company, "and that totally astounded us," Ron noted. "I thought, holy Toledo, what are we in for here?"

When Rio Grande started divesting itself of non-core businesses several years later, they let it be known that Arrow was for sale. Several companies came to look over the facilities, Ron recalls. "I remember when Klaus (Huss) came in and looked around and showed some interest in buying Arrow, I thought to myself, my gosh, maybe we'll get somebody in here that really knows something about the amusement industry. That would be a nice change." The Huss plant in Bremen, Germany, already had a stellar reputation for building amusement rides.

Huss made it official and signed papers to buy Arrow on Nov. 22, 1981. The Germans got rid of the muffler man and hired Dana Morgan, Ed's son, who had been running the Santa Cruz Beach Boardwalk, to be president of Arrow. Morgan worked out of the mountain view office with the other executives and engineers, while the manufacturing plant remained in Clearfield, Utah.

Klaus Huss highly respected Ron and wanted him to accompany him on sales and marketing trips. "We'd travel everywhere. I'd go to Germany for Octoberfest and come home and the next day, he'd call and tell me to meet him in Tokyo. He always kept me moving but I didn't mind it at all."

Ron said all the traveling was "one of the benefits" that he appreciated most during his years with Arrow. "I traveled all over the world and got to see amazing things and meet fascinating people. I still look back and think fondly of all those friendships I made."

On one of his 25 trips to Tokyo, Ron was told that Dana Morgan was no longer president and that a former Arrow executive Dean Schallen was brought back to run the company. He didn't last long either. He left and Peter Zwickau, a German, was made president and remained in that position until shortly after the company went into its first bankruptcy in late 1984. The financial problem was caused indirectly by Huss's large investment (and resulting debt load) in Darien Lake amusement park in Darien, New York, and its ride concessions business at the Louisiana World Expo in New Orleans. Ron points out that the financial problems were not caused by the performance of the ride building company.

Arrow-Huss, or "what was left of it," according to Ron, was consolidated to the Utah location in 1984. "I really debated whether I wanted to move to Utah. But, I decided I'd go because I really believed in what our company was doing." Ron moved his family to Utah during the first week of November and by the time he went to the IAAPA trade show in Dallas two weeks later, the company had been put into involuntary Chapter 11 bankruptcy. Arrow did not take a booth that year at the trade show which in itself created quite a bit of talk within the industry about the future of the company. Rumors ran rampant – would Arrow ever be able to make a comeback?

Ron's Road to Ownership

The bank was deeply involved in the company by this time and during a meeting with the bankers, Arrow's attorney told the group that if the owner (Huss) went 120 days without filing a reorganization plan, the management team could file its own plan, and if approved, take over the company. That's what Ron, Norm Scott, Bob Hughes, and 10 other long time employees of Arrow set out to do.

They hired an attorney and started writing their own plan for reorganization. "The rest of 1984 and into 1985 was kind of a nasty. We had all kinds of meetings and finally in November 1985, a year later, we all met down in Salt Lake City with the attorney representing Klaus Huss. The attorney said it looked like Huss's plan had no chance of being approved, but that our plan did."

A Great Kudo!

"Mr. Toomer is the unquestioned king of coaster design."

NEW YORK TIMES, 1989

The new company, to be known as Arrow Dynamics, was required to renegotiate and be responsible to all creditors. With no capital

226

Ron and Betty Toomer, June 1997

behind it, the company's plan was centered on the need to operate strictly on cash flow. They were able to negotiate favorably with the bank creditors and ended up owing $4 million as part of the deal. Out of cash flow, they started paying off the debts and were able to repay $2 million of it during the first three years.

"We took over officially in January 1986 and elected Norm Scott as president and asked him to lead the charge for us. We started calling everyone we knew to tell them that we were back and we were ready," Ron notes. Right away they received an order from Lew Hooper at Kings Island for the Vortex, a custom looping coaster, with a price tag of $4 million. It was built on the same site where the ill-fated Bat had been. "We had a pretty good year in 1986."

Ron Becomes President

Norm Scott died unexpectedly on July 1, 1986 and Ron stepped in as president. Despite the setbacks, its previous financial problems, and a huge debt for an under capitalized company, Arrow Dynamics got off to a strong rebound. Ron thinks the first six to eight years of his team's ownership were the most productive and the most creative in the company's checkered history.

Ever the hands-on man, Ron remained responsible for all coaster designs coming out of Arrow, even after he became president. He had a drafting table in his office and he continued to do most of the

Coasters Forever!

"Roller coasters will remain viable and will continue to be the centerpiece of a park's offering. People want a challenge and the fear of danger - yet the knowledge that they will come back and everything will be OK. People will line up to be scared because they know, deep down, that coasters are safe."

RON TOOMER

original layouts and profiles. The engineering and design duties of his job remained the same; he created the visuals of the rides, the layout of the ground and the basic profile - all the hills and the ups and downs. He performed all the calculations to make sure that everything would work before presenting the concept to a potential customer. Once the buyer agreed on the ride, Ron would turn the work over to the engineers who would make the shop drawings and then make the ride happen.

The years 1980 to 1986, before he became president, were interesting, challenging, and eventful for Ron and his sagacity and his positive attitude kept him going. Many wondered why he stayed around. "I just kept doing what I was doing and tried not to get involved in other stuff. We had enough work to keep me busy."

Maybe It's Time

By the early 1990s, Ron started thinking about retiring and started looking around for someone who might be able to take over the company. While not officially in financial trouble, the company needed more money for research and development than cash flow would allow. Arrow was in dire need of new rides to stay competitive. "We thought we might be able to sell part of the company and use that cash to develop new rides," Ron said. "Eventually, we did find a group that would put some money into the company."

In 1994, Ron found an international investor group who took control by investing more than $3.5 million in the company. "One of the first things they decided was that we should make an offer to pay off all the rest of the creditors, approximately $1.5 million. An offer was made to the creditors and most of them accepted. It was nice getting out of debt."

Ron said the more he thought about retiring, the sadder he became. "The unfortunate thing about it is that for nearly 30 years, I had been the face of the company all over the world and everybody knew me and trusted me." When the investment group took over, Ron was promoted to chairman and a new president was brought in. After a false and very short start with a new president that didn't work out, the group brought in Alan Harris, who had previously represented Arrow's international interests in Europe.

Things didn't improve and management and stockholders became restless. With no new product and with the new, more caustic attitude of top management, the marketplace was quickly losing faith in Arrow, going elsewhere for new rides. "During all my years with Arrow, I truly believed I had to do whatever I could to keep the customer happy,"

**Ron Toomer and Jim Rowland, right, of
Blackpool Pleasure Beach at the 1995 IAAPA convention.**

Ron points out. "If something went wrong, well I was there almost immediately to fix it. But the attitude of the new group was one of let's make as much money as possible and to hell with the customer. It didn't take long for my friends out there to see the drastic change in management style."

One day Ron received a call from another ride manufacturer who was interested in buying Arrow, lock, stock and barrel. "I thought what the heck, it couldn't get any worse than it was, so I passed along our board members names and phone numbers and when Alan (Harris) found out about it, he got quite angry with me for divulging that information."

That run-in with Harris helped Ron make an ever-important decision. "That's what made me leave the company. They mistakenly thought I had tried to screw them, so with their encouragement and blessing, I packed up and left the following week." He has never looked back or regretted making that decision. "I couldn't be a part of where they were headed. It was against everything that I had worked so hard for so many years. I had to do something and I gave up my job for it."

The amusement park industry is a business of personalities and the basics behind Arrow for so many years was that all dealings were based on the customer's trust and faith in Ron. "After other people got in here, they didn't understand that this was a personality based and person to person business," Ron said, noting that one of the first things Alan Harris said to him was, "You guys need to start running this like a business."

Ron says he doesn't know what he could have done in 1998 to save the company. "You know, hindsight is great and I can say to myself that we shouldn't have gone out looking for money and just kept doing what we were doing, but that's not what we elected to do, so I have to live with that decision."

Never regaining its once-noble position, Arrow struggled for several years after Ron retired, selling a few rides and living off its parts business and its refurbishment work. Suffering from the creation of the expensive X coaster at Six Flags Magic Mountain, the company declared bankruptcy on Dec. 3, 2001 and went searching again for a "strategic partner," to purchase all assets of the company. On Oct. 28, 2002, S&S Power won court approval to acquire Arrow out of bankruptcy. In the years to follow, S&S used the technology and a few of the other assets of the acquired company, but the name Arrow slowly lost its magic and by 2006 was rarely if ever used on new rides.

The Down Side of an Up and Down Business

"Ron Toomer's Job Makes him Sick to his Stomach."

FINANCIAL POST, JUNE 1989

Ron the Man

In addition to his remarkable contribution to the coaster industry, Ron has impacted the industry in many ways, including his service on the IAAPA Board of Directors. He has lectured to worldwide engineering associations, including the National Geographic Explorer, and has spoken to literally hundreds of science classes. He feels he has a "duty" to share his experience and his passion, especially with the younger set.

In 2000, Ron was voted into the IAAPA Hall of Fame as a Living Legend. "There is no better illustration of a pioneer in the roller coaster field than Ron Toomer," wrote Premier Rides president Jim Seay, a pioneer in his own right, on his IAAPA Hall of Fame nomination for Ron.

Ron has achieved a celebrity status worldwide and remains amazed at the amount of interest there has been in him and his work. *Readers Digest* once called him the chief arms supplier of the coaster wars. Ron shakes off his celebrity status. "The media is something that naturally happens when you do weird stuff," he notes. "It was nice, but I don't think I ever got carried away. I enjoyed sharing my ideas and feelings with others, and of course the publicity certainly didn't hurt our business."

Following 20 years in Utah, Ron and Betty moved to the Dallas-Ft. Worth area of Texas in 2004 where they plan to spend their retirement years. Never a workaholic, Ron said he has had no problem slowing down. "No, I just had to let it go, I couldn't devote too much time to being angry or disappointed," he said. He has returned to one

Quietly Effective

"While Ron is not a very vocal and outgoing person, he is a deep thinker and a visionary. I served with him on the IAAPA Space Allocation Committee and his comments were always well thought out and appropriate to the subject matter. Ron does not waste words - he says what is necessary - but he is always right on."

BILL ALTER, LONG TIME INDUSTRY SUPPLIER OF GAMES AND TICKETS of his earlier passions, woodworking and has carved a few decoys since retiring. He and Betty travel a bit, mostly by car, and because of his motion sickness Ron insists on driving.

Their home humbly showcases the industry from which he retired. There are several roller coaster pictures on the wall, a carousel horse his employees created as a gift for him and Betty in 1991 and his Hall of Fame award displayed on a table. "Anybody who doesn't know me would come in here, look around and think I'm some kind of a roller coaster freak," he laughed.

If only they knew.

BIBLIOGRAPHY

ARTICLES & INTERVIEWS

All Aboard, *Forbes*, by Kerry Hannon, Aug. 10, 1987

Amusement Parks Go Head Over Heels for New Thrills: Coasters Climb to New Heights, *USA Today*, by Jefferson Graham, May 14, 1990

Anatomy of a Thrill Seeker, *Funworld*, by Kathleen Cassedy, November 1987

Arrow, *NAPHA News*, March/April 1999

Arrow Advertisement, *Inside Track*, November 1996

Arrow's Corkscrew Coaster; As Successful as the Flume? *Amusement Business*, by Paul Curran, July 19, 1975

Arrow Dynamics, *Amusement Park Journal*, by Charles Jacques, Jr., December 1986

Arrow Dynamics, *The Loop*, Aug. 23, 2002

Arrow Dynamics Mine Train Coasters, *Amusement Today*, June 1997

Arrow Dynamics News, in-house publication, 1991-1992

Arrow's Mine Train Coaster, *Amusement Park Journal*, by Charles Jacques, Jr., June 1985

Arrow's Suspended Coasters Remain Popular with Guests, *Amusement Today*, by Scott Rutherford, November 2004

Fantastic Flumes, *Inside Track*, by Gary Slade and Larry Minor, July 1993

From Disney to Desperado, the Straight Story on Arrow, *Inside Track*, November 1994

Hall of Fame, *Funworld*, January 2001

Here We Go Loop-the-Loop, *The Toronto Sun*, by Steve Payne, July 29, 1995

Huss Newsletter, November 1984

If The Riders Scream "We're Going to Die!" Then It's a Success, *The Wall Street Journal*, by Robert Johnson, May 28, 1992

Interview with Jim Palmer, by Tim O'Brien, March 13, 2006

Interview with Peter Zwickau, by Tim O'Brien, March 13, 2006

Interviews with Ron Toomer, by Tim O'Brien, Oct. 10, 2005; Feb. 22, 2006; April 25, 2006; May 17, 2006

Roller Coaster King Ron Toomer Has a Job He Can't Stomach, *People*, July 24, 1989

Ron Toomer Interview with Sam Donaldson, Primetime Live ABC News, July 5, 1990

Style Makers, *New York Times*, by Andrew L. Yarrow, July 2, 1989

The Five Month Failure: An Amusement Park's Quick Death, *Amusement Park Annual*, March 1980

The Thrill Maker, *Funworld*, by Keith Miller, October 2005

This Company's Specialty: Terror on Wheels, *The Financial Post* (Toronto, Canada), by Jamie Wayne, June 19, 1989

Twenty Questions With Arrow Chairman Ron Toomer, *Inside Track,* by Gary Slade
and Mark Wyatt, November 1994
Venerable Corkscrew: End of a Long Ride, *Los Angeles Times,* by Zan Dubin,
Sept. 17, 1989

BOOKS & INTERNET
The Incredible Scream Machine, A History of the Roller Coaster, Amusement Park
Books/Bowling Green State University Popular Press, 1987, by Robert
Cartmell
Roller Coaster, Chartwell Books, 1998, by David Bennett
Roller Coasters, Lowe & B. Hould Publishers, 2003, by Scott Rutherford
*Roller Coasters: An Illustrated Guide to the Rides in the United States and Canada,
With a History,* McFarland & Company, Inc. Publishers, 1993, by Todd H.
Throgmorton
*Roller Coasters, Flumes and Flying Saucers: The Story of Ed Morgan and Karl Bacon,
Ride Inventors of the Modern Amusement Parks,* Northern Lights Publishing,
1999, by Robert R. Reynolds
White Knuckle Ride, Salamander Books Limited, 1996, by Mark Wyatt
www.rcdb.com

JEFF HENRY

"I have no interest in the readily achievable."

Jeff Henry is a successful pioneer at age 51. He is recognized worldwide for his groundbreaking lineup of creative waterpark rides, slides and attractions.

No one would argue that he's a true pioneer and has already created more innovative rides than do most people in a lifetime. But at his age, isn't he really too young to be considered an "official" legend? Pioneers who have blazed their unique trails and have lived long and creative lives or have passed away can be considered legends. But can an active 51 year old pioneer be put into that same category?

To solve that quandry, the author has created a new category and has given Jeff the distinction of being the first ever "Legend-in-Progress." It's something like a work in progress – one never knows exactly how it will turn out but it sure looks grand so far. Jeff's greatest work could very well be in the future. He's still creating and working daily and he says he has no plans to slow down as long as the creative juices continue to flow. He has a black book full of creative ideas and he has much more planned.

In early 2006, after having just completed the construction of a new Schlitterbahn on Galveston (Texas) Island, his family's third Texas waterpark, Jeff claimed that he was "having too much fun" to ever think of slowing down. "I am having a ball. I never in my life have had as much fun as I'm having now. We just go around creating new stuff."

The waterpark industry is not a job or an occupation for Jeff – it's a lifestyle, a mindset one finds in all legends. Another attribute Jeff shares with the older pioneers is his ability to see the big picture and then through hard work and dedication realize that vision.

The HENRY File

JEFFREY WAYNE HENRY

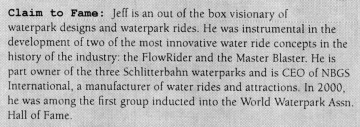

Born: Houston, Texas, Aug. 2, 1955

Married: Now single.

Children: Amber and Jeff Jr.

Education: One week at Southwest Texas State University.

Claim to Fame: Jeff is an out of the box visionary of waterpark designs and waterpark rides. He was instrumental in the development of two of the most innovative water ride concepts in the history of the industry: the FlowRider and the Master Blaster. He is part owner of the three Schlitterbahn waterparks and is CEO of NBGS International, a manufacturer of water rides and attractions. In 2000, he was among the first group inducted into the World Waterpark Assn. Hall of Fame.

Mentor: Bob Henry. "My father is my teacher and my master, and I've always been an apprentice to him. He taught me accounting. He taught me building and construction. He taught me excavation and he taught me engineering and design. The guy literally put me through every single discipline there was."

First job in the industry: At age 11, sweeping streets at Camp Landa, for 25-cents an hour.

Business philosophy: B.I.S. Bundle, Integrate, Synergy. "I take what others are doing, bundle it up and integrate it with what I know needs to be accomplished and then I create a synergy to make it happen."

Hobbies: Flow riding, tubing, scuba diving, and deep sea fishing.

On the FlowRider: "I am addicted to it and it's the only form of exercise I get. All I want to do is flow ride. It is completely cardiovascular and is actually the hardest thing I have ever done. I'm the best 51-year-old in the world right now. I am building a FlowRider at my home, and I'll be the only guy in the world that has a FlowRider in his backyard for his own personal use."

On reading: "I am a consummate reader and I listen to books on tape when I travel. During the past decade I have probably listened to 5,000 books on tape."

Advice: "Being a success is all about productivity. If you can be more productive than the rest of the people around you, you will get to the top and be successful. That works for any field or occupation that you choose."

JEFF HENRY

As CEO of NBGS and part-owner of Schlitterbahn waterparks, this Legend-In-Progress is not a typical businessman - Jeff is different. He is often controversial, he is fun-loving, he doesn't like to wear shoes at conventions, and it's usually difficult to figure out whether his comments come from his heart, his experience or his orneriness. The breadth of his vision is different than most and it could be said that Jeff may be the most misunderstood and under-appreciated legend still in business today.

Jeff Henry moved from Houston to New Braunfels, Texas in 1966 when his parents purchased Camp Landa, a small resort on the Comal River. He was 11 years old at the time and was soon so smitten with water's potential as a recreational element, that he decided there and then that it would be his life's work.

He lived next to the river. He swam in it, played in it, and floated on it. He would stare at the moving water for hours coming up with ideas that would one day make him one of the most creative waterpark and ride designers the industry has ever known. "I learned everything I know about water by looking at it, watching it," he notes.

He claims to have started having visions and dreams of building water rides shortly after moving to Camp Landa. "By the time I was 15, I was building rides and I have never stopped nor do I plan to stop. This is a life's work for me." He doesn't know how many rides and attractions he has built. "In the thousands, I'm sure," he figures.

Jeff doesn't make it a practice to second guess himself and his confidence is second to none. "I have always felt I had the ideas and the knowledge to build waterparks and water rides and I have always believed that I could build a better park than anyone else."

He says he has gained that confidence because of the success he has already experienced and the fact that he works hard at what he does – constantly experimenting with new technology and new approaches. Most importantly his success can be attributed to the fact that he always remembers who the product is for that he is creating – families spending hard-earned money to have a good time.

In today's world as people try hard to think outside "the box," Jeff doesn't have to worry - he has never been IN that box. Much of what he has created is outside the paradigm of not only waterpark attractions but of waterpark manufacturers and developers as well. He is successful because he grew up with few if any restraints. He never let educational expectations, self image or the fear of failure restrain his active and visionary mind.

The World Waterpark Assn. (WWA) recognized Jeff's significant contributions in the industry and inducted him into their Hall of Fame

237

in 2000. His notoriety has grown since and he has appeared on countless TV shows and in articles written about his creative concepts. He has been acknowledged as a waterpark innovator; the likes of which the industry has not seen since George Millay, the "Father of the Waterpark Industry," created the original Wet'n Wild waterpark in 1977.

Jeff's pioneering efforts came early because he was deeply involved in virtually every aspect of the business at a very young age. First as a person who truly understood the appeal and the power of water as a family recreational activity and secondly as an operator, designer, builder, and an artist who creates unique watery environments for family fun.

Jeff Establishes Himself as a Pioneer

In 1979, Schlitterbahn the waterpark opened at Camp Landa creating the world's first waterpark resort. Paid attendance that first year was approximately 10,000, according to Jeff, who helped build nearly all the original attractions with his father. In 1984 Jeff founded New Braunfels General Store (NBGS), a water ride manufacturer that would eventually build innovative rides for waterparks across the planet.

In 1991, Jeff collaborated with Tom Lochtefeld in the research and development of the FlowRider wave surfing ride, and three years later, he took another one of Lochtefeld's ideas and developed the Master Blaster, the world's first uphill water coaster. Both products were innovative and are found in waterparks, cruise ships, and resorts throughout the world. Both took "Best New Product" honors in their inaugural years at the International Assn. of Amusement Parks & Attractions annual convention and trade show.

The Master Blaster is the only ride that has ever swept the best new product awards at the trade show. In 1993 it took home "Best New Major Ride," "Best New Technology," and "Best New Water Ride." By 2006, nearly 100 Master Blasters had been installed throughout the world.

The FlowRider and the Master Blaster helped put Jeff, Schlitterbahn, and NBGS on the international map for the first time.

Jeff Builds a River

In 2001, Jeff developed the Transportainment River System, a high capacity man-made river with technology that transports guests from one attraction to another without them having to get out of the water, eliminating the need to stand in line. The creation of the Master Blaster which solved the problem of getting people up hills while in a tube, made Jeff's idea possible. The river system serves as the backbone to Schlitterbahn South Padre Island Waterpark, which he designed and opened in 2001, and Schlitterbahn Galveston Island Waterpark that opened in 2006.

The Transportainment River System was named "Best New Waterpark Product" at the IAAPA Trade Show in 2001 and NBGS International was named the "Impact Award" winner for that innovation, signifying that the product was judged to have the most impact on the future of the amusement industry. The new technology used in the Transportainment River System earned the World Waterpark Assn.'s "Industry Leadership & Innovation Award" that same year.

**The Henry family at Schlitterbahn,
Jeff, Bob, Billye, Jana and Gary, 1998.**

An Early Passion

Jeff was one of the lucky ones who knew at an early age what he wanted to do when he grew up. "When I was 14 years old I told my dad that I wasn't ever going to leave (Camp Landa). I was going to stay with him, stay in the business and that someday I was going to develop water rides and resort and recreational properties," he recalls.

The Henry siblings, Jana, Jeff and Gary, 1959.

How was he able to identify a career path so early in life? He thought it through and realized that his dad had spent the first 20 years or so of his life growing up and getting through college. Then for the next 20 years he worked for other people in order to save enough money to start a business for himself. Bob Henry was determined that he wouldn't have to work for others his entire life.

Since Jeff knew what he wanted to do in life, he didn't feel he needed to attend college. "There was no sense in wasting the time. My father is my teacher and my master, and I've always been an apprentice to him. He taught me accounting. He taught me building and construction. He taught me excavation and he taught me engineering and design. The guy literally put me through every single discipline there was."

His father felt that by going into business for himself that he was "retiring" because he no longer was working for someone else. If that's the case, Jeff retired when he was 14. He "never had a job" in his life. He never filled out a job application and he never had to work for anybody except for his family in the family business.

He notes that in addition to finding his passion early and making life-long decisions at 14, the opportunity to be with his family through the years has been a great benefit and a wonderful experience. "Keeping my brother and sister, mom and dad all together was my dad's greatest wish. That's why I tried very hard to get my brother and sister to come back to the business after they graduated from college, and then holding them together and trying to keep them here along with my dad and me, giving them opportunity, love and friendship. I'm over 50 and my sister Jana, brother Gary, my father Bob, and my mother Billye have all stayed and worked together as a family. We've never been apart."

Before There was a Waterpark

The waterpark industry had not officially commenced when the Henry family started building rides and slides at their resort. His father built the first waterslide there in 1967, which was a green 80-foot long fiberglass flume. It was a straight shot with a big drop in it. "I built the first channel down to the Comal River in 1971. It was a 100-foot long concrete river ride and it took me about eight months to dig it out with a shovel. I mixed the cement by hand, and built the whole thing. We rented inner tubes for people to float through it."

He Did it His Way!

In today's world as people try hard to think outside "the box," Jeff doesn't have to worry - he has never been IN that box. Much of what he has created is outside the paradigm of not only waterpark attractions but of waterpark manufacturers and developers as well. He is successful because he grew up with few if any restraints. He never let educational expectations, self image or the fear of failure restrain his active and visionary mind.

The family had begun enhancing their resort with waterpark rides, slides and attractions at least 10 years before Wet'n Wild Orlando (considered to be the first "official" waterpark) opened in 1977.

But the Henry family wasn't trying to build a park per se; they were creating Schlitterbahn the resort, and saw the water elements as resort amenities, not as stand-alone attractions. It has been the lodging element at Schlitterbahn that has remained the economic driver through the years and lodging is what funded the creation of the waterpark.

Jeff laughs when people today talk about the "new" waterpark resorts springing up across the world.

"For the past 10 years people have been talking about how lodging and water attractions can work so well together. People now seem to have that concept figured out, but it's funny how we had it figured out in 1967. My father was at least 20 years ahead of everybody."

Jeff believes his dad, Bob Henry, is the true father of the waterpark industry, not George Millay, and he believes that Schlitterbahn is the world's oldest waterpark, not Wet'n Wild. "It all began here in 1967, way before anybody else even dreamed of something like this and 10 years before the next park opened. Dad never got any credit for that, but he really didn't care about credit."

Building Everything from Scratch

Jeff said everything that was created, first at the resort and then at the waterpark, was built by himself, his father and his brother Gary; all by trial and error because no models of what was "supposed" to be done existed at the time. When Jeff takes people on a tour of Schlitterbahn, he enjoys pointing out his three decades of mistakes. "Every single place we go in the park, I can point at something and say, that's a mistake there, and over there, that's another mistake. Nope, shouldn't have built that one that way. But, you go back, you fix it, you make it work, you keep it safe."

In addition to creating and physically helping build most of the early rides at Schlitterbahn, Jeff was that park's general manager and its first lifeguard. After he created and built the second Schlitterbahn on South Padre Island in 2001, he stayed there as general manager for four years. He hired a full time manager for Schlitterbahn Galveston Island Waterpark when it opened in 2006.

He smiles when he recalls his short-lived career as GM of the original Schlitterbahn. "Everybody got mad at me; I got mad at everybody. So my sister became the general manager, and then everybody got mad at her. Then my brother became the general manager, and everybody got mad at him, and then Rick Faber (Jana's husband) became the general manager and everybody got mad at him, and then Terri Adams became the general manager and she's managed to keep her job and get promoted a couple times."

Jeff Develops the Schlitterbahn Difference

"We're now aggressively developing, expanding and building our waterpark model, the evolved model that we started with in 1966," Jeff pointed out. "You know, today's model is not really much different than it was then, just bigger and meaner - kind of like a river on steroids."

There is a big difference between the Schlitterbahn waterparks and the rest of the industry, according to Jeff. "The reason we've done so well is because we are not a waterslide park - we are a river park. We have river rides, which make up the predominate number of entertainment minutes that we offer our guests. Of course waterslides are necessary and you need to have them, but slides without all the other rides and attractions set you up for failure. You need the full mix, and a critical mass to have a really great park."

By regularly reinvesting in lodging, rides, slides and unique experiences, Schlitterbahn grew to 65 acres by 2006 and was hosting nearly a million people each year, making it the most attended seasonal waterpark in North America.

Jeff testing a ride at NBGS, 1983.

The Builder as an Artist

"I think of myself as an artist. I take a piece of property and I sculpt it into a water family entertainment facility. I think it is true visual art and it lives and breathes as it is being created - just ask the crews I work with. They get so frustrated with me because I change my mind every 12 seconds about what I want. I think of a way to do something and if I stop there, it's over. Instead, I just keep looking at it and keep studying and making it better."

One of the competitive advantages Jeff has over other waterpark developers is the longevity and the resulting expertise of his crew. For the Galveston Island project in 2005/2006, he and his seven top guys represented 250 years of combined experience of working together on waterparks. "Once we figured that out, we began figuring how much total experience we have on the entire team. Everybody has at least 10 years and some people have 25 years. It averaged 15 years per man and we had 100 people on that job. That's 1,500 years of waterpark experience on just my team."

Jeff on the FlowRider in Schlitterbahn's Surfenburg area, 1991.

He said it's that team experience of working together that has created the success the company is now enjoying. "We build good things that are successful and it's because we're a team, not because I'm a great individual or that any of these people are great individuals. We're all independently great at something, but by ourselves none of us stand out above the rest. When you put us all together, collectively, we probably have the most experienced group of water resort people on the face of the earth working together and we've all been together for virtually all of our lives."

Jeff notes that he is now seeing the second generation coming of age and staying around to work in the same business. "We've got this new generation of these 21 and 22 year old guys and girls who already have five to 10 years of experience! They're already very good and they are kicking our butts. I mean us old guys aren't even in their league."

However, he still has the edge over the youngsters - he has more experience and he still has better ideas. "But at this point, it's almost over. I'm training them as fast as I can and giving them as much of my knowledge as fast as I can so they will be ready to take over. We're finding the young people today can absorb knowledge faster than we ever dreamed of when we were that age."

He hopes all the Henry kids now running around doing a variety of different jobs for the family eventually come into the business. Jeff,

Retaining the Team

"If you don't retain your best people and take care of them, you will lose them and if that happens, you'll lose all of that accumulated knowledge. The success of our family business has been that we don't lose people and as a result, we maintain a brain trust that allows us to ratchet up to the next level every time we do something."

JEFF HENRY, ON THE IMPORTANCE OF KEEPING A TEAM TOGETHER

Gary and Jana are counting on them in the transition plan. In 2005, they finished the 40-year plan their dad had put together and at the beginning of 2006, they began a new 20-year plan that they themselves created. Jeff recognizes that the three of them, as well as the rest of the senior group now running things, will all be retired when the current plan ends. Part of the new 20-year blueprint is to get the future leaders picked and have them trained and ready for the job. "Of course we'd like to have our own families running the company in the future, if that's possible."

Jeff's the Boss Man

While Jeff is quick to hand out praise to his team, he remains the brains behind the design and layout of all the parks. "I have a lot of great ideas and most of the things we do are totally my idea; however, the execution of those ideas is 99% in the hands of the 100 people that make up our development team."

One of Jeff's top lieutenants is John Schooley, his partner in Henry-Schooley & Associates. Jeff explains how well the two work together. "I work on white boards mostly, not on computer. I put my ideas up on those boards with sketches and drawings and write hundreds of points about what it does, why it does it and how it works. John will then take it and he'll put it into a form that others can understand."

SOME MODELS NEVER CHANGE

"Our waterpark model today is not really much different than it was then, just bigger and meaner – kind of like a river on steroids."

JEFF HENRY, ON HOW HIS PARK DESIGNS HAVE CHANGED OVER THE YEARS

He notes that it's hard for most people to comprehend his original concepts. "John is able to decipher what I'm saying and can put it into an organized, written format that everybody can recognize. At that point, the rest of the team can take it and develop it and run with it, and the lawyers can patent it."

When Jeff and his team create rides, they do virtually everything up to the actual engineering. They complete their own mockups and their own hydraulic model testing. Once that is accomplished, they typically put it into a drawing via AutoCAD. It is then handed over to "a competent" engineering firm, Jeff explains. "We present it to them and tell them that this is what it looks like, here is where the slopes are and here is what the gradients are and here's how it's going to work. Now draw it, stamp it and seal it. Tell us what size rebar it needs to be and what the concrete needs are, and off we go to build it."

A General Store Opening

Jeff founded the New Braunfels General Store (NBGS) following multiple requests from other parks and developers to purchase the unique attractions and rides that he was creating for Schlitterbahn. The waterpark proved to be a great testing ground for the new technology that he was developing.

According to Jeff, NBGS was founded for two reasons: First, to market the water play products that he had developed for his own kids, such as frogs, turtles, alligators; and secondly, to provide stable employment for his crew. "When I first started building stuff, unique stuff, there wasn't anything similar to it for sale in the industry. We were building our own water slides, and I had little kids, so I wanted to build fun stuff for them. They were beautiful toys. I sold a lot of them and you'll see them in waterparks all over the world today."

Jeff said it was the desire to keep his crew together that served as the real catalyst for the creation of NBGS. "We had built the (original) Schlitterbahn waterpark and we were out of money. I had two choices. Either cut my construction crew during the off season or find something for them to do. I decided that it was absolutely essential that I keep all of these people together because I believed then and I still do, that they are vital to the long-term success of our company. If you don't retain your best people and take care of them, you will lose them and if that happens, you'll lose all of that accumulated knowledge. The success of our family business has been that we don't lose people and as a result, we maintain a brain trust that allows us to ratchet up to the next level every time we do something."

Following a Different Path

Jeff is not a typical businessman - Jeff is different. He is often controversial, he is fun-loving, he doesn't like to wear shoes at conventions, and it's usually difficult to figure out whether his comments come from his heart, his experience or his orneriness. The breadth of his vision is different than most and it could be said that Jeff may be the most misunderstood and under-appreciated waterpark pioneer still in business today.

In its early years, NBGS was performing 50% of its work for other parks and 50% for their own park. All research and development was funded by the family's Schlitterbahn waterpark. To get some of that R&D money back, Jeff found it was both efficient and essential to go out and sell the NBGS products once they were tested and proven at Schlitterbahn.

Former Schlitterbahn PR director Sherrie Brammall is flanked by Jeff on the left, and former NBGS President, Mike Jaroszewski as they stand in a Master Blaster flume at NBGS in 1993.

"My goal was to go out into the marketplace and sell enough product to get the R&D money and the cost of that first ride back," he said, but admitted another, up until now untold and more personal reason for the manufacturing company. "OK, to be honest, I created NBGS so I could travel and see the world. That's the basic truth. But I had to do well and sell something along the way because I didn't have any money and I couldn't go see the world unless I had somebody paying my plane ticket, and my hotel room, and my per diem. We never made a lot of money at NBGS and it was not a profitable entity for my family, but I was able to learn a great deal about the business by traveling the world and that in turn greatly helped our waterpark development business."

During his travels he met virtually every person involved in the waterpark industry. He met the major design and development guys and got to see what everybody was doing. He was able to pick up an incredible amount of knowledge and was able to "borrow thousands of ideas" from his travels. He estimates he traveled to more than 100 countries and worked on more than 1,000 parks.

The Splashmaster

"He builds it, and they come. Waterpark phenom Jeff Henry thrives as the wizard of wet."

PEOPLE, AUG. 19, 2002

By late 2005 Jeff had booked 100% of the production capacity at NBGS solely for rides and attractions for the Schlitterbahn parks. In early 2006, Jeff and the family made a decision to stop taking orders from outside businesses and to concentrate on the manufacture of products only for their Schlitterbahn parks. The company licensed several U.S. and international companies to manufacture and market the NBGS product line.

Jeff Puts Schlitterbahn on the Map

Tom Lochtefeld originally contacted Jeff for advice about putting soft foam on a new ride that he was developing. "It was an amazing concept and he got my attention immediately," he recalls.

Jeff was so enamored with the ride that he went to his brother Gary and told him that "we absolutely need to have that ride." When Gary asked why, Jeff simply replied that it was "going to be the best thing ever built." Gary said OK and the brothers plopped $50,000 on the table to further Lochtefeld's R&D and to build a model.

They flew to Scripps Institute of Oceanography in La Jolla, Calif. where they worked with Dr. John Powell, who had earlier helped George Millay and Wet'n Wild create several rides. Millay described Powell as a "genius" and as "a rare breed of scientist, engineer and backyard rigger and manufacturer." Powell worked his wonders for Jeff and Lochtefeld and created a working model of the FlowRider and tested it successfully. Jeff built Boogie Bahn, the first fully operational FlowRider at Schlitterbahn in 1991, the following year.

The FlowRider opened as the centerpiece of Surfenburg, a newly developed area of Schlitterbahn. "It's what put us on the map," he said. "It was Tom who made it all possible, thanks to his invention."

Surfenburg premiered in late June 1991, about a month after the rest of Schlitterbahn had opened, but by season's end, the FlowRider had helped overall attendance jump by 24%, which, according to Jeff meant that he had paid for the entire new area of the park in less than 100 days.

The FlowRider is a continuous wave surfing machine. It provides the action of surfing and the feeling that one gets when they're on top of a wave. Anyone can experience the feeling of surfing by riding and/or falling off the consistent wave created by that ride.

A True Innovator

"Jeff is one of the waterpark industry's true visionaries. For more than two decades, he has challenged conventional wisdom and driven industry innovation. As an operator and supplier, his parks and products continue to raise the bar and make the waterpark experience better for millions of our industry's guests."

RICK ROOT, PRESIDENT, WORLD WATERPARK ASSN.

"When we started working on it, Tom had agreed to give me the exclusive distributorship in the U.S. When we finished it, I told Tom that I couldn't accept that and I gave him back those rights."

Jeff said the ride turned out so good and that Tom had so much passion for it that neither he nor NBGS could ever do it justice. "I could never sell it the way he could. It's really not a ride; it's a sport. It has a whole life to it. Someday I believe there will be an Olympic medal on the FlowRider. To me, it's the only thing in the world I like more than good sex. I mean it's that good, it's addictive."

Jeff Henry, 1978.

Jeff Brags on the FlowRider

"For a moment in time you are up there surfing and you are in a euphoric place, in a state that is only known to surfers. The FlowRider provides that to every single person who rides it." And yes, Jeff admits that he is addicted to the ride.

"That's the only form of exercise I get. All I want to do is flow ride. It is completely cardiovascular and is actually the hardest thing I have ever done. I'm the best 51-year-old in the world right now. I am building a FlowRider at my home, and I'll be the only guy in the world that has a FlowRider in his backyard for his own personal use."

According to Jeff, the FlowRider was the first totally new ride experience introduced to the industry for more than a decade. "It was a good example of what a major new, hot innovative product could do for the bottom line," he notes.

Along Came the Master Blaster

Once the FlowRider was established and Jeff had returned all exclusive rights to sell the ride, Lochtefeld was back in Jeff's office handing over another innovative idea. "He walked in, thanked me for my help with the FlowRider and tossed a two inch thick package on my desk," Jeff said.

Lochtefeld told Jeff that if he liked it, he could develop, build, and market it and have the exclusive rights worldwide. All Lochtefeld wanted was a royalty on each one sold. It was a thank you for Jeff's generosity with the FlowRider. The name of the new invention was the Master Blaster, an uphill water roller coaster.

He knew that if Jeff liked the idea, he would grab hold of it and stay with it until he got it right. When the Master Blaster was put on the market, it took the industry by storm. It was the first waterpark ride that could actually take riders up hill. Today, several companies have created similar rides that are generically called water roller coasters.

Jeff, in the center with a shovel and no shirt, and part of his crew as they built Schlitterbahn in 1978.

Jeff Works for His Guests

His next major impact on the industry came as a result of talking with his guests and finding out what they wanted most in a waterpark. "I work for the people who buy my tickets and I want to give them what they want."

During those talks, he found that the one thing above everything else that his patrons wanted were shorter lines for the attractions. He thought long and hard about the problem of long lines and came up with an innovation he calls the Transportainment River System.

"It's very simple. You need a lot of rides in a waterpark and they all need to be hooked together in a continuous, endless fashion. You float down a river channel that utilizes our technology that simulates hydraulic flow patterns found in natural rivers." During the journey riders go down a slide, then up a hill on a water coaster and then maybe into a pool and then down the river to another slide until they experience all the attractions, all while they remain in the water floating on a tube.

His objective is to build a lineless waterpark where there is never a queue. He began the concept at the South Padre Schlitterbahn, where he combined a downhill, fast-flow rapids river with a momentum river (a fast-flow river driven by the waters coming from a FlowRider), with a tidal wave river (a river with waves in it), and he interconnected all of them. He put a Master Blaster at the bottom of the lowest point of the river to carry people back to the highest point of the river so that it became an endless river.

In Galveston he took the concept a bit further with a river nearly a mile long connecting all the outdoor attractions. While it's the best example yet, it is not the perfect lineless park that he wants. That will be Jeff's next generation of Transportainment which is set to premiere at the next Schlitterbahn in Kansas City, Kans., expected to open in early 2008. He sees that one as a 100% lineless park, which has been his goal for the last 10 years, a vision that has cost his company nearly $10 million to fund.

Team Work

"I have a lot of great ideas and most of the things we do are totally my idea; however, the execution of those ideas is 99% in the hands of the 100 people that make up our development team."

JEFF HENRY

The Convertible Waterpark

In Galveston, to help make the $34 million waterpark a year-round facility, Jeff introduced what he calls a "convertible waterpark" whose roof opens and closes with the push of a button. The 70,000 square foot area under the retractable roof is known as Wasserfest. The 16 adjacent outside attractions are located in an area known as Surfenburg.

The reason he created the convertible waterpark was twofold. 1) He wanted a year-round park that could operate when it was cold, and 2) He wanted to cut down the number of days lost to inclement weather. "Over a 25 year period at Schlitterbahn, we lost an average of 13 days of business a year to rain and bad weather during our 100 day season. That's 13% of our season," Jeff points out.

As long as those days are in May and April or September, it doesn't affect the bottom line much, but when those 13 days are in July or August, it can be a 20% hit on the overall bottom line of the company, he estimates. "I decided to minimize that hit and create a way to operate at least part of the park in the rain as well as during winter."

The roof is simpler than the kind you find on a retractable baseball stadium. "Remember I come from simplicity. I am not into building things that are hard or expensive to operate," he said, noting that the indoor waterpark has the feel of an outdoor park when the roof is open, differing it from a traditional indoor waterpark. "The problem with a totally indoor waterpark is that during the summer you've got to cool it and most people don't want to be inside. So to serve your guests, you also need to build an outside waterpark and when you do that you end up with two of everything. You have two sets of capital. You have two crews and two sets of maintenance. With my concept, you end up with one, so it cuts your costs in half. It's far more efficient."

Jeff, the Idea Machine

Where does he get all those creative ideas? "I don't really know. Maybe I'm crazy, but they pop into my head all day." When he gets an idea, he doesn't rely on his memory to keep it alive. He has a black book, a journal in which he jots them down. He's been carrying a journal for 25 years.

"I think every person on earth should journal, and you should write down every idea that comes into your head, every thought you have, all the good things that happen to you each day. Then at the end of the year you should go back and read those books. You should make a list of the things that you got done or you didn't get done that you had listed in there. By checking your journal like that, you can dramatically increase your productivity."

Creative ideas and innovation are critical to keep any industry alive and vibrant and that reality has Jeff worried. He doesn't think the waterpark industry is being cared for today by creative, innovative people or companies. He doesn't think the industry as a whole is in good hands.

"Nearly all of the innovation in the waterpark industry through the years has come from a small number of entrepreneurs, such as George Millay, Rick Briggs, Greg Mastrianni, Rick Faber, and Jack and Turk Waterman. These guys loved the business during their peak years and they had a deep passion for it. They weren't in it solely to make money so it wasn't always about a profit or loss. It was about fun. It was about, 'man let's do this slide cause it's going to be cool.' They all needed to make money at the end of the day of course, but it wasn't primarily about money, which it appears to be today."

Consulting When Not Building

In addition to creating rides and Schlitterbahn waterparks and spending time on his FlowRider, Jeff has kept busy consulting on waterpark projects around the world. He pointed out a couple of those projects of which he is especially proud.

One is Destiny USA, a proposed 800-acre domed destination resort in Syracuse, N.Y. The project was imagineered to create awareness of renewable energy sources and to potentially change America's

Water+Lodging=Cool Resort

"For the past 10 years people have been talking about how lodging and water attractions can work so well together. People now seem to have that concept figured out, but it's funny how we had it figured out in 1967. My father was 20 years ahead of everybody."

JEFF HENRY,
ON HIS
FATHER'S
RESORT
CONCEPT

Jeff and his father Bob Henry, 1997.

**Jeff and his granddaughter afloat
at Schlitterbahn South Padre Island, 2001.**

dependence on foreign oil. Totally dependent on sustainable design innovations, Jeff's challenge was to design an indoor five-mile long river system that would float tube riders through an aquarium, past entertainment stages, and through different sculpted landscapes and environments.

The owners of Destiny USA are Bob and Steve Congel, both good friends of Jeff. What the Congels are trying to do is get the United States off oil. They are trying to demonstrate to America as a country that "we can build a $20 billion dollar resort product and use no fossil fuels at all. I was only one of their consultants and I'll continue to work for them because I believe in their mission. Their mission is to make this a better world."

In the beginning, Bob Congel told Jeff, "I want to save the United States of America by showing that we don't have to have this damn foreign oil." Jeff liked what he heard and thought, "This guy, I'll work for."

He was also on the design team for Kerzner International, the developers of the water-themed Atlantis resort in Nassau. He was on the team that created the river system at the resort hotel and later he served on the design team and provided the technology for a river system at the Atlantis in Dubai. He likes working with Sol Kerzner because Sol is an innovator.

"We won't work for corporate parks because their goal is to solely make money. They don't want innovation. They don't have the heart, they don't have the soul or passion and that attitude is contrary to my main mission of providing fresh, innovative family entertainment," Jeff said. "They only care about one thing and that's their return on investment. But you know, that's not what our customers care about."

He also points out that on top of everything else, the "big guys" aren't fun to work for anymore. "They have way too many rules. It's very difficult to bring fresh new ideas to the marketplace when you work with so many rules."

The Epiphany

During a severe bout with ulcerative colitis in 1984 when he was 29, Jeff had a proctocolectomy and his entire colon was removed. He then underwent an ileostomy, which left him in a condition in which he must wear a bag for the rest of his life. He was quite ill for several months and was in the hospital for more than six weeks. He recalls the day he was released from the hospital.

The Name Says it All

Schlitterbahn (SH-litter-bon) is a German hybrid name meaning "slippery slopes."

"I was in a wheelchair and as they wheeled me out of the hospital, the first thing I saw was the color green. Green like I had never seen it before. I guess I had never taken the time to appreciate the art of a fresh new green spring."

He asked his attendant to take him to Schlitterbahn before taking him home. "I asked to be wheeled down to the kiddie pool I had built years before. I still don't know why, but I felt I wanted to be down there alone. I fell asleep and woke up about an hour later and the park had opened."

Jeff recalls that the park was busy that morning and there were families "just milling about." He remembers that moms and dads and kids were all playing together and having a good time. "I realized right then what my purpose was on earth. It came to me as I sat there and watched everyone. It felt good." That purpose, he waxed, is to "provide a place of recreation where families can bond," and to "create happiness that will help tie family units together."

Waterparks as a Mission

He thinks good waterpark operators fit into a special "doing good things for other people" category. "We do good things for people by providing quality and innovative recreation. People work 50 weeks a year to take two weeks off. Where do many of them go during those two weeks? They come to our parks and our resorts to enjoy life as a family and to strengthen family bonds. I think that service is pretty damn important in the world today."

It was thumbs up following Jeff's first ride on the Transportainment River System at Schlitterbahn South Padre Island in 2001.

In today's environment, Jeff thinks it's a pity that few entrepreneurial family operators are still in the waterpark business. "There are only a handful of us left. As a result, there has been little innovation coming out of the parks themselves and that's why many parks are now having financial problems or have already gone broke."

Busy Boy Jeff

Schlitterbahn's aggressive expansion plans are taking up all of Jeff's efforts and time and he is incredibly excited about working on his next park, the Schlitterbahn Vacation Village in Kansas City. He notes that he is adding all kinds of "new stuff" to that project, which will turn Schlitterbahn's current model of a seasonal park into a year-round product. It also converts it from a waterpark and amusement attraction to a full blown, contemporary resort with accommodations, restaurants, retail outlets, residential areas and a wide variety of family experiences.

"We've jumped to a new level. We're going to lead the industry out of what I see as a slump and head it into a new direction. Whether we're the sole leader or we're not, we are going to lead in a way that is different from everyone else."

Losing the ability to help families bond and enjoy each other in a family-friendly, innovative and affordable environment is what put the industry in its current slump, according to Jeff.

"When we lost that, we lost the vision of what we should be about. Now, it's time to get it back. It's time for all waterpark companies to realize that we all have to make some changes. We must pay more attention to what we are doing and must focus more on providing family fun. Everyone in this business must focus on creating new, exciting, educational value entertainment so that we as an industry can grow and be healthy again."

Pay attention and focus on family values. It's that simple.

"Living Outside the Box

"The beauty of Jeff is that he has always lived and worked outside the accepted parameters of the waterpark industry. He has used his creative skills, unique personality and his energy to always not do what all the others were doing. I have to salute him. While the rest of us were figuring out different ways for people to climb to the top of a tower and slide down, he was way out there coming up with innovative products."

CHIP CLEARY, SENIOR VP, PALACE ENTERTAINMENT

BIBLIOGRAPHY

ARTICLES & INTERVIEWS

A Day at the Beach, Schlitterbahn Beach, *Funworld,* September 2001

Destiny's Latest Plan is Largest Waterpark, *The (Syracuse) Post-Standard,* by Bob Niedt, Dec. 9, 2002

Face to Face With Jeff Henry, *Attractions Management,* by Roger Currie, September/October 2001

First Master Blaster Water Roller Coaster to Debut Next Spring, *Inside Track,* by Mark Wyatt, July 1993

Henry's New Ideas Put into Action in Texas, *Amusement Business,* by Tim O'Brien, Dec. 24, 2001

Henry & Langford Join Forces, NBGS ReSource newsletter, March 1998

Interviews with Jeff Henry, by Tim O'Brien: June, 2001; Feb. 21, 2006; Aug. 28, 2006

Interview with Tom Lochtefeld, by Tim O'Brien: Sept. 12, 1995

Just Add Water, *Houston Chronicle,* by Louis B. Parks, July 18, 2004

1997 Was the Year of the Master Blaster, *Amusement Today,* October 1997

NBGS Introduces New Transportainment System, *Amusement Today,* Feb. 2001

NBGS Master Blasters Go International in '97, *Amusement Today,* July 1997

NBGS Pitches River Walk, *New Braunfels Herald Zeitung,* by Jo Lee Ferguson, Sept. 12, 2000

Perspective: Shoeless Jeff, *Funworld,* by Meg Hartman, January 1997

Quite a Splash for Waterpark, *Kansas City Star,* by Rick Alm, Sept. 16, 2005

Ready to Make a Splash, *Houston Chronicle,* by Jon Paul Morosi, March 3, 2006

Schlitterbahn Galveston Island Plans Unveiled, *Amusement Today,* July 2005

Schlitterbahn Park Planned for Galveston, *Houston Chronicle,* by Richard Stewart, Aug. 29, 2003

Schlitterbahn/NBGS Press Releases, 1989-2006

Schlitterbahn to Build Second Texas Park, *Amusement Today,* May 1997

Schlitterbahn Transportainment a Hit, *Amusement Business,* by Tim O'Brien, July 2, 2001

Schlitterbahn Waterpark: Lone Star Maverick on the Rise, *Funworld,* by Sherrie Brammall, November 1991

Splashmaster, *People,* Aug. 19, 2002

Texas Size Fun in Schlitterbahn Waterpark Resort, *Funworld,* September 1999

Theming, Resorts Seen as Trends, *Amusement Business,* by Tim O'Brien, Oct. 4, 1999

Waterpark Plans Expand Substantially, *Basehor Sentinel,* by Joshua Roberts, Jan. 12, 2006

Waterpark Report: The Total Immersion Theory, *Funworld,* by Norm Matzl, August 2001

Waterparks in the 21st Century, NBGS advertising supplement in *Amusement Today,* June 1999

INDEX

Harrison "Buzz" Price and Tim O'Brien,
March 3, 2007

Tim O'Brien has spent more than two decades chronicling the amusement industry, during which time the award winning photojournalist has had more than 5,000 articles and more than 3,000 photos published. He has appeared in numerous theme park documentaries on national and international TV and has authored 10 books, including "The Amusement Park Guide," considered the Bible of theme park and amusement park guidebooks.

He has written two other books for Ripley Publishing: *Ripley's Believe It or Not! 2005 Baseball Media Guide,* and *The Wave Maker – The Story of Theme Park Pioneer George Millay.*

Tim is VP Publishing & Communications for Ripley Entertainment and is responsible for generating corporate publicity while serving as the international corporate spokesperson. He lives and works in Nashville, Tenn., where he enjoys life with his wife Kathleen and their two amazing cats, George Harrison and Petula Clark.

Printed in the United States
90369LV00002B/331-348/A